# The Historical World of Frederick Jackson Turner

Narrative by Wilbur R. Jacobs

"There is vitality, vigor, initiative in the men out here . . . ."
*(Turner to Max Farrand, March 1, 1927)*

Turner at the Huntington Library, San Marino Ranch, California, *c.*1927
*Courtesy of the Huntington Library*

THE HISTORICAL WORLD OF

# *Frederick Jackson Turner*

WITH SELECTIONS FROM HIS CORRESPONDENCE

*Narrative by Wilbur R. Jacobs*

NEW HAVEN AND LONDON | YALE UNIVERSITY PRESS

1968

Library of Congress catalog card number: 68–27757

Designed by John O. C. McCrillis, set in Granjon type, and printed in the United States of America by Connecticut Printers, Inc., Hartford, Connecticut. Distributed in Great Britain, Europe, Asia, and Africa by Yale University Press Ltd., London; in Canada by McGill University Press, Montreal; and in Latin America by Centro Interamericano de Libros Académicos, Mexico City.

*FOR RAY A. BILLINGTON*

*Friend and Scholar of the American Frontier*

*We must not lose our past. Our libraries hold histories; but without recognition who will read them, and what kind of men will choose the calling?*

Frederick Jackson Turner to Guy Emerson
June 30, 1926

# Preface

Frederick Jackson Turner has long been recognized as one of our most distinguished historians, a scholar whose work on the phenomenon of the frontier and on sectional development helped transform the teaching and writing of American history. At the University of Wisconsin and at Harvard he gained a reputation as a man of ideas, a brilliant teacher who probed the origins of the American character and the emergence of democracy in American society. At a time when university scholars were more and more narrowing their fields of specialization, Turner was moving in the opposite direction, toward broad interdisciplinary and comparative study. Turner stressed the interplay between history and economics, as well as the relevance of history to sociology, geography, geology, and other social and physical sciences. In both his published work and his correspondence he moved freely across the barriers separating the disciplines. He concerned himself with the present as well as with the past, and thought of himself as both sociologist and historian. In his letters Turner gives us a firsthand view of his approach to the writing and teaching of history. They show that he belonged to that rare class of scholar, the original thinker.

The more than one-hundred-and-fifty-odd letters excerpted or given in full in this book have been selected from several thousand letters that Turner wrote to friends, colleagues, students, and others. Some fifteen hundred typescript pages were combed for important, or interesting, or characteristic passages. In some cases, where the publication of the complete letter seemed pointless, significant extracts have been selected.

I have of course attempted to include the letters of intrinsic value—those in which Turner states his beliefs, talks about himself, or discloses some aspect of his own character. Repetitious letters and those in which he merely lists acquaintances present at a professional meeting, issues or accepts invitations, or recommends a student or scholar in routine terms have been excluded. Through the letters and the connecting commentary I have tried to present a portrait of the man himself, one drawn mainly by Turner's own words. I have made every effort to make this selection of Turner's letters representative of his own interests and concerns in the changing world of the historical scholarship of his time.

Not all of the letters included in this selection would be judged worthy of publication if the inherent interest of the individual letter were the only criterion for selection. Taken together however they provide an autobiographical account of Turner's career and give us insight into Turner's temper and spirit—an insight we could never hope to gain from his published works alone. His letters reveal his educational concerns, his views on history and politics and the problems of writing history. They also give the reader an appreciation of his generosity to fellow scholars and former students.

Most of the originals of Turner's letters are in the collection of his papers at the Henry E. Huntington Library in San Marino, California. After Turner's death in 1932, Max Farrand, Director of the Library, wrote to many recipients of Turner's letters requesting that extant letters be deposited with his other papers at the library. A large number were given outright to the library, but a few, such as Turner's letters to Carl Becker (Becker pleaded that he could not part with them at the time) were lent to the library on a temporary basis, so that transcript copies could be made. These were then collated by Merrill H. Crissey, Turner's secretary. Later, photostatic and film copies swelled the collection, and early in the 1960s Ray A. Billington and I discovered additional batches of letters which have since been deposited at the Huntington Library. These materials were supplemented by handwritten letters, typed carbons (most without a signature), and drafts of letters which Turner himself preserved. He also kept almost all of his incoming correspondence. Despite the relative completeness of the Huntington collection, however, a number of letters remain in other depositories or in the hands of individuals. Photocopies of these have been added to the Huntington collection, and the complete correspondence collection has been chronologically arranged and expertly indexed by the library's Department of Manuscripts staff. By the winter of 1968, most of the recent additions of Turner correspondence had been incorporated into the collection and included in the comprehensive index which was originally made by Norma C. Cuthbert and later expanded by Barbara P. Boucot. The general correspondence, together with emphemera (clippings, pocket diary pages, fragments) is housed in some seventy boxes. Family correspondence and Turner's correspondence with Mrs. Alice Forbes Perkins Hooper, a close friend and the benefactress of Turner's Harvard Commission on Western history, are in a separate series of boxes. More detailed information concerning the method of classification is to be found in the Bibliographical Note. All the letters and extracts of letters in this volume are from the Huntington collection.

I have attempted to spare the reader the distraction of footnotes, and wherever possible references have been incorporated into the text. Biographical data on most of Turner's correspondents has been obtained from such generally available reference works as the *Dictionary of American Biography, Who's Who,* or the alumni directories of the Universities of Wisconsin and Harvard. The Bibliographical Note at the end of this volume mentions other relevant reference materials.

The letters and extracts printed here have been only minimally edited. The "e" in "the," for instance, which Turner frequently left out when he was writing by hand, has been replaced. Similarly certain errors of punctuation have been corrected: where no mark of punctuation appears at the end of a sentence, I have inserted a period. Bothersome commas not in accord with Turner's normal usage have been omitted; and if a comma is lacking where we would expect to find one and where Turner himself would normally use one, then a comma has been inserted. Obvious slips of the pen or, in the case of typed manuscripts, typographical errors, have been corrected. No further attempt has been made to make Turner's letters either consistent or modern or correct. Occasionally I have supplied explanatory material in brackets. Where Turner himself used brackets, they are identified as his.

Only rarely does one have difficulty in reading Turner's excellent handwriting, with its occasional decorative flourish, although in later years, and especially during periods of illness, there are passages that degenerate into a scribble. Such passages are however few in number, for in the 1920s and 1930s Turner dictated many of his letters and had them typed.

This volume is the middle part of a Turner trilogy; the first volume, a collection of Turner's unpublished writings on American history, appeared in 1965 under the imprint of the Huntington Library with the title *Frederick Jackson Turner's Legacy*. The third volume, now under way, is a brief biographical study of Turner in which I attempt to assess his significance as a writer and a teacher against the background of twentieth-century developments in historiography and historical method.

*Santa Barbara, California*
*March, 1968*

W. R. J.

# Acknowledgments

During the fifteen years I have concerned myself with Turner and his writings I have incurred many intellectual debts that are difficult to acknowledge. I am especially grateful to those who have written so penetratingly on Turner: Carl Becker, Merle Curti, Avery Craven, Fulmer Mood, Ray A. Billington, and Norman Harper. Many of Turner's former students, some of them now no longer living, helped me with their counsel, and I take this opportunity to acknowledge their assistance. Edgar Eugene Robinson, Herbert Eugene Bolton, Homer C. Hockett, Guy Stanton Ford, Edward Everett Dale, Thomas P. Martin, Frederick Merk, James A. James, and Colin B. Goodykoontz all gave me aid and encouragement.

Without the assistance of Norma B. Cuthbert and Barbara P. Boucot, who cataloged and classified the Huntington Library Turner Collection, my work might never have been completed. Other members of the Huntington Library staff—Mary Isabel Fry, Cary S. Bliss, Edwin H. Carpenter, Herbert C. Schulz, Haydée Noya, William A. Parish, Erwin F. Morkisch, and James Thorpe—have given me the benefit of their knowledge of the Library's resources. I am grateful to David C. Mearns for assistance in using the Turner letters in the Woodrow Wilson Collection at the Library of Congress. For help in examining Turner materials at the University of Wisconsin and the Wisconsin State Historical Society I am indebted to Josephine L. Harper. Officers and librarians of the Harvard College Library extended every courtesy in permitting me to consult Turner materials in the Houghton and Widener Libraries. I am especially obligated to the late William A. Jackson and to Carolyn E. Jakeman. Charles A. Barker and the late Sidney Painter, my former teachers, made it possible for me to use the papers of Herbert Baxter Adams at Johns Hopkins University. Robert Burke and George P. Hammond helped me gain access to Turner's letters among the Herbert Eugene Bolton papers at the Bancroft Library at the University of California, in

Berkeley. My thanks also go to Mrs. Theodore Calvin Pease, who located the letters written by Turner to Clarence W. Alvord, which were preserved in the library of the University of Illinois. Robert Rosenthal helped me locate materials in the Hermann von Holst and William Rainey Harper Collections housed in the University of Chicago library. Donald C. Davidson and Martha H. Peterson of the library of the University of California at Santa Barbara obtained key reference works for my use. I am also grateful for help given me by staff members of libraries at Princeton University, the University of Minnesota, and the University of California at Los Angeles.

My deepest debt is to my wife, who spent many long hours collating Turner's letters, and more than one summer traveling across the continent in the search for Turner materials. I am also deeply indebted to Jean Bonheim, John E. Pomfret, Ray A. Billington, and Alexander DeConde for their valuable editorial suggestions.

Financial assistance provided by the committees on research of the American Philosophical Society and the University of California at Santa Barbara and by the Trustees of the Huntington Library have helped defray the cost of an expensive project.

One who works on a book of this kind is most grateful to those whose counsel saves him from error. This study owes many of its virtues to such counselors, but I am responsible for all of its defects. For permission to publish Turner's letters my sincere thanks go to Jackson Turner Main and officers of the Henry E. Huntington Library.

# Contents

| | | Page |
|---|---|---|
| Preface | | ix |
| Acknowledgments | | xiii |
| Chronology | | xix |
| 1. | Prologue: Turner's Visit to Chicago in 1893 | 1 |
| 2. | Turner's Life and Affairs | 6 |
| | Beginnings of a Career | 21 |
| | The Princeton Offer | 25 |
| | The Year in Europe | 32 |
| | The Stanford Offer | 35 |
| | Intercollegiate Athletics | 37 |
| | A Trip through the Wilderness | 40 |
| | The Move to Harvard | 44 |
| | The American Historical Association Reform Movement | 49 |
| | In a Lighter Vein | 51 |
| | An Autobiographical Letter | 54 |
| | The Huntington Library Years | 62 |
| 3. | Turner's Educational Concerns | 67 |
| | Turner at Johns Hopkins | 73 |
| | Turner at Wisconsin | 81 |
| | The University Library | 90 |
| | The University and the State | 94 |
| | Turner at Harvard | 100 |
| | The Harvard Commission on Western History | 101 |
| | Lectures at Berkeley | 106 |
| | Editorial Policies | 110 |

Page

The Philanthropic Foundation 111
Popular Education 113
Young Historians 114
The Huntington Library 117

4. Social History and Politics 124
Social Forces in America 130
Politics and the Progressives 136
Historical Misconceptions 137
Turner and World War I 143
The Complexity of History 149
America and Europe 156
The Frontier Theory: Favorable and Adverse Criticism 163

5. Problems in Writing History 174
Turner's Publications 181

6. The Generous Critic 193
Letters to Woodrow Wilson 197
Letters of Advice 200
Tokens of Esteem 206
Praise and Criticism 210
The Case of Arthur H. Buffinton 221
Turner's Later Years 228

7. Epilogue: Turner's Accomplishments 251

Bibliographical Note 256

Index 275

# Illustrations

FRONTISPIECE Turner at the Huntington Library

Turner's Parents *Following page 136*
Herbert Baxter Adams' Seminary
Woodrow Wilson in 1897
A Wilderness Trip in 1908
The University of Wisconsin in 1884. Turner's Room at Johns Hopkins
Two of Turner's Teachers, William F. Allen and Richard T. Ely
Founding Fathers of the State Historical Society of Wisconsin, Lyman C. Draper and Reuben Gold Thwaites
Henry Morse Stephens, Turner's friend at the University of California
Turner's Lifelong Friend, Max Farrand, about 1931
Turner and His Wife c. 1893
Turner at the University of Wisconsin in 1887
Turner's College History Textbook
Herbert Eugene Bolton on the Trail
Turner and His Cambridge Home, 1923–24
Carl Becker c. 1930

# Chronology

| | |
|---|---|
| 1861 | November 14: Frederick Jackson Turner born at Portage, Wisconsin. Parents: Andrew Jackson Turner, 1832–1905, newspaper editor; and Mary Hanford Turner, 1834–1906. |
| 1878 | Graduated from Portage High School. Awarded prize for graduation oration, "Power of the Press." |
| 1878–80 | Worked as typesetter in father's newspaper office. |
| 1880 | Entered University of Wisconsin. As undergraduate begins study of Wisconsin history using original materials from the Draper Collection at the State Historical Society of Wisconsin. |
| 1884 | A.B., University of Wisconsin. |
| 1884–85 | Newspaper correspondent for Chicago and Milwaukee papers. |
| 1885–88 | Tutor of rhetoric and oratory, University of Wisconsin. |
| 1888 | A.M., University of Wisconsin. M.A. thesis on the Indian trade in Wisconsin. |
| 1888–89 | Graduate student, Johns Hopkins University. |
| 1889 | November 7: married Caroline Mae Sherwood in Chicago. Children: Jackson Allen Turner, 1892–99; Mae Sherwood Turner, 1894–99; Dorothy Kinsley Turner (Mrs. John S. Main), 1890– .<br>December 9: death of William F. Allen, Turner's friend and former teacher. |
| 1889–91 | Assistant Professor of History, University of Wisconsin. |
| 1890 | Ph.D., Johns Hopkins University. |

| | |
|---|---|
| 1891 | Publication of doctoral dissertation, *The Character and Influence of the Indian Trade in Wisconsin.* |
| 1891–92 | Professor of History, University of Wisconsin. |
| 1892–1910 | Professor of American History, University of Wisconsin. |
| 1893 | Read paper on "The Significance of the Frontier in American History" at Chicago meeting of American Historical Association. |
| 1896 | Received offer from Princeton. |
| 1900 | Invited to head the Department of History at the University of Chicago. |
| 1900–01 | Turner, his wife, and daughter spend a half year in Europe (August–February). |
| 1904 | Visiting professor at Harvard for one term. |
| 1905 | Received offer from Stanford. |
| 1906 | Publication of *The Rise of the New West, 1819–1829.* |
| 1908 | LL.D., University of Illinois. |
| 1908 | Refuted criticism from regents of the University of Wisconsin. |
| 1909 | Accepted offer from Harvard.<br>Litt.D., Harvard University. |
| 1910 | Began teaching at Harvard as Professor of History. |
| 1910–11 | President, American Historical Association. |
| 1910–15 | Member, Board of Editors, *American Historical Review.* |
| 1911 | Publication of first edition of *List of References on History of the West.* |

| | |
|---|---|
| 1912 | Publication of *Guide to the Study and Reading of American History,* edited with Edward Channing and Albert Bushnell Hart. |
| 1914 | Summer lectures, University of Washington and University of Oregon. |
| 1914–16 | President, Colonial Society of Massachusetts. |
| 1915 | University of California summer session lectures. |
| 1916–17 | Research Associate, Department of Historical Research, Carnegie Institution. |
| 1917 | Member, National Board for Historical Service.<br>Delivered Lowell Lectures, Boston, Massachusetts. |
| 1920 | Publication of *The Frontier in American History.* |
| 1921 | Litt.D., University of Wisconsin. |
| 1922 | Published "Sections and the Nation" in the *Yale Review.* |
| 1924 | Retired from Harvard University.<br>Summer lectures, Utah State Agricultural College, Logan, Utah. |
| 1924–1926 | Lectured at University of Wisconsin while living in Madison. |
| 1925 | Summer lectures, Utah State Agricultural College, Logan, Utah. |
| 1927–32 | Research Associate, Henry E. Huntington Library, San Marino, California. |
| 1932 | March 14: died in Pasadena, California.<br>Publication of *The Significance of Sections in American History* (introduction by Max Farrand).<br>Awarded, posthumously, a Pulitzer Prize. |

1935 Publication of *The United States, 1830–1850: The Nation and Its Sections* (introduction by Avery Craven).

1938 Publication of *The Early Writings of Frederick Jackson Turner* (comp. Everett E. Edwards with an intro. by Fulmer Mood).

1966 Publication of *Frederick Jackson Turner's Legacy: Unpublished Writings in American History* (introduction by Wilbur R. Jacobs).

# I

# Prologue: Turner's Visit to Chicago in 1893

The year 1893 is an important one in the annals of American historiography. In that year at a meeting of the American Historical Association in Chicago, a thirty-two-year-old professor of history from the University of Wisconsin, Frederick Jackson Turner, read a paper entitled "The Significance of the Frontier in American History." From Turner's correspondence we can gather something about the circumstances leading up to the event.

We know that Herbert Baxter Adams, under whom Turner studied at Johns Hopkins University, was so impressed by his former pupil's essay, "Problems in American History," that he suggested to Turner in a letter of November 28, 1892, that he prepare another "such paper" to present at the summer meeting of the American Historical Association to be held in Chicago. This meeting was to constitute one of the "Congresses" of the World's Columbian Exposition (the impressive name given the Chicago World's Fair).

Turner's formal invitation to present the paper came from Charles Kendall Adams, member of the Association's Council and President of the University of Wisconsin, where Turner began his career in 1889. Turner had risen quickly on the academic ladder at Wisconsin and within a few years assumed the leadership in building a strong department that attracted graduate students. He requested that one of his advanced students, Orin Grant Libby, be permitted to read a paper at the Chicago meeting on the topic, "Distribution of the Vote on the Ratification of the Constitution." "If there is any doubt about it appearing," Turner wrote the program chairman, "kindly put it in place of my own paper on the 'Significance of the Frontier in American History'" (Turner to William F. Poole, May 10, 1893). Turner's generous proposal was however not accepted. His paper was scheduled for the program and Libby's was not.

Even before the Congress convened there was criticism on the decision to hold an academic meeting amid the hoopla of a Midwestern fair. The eminent Boston historian and librarian, Justin Winsor, wrote Herbert Baxter Adams (March 22, 1893) that the list of participants promised only a "pitiful show." Winsor assumed that "any reputable writer" would refuse to be a part of the affair, recognizing that "conditions are not favorable . . . for a creditable show for American scholarship."

Despite this gloomy forecast, the report on proceedings of the meeting suggests that it was at least moderately successful. A highlight was the "social reception" held at the newly built Art Institute building on the lake front. Those who gave luster to the program were such veteran historians as James Schouler, J. Franklin Jameson, and Reuben Gold Thwaites, and Ainsworth R. Spofford, Librarian of Congress. Among the capable younger men present at the meeting was Turner's Wisconsin colleague, twenty-three-year-old Charles Homer Haskins, destined to become a distinguished medievalist. Both Haskins and Turner seem to have looked forward to the event which gave them an opportunity to talk to other historians and to former Johns Hopkins teachers and associates.

From family correspondence we know that Turner's parents also arrived at the Fair about this time, although they apparently did not hear his paper. His father, whose special interest was the history of Wisconsin politics, would certainly have commented on his son's part in the proceedings had he been in the audience. Instead, he reported (Andrew Jackson Turner to Helen M. Turner, July 23, 1893) that his son had arrived in Chicago a week before his parents and had helped them in "getting started" on their sightseeing program—they visited White City and saw the marvels of the "electric display."

Turner read his paper on July 12, 1893. According to the report of the proceedings, he was the last of five speakers scheduled for an evening session at the Art Institute building. The speaker to precede Turner was his friend, Reuben Gold Thwaites, who spoke on the prosaic topic of "Early Lead Mining in Illinois and Wisconsin." Turner's paper on "The Significance of the Frontier in American History," although lengthy, was far from humdrum, and his language had a rhythmic flow. Moreover Turner was an experienced lecturer with a pleasant, well-modulated voice. The audience however had already heard four papers, so Turner's words may have fallen upon deaf ears.

The greater part of the American Historical Association's published report on that evening's program was devoted to Turner's paper. The report was written by Herbert Baxter Adams and included a number of quotations from Turner's address: "Up to our own day . . . American history has been in large degree the history of colonization of the great west. This ever-retreating frontier of unoccupied land is the key to our development." Yet despite quotations Adams seems to have missed the broader implications of the frontier theory—the idea, for example, that the immigrant had a chance to turn his back on a decadent Europe, to make a fresh start in a society impatient of the traditions, restraints, and social inequalities of Europe. Turner, at heart a patriot, had viewed the American wilderness as the great force molding the American character and dictating, ultimately, many of the directions in which American society evolved. This aspect of Turner's thought finds no real place in Adams' account of the proceedings.

Although we do not know how Turner's audience reacted to his paper, we have a number of comments from those to whom Turner sent offprints. The economist Francis A. Walker, whose examination of census data had led him to conclusions not dissimilar from Turner's, commented in writing to Turner (January 31, 1894), that "the subject is a fascinating one." Historian John Fiske sent a postcard to Turner on February 6, 1894, saying it was an "excellent admirable essay" and that he had been "working toward that same *perspective,* and it is growing more fruitful, if a mixture of metaphors be allowed." Edward Everett Hale, Unitarian clergyman of Boston, was less enthusiastic; on April 21, 1894, he wrote to Turner coldly acknowledging the receipt of this "curious and interesting paper." Theodore Roosevelt, at the time a civil service commissioner, wrote Turner on February 10, 1894, that he planned to "make use" of the "pamphlet" in his third volume on *The Winning of the West.* Roosevelt added, "I think you have struck some first class ideas, and have put into definite shape a good deal of thought which has been floating around rather loosely."

Certain themes developed by Turner had already been touched upon by some of his contemporaries. Francis A. Walker, for instance, in a Phi Beta Kappa address of 1889 (Turner covered his copy with marginal notations and underlining [Turner Collection, Huntington Library, File Drawer 15]), talked about the mingling of frontiersmen in the "vast territory" of the West. Here Walker said, one found an energetic, inventive people fired with "Americanism." And the first volume of Theodore Roosevelt's *The Winning of the West* contained passages (marked by Turner in his personal copy of the book) describing "the true significance" of "the vast movement by which this continent was conquered and peopled." Turner's unpublished essay "The Hunter Type," written about 1890 (File Drawer 15), is based almost entirely upon the early volumes of *The Winning of the West.* Indeed, the first two volumes of this work may well have provided the inspiration for his frontier hypothesis, for "The Hunter Type" paints a heroic portrait of the border warrior and advances the idea that this particular type of man marked a stage in the evolutionary process of society's development. Study of the type, Turner implies, is more important than study of the individual, a theme that was to appear in later published essays.

After 1893 Turner both amplified and modified his frontier theory. He stressed the importance of the European cultural inheritance and the persistence of older habits of thought and action; he showed how settlers moved into "physiographic provinces" and how, when the frontier moved westward, sectional rivalries appeared. The "frontier process," as Turner called it, was infinitely complex, and the historian who hoped to understand its workings must be prepared to carry on his investigations in areas previously strange to him; social, economic, and political forces needed to be given due weight in historical analysis. Such an approach to history would, Turner hoped, make local history more interesting to professional historians, and thus rescue it from amateur enthusiasts. The conflicting interests that had developed between different localities resulted eventually in the division of the United States into a mosaic of geographical "provinces," or sections; these were held together by the political parties. The American character, what Turner called "Uncle Sam's Psychology," was yet another suprasectional binding element.

Turner's ideas about what is important in history and how historical investigation should be carried on were immensely influential. Historians began to pay more attention to what men did rather than what they said; they were readier to include economic and social forces in their considerations; they were more prepared to look beyond character and event in order to locate what Turner called "the forces of historic change." There was much beyond the overt record to challenge the investigator.

# 2

# Turner's Life and Affairs

## *Introduction*

Turner's papers tell us little about his early life. He was born in Portage, Wisconsin, on November 14, 1861, oldest of three children. Both parents were born in New York, and both could trace their lineage back to English Puritan families of seventeenth-century New England. In his autobiographical notes Turner explains that his father, Andrew Jackson Turner, had met his future wife, Mary Hanford, in Friendship, Adams County, Wisconsin. Both families had moved to Wisconsin from New York: "My mother was the village school-ma'am," he wrote, "when my father, as a newspaper compositor, met her." Turner notes what his father is reputed to have said on the occasion: "I'm going to marry that red-headed girl." Actually, Turner said, "my mother's hair was rich brown rather than red."

Turner spoke of his father with deep affection. In a letter of November 16, 1908, to his friend Max Farrand, Turner recalled: "My father died so recently that it is hard for me to realize that I have no longer his strong gentle presence near me. He . . . lived the allotted age, and was a man whom people like to speak of as one who helped his fellows, and stood for good things. That is the kind of legacy that is best worth having." Turner himself is remembered for just such traits. Writing to Merle Curti twenty years later (on August 8, 1928), Turner draws attention to the advantages for a historian of having a newspaper editor for a father: "My practical experience in newspaper work, and in contact with politics through my father probably gave me a sense of realities which affected my work and my influence. I had to see the connections of many factors with the purely political. I couldn't view things in the purely 'academic' way."

In his autobiographical notes Turner recorded many highlights of his life. Beginning with his entrance to the University of Wisconsin in 1880, he wrote: "I was a freshman—Had been typesetter in a small newspaper office—my father Edr. & politician of New York stock—A Republican who had been brought up as a Dem." Turner kept track of his own voting record; he voted for both Democratic and Republican presidential candidates, was in later years an enthusiastic supporter of Woodrow Wilson, but had a low opinion of the Warren Harding administration that followed.

Turner graduated from the University of Wisconsin in 1884 and for a brief period was a newspaper correspondent for Chicago and Milwaukee papers. In 1885 he accepted the post of university instructor in rhetoric and oratory, resisting the temptation of a trip to the West with Reuben Gold Thwaites, who planned to write an account of exploration in the Colorado Rockies. Turner was exceptionally well qualified to teach oratory, for his own efforts in that direction were, according to a former classmate, "never equalled by any professional actor I have ever heard."

Turner's main interest however was history, an interest which had been sparked by his father's writings in local history. At Wisconsin, Turner studied under William F. Allen, a gifted teacher who trained his students to use the modern and more scientific methods of historical investigation with which he had become acquainted in Germany. In particular Allen stressed the critical use of sources; but he also passed on to Turner his own belief that societal institutions are in part shaped by the broader forces and tendencies underlying particular events—forces which were too often ignored in historical analysis. Turner's M.A. thesis on the Indian trade in Wisconsin, which he eventually expanded into a doctoral dissertation, was of course much influenced by Allen's teachings. Recognizing the unusual promise of his student, Allen gave him special assignments involving investigation of manuscript collections amassed by Lyman C. Draper in the State Historical Society of Wisconsin. Turner described this period in his life in a letter to Constance Lindsay Skinner (March 15, 1922; see below, pages 55–62, for the complete text of this letter):

> I was, as an undergraduate in Madison, given the freedom of the Draper Collection (with limitations! I had only a third of one year in Am. History) and the other western manuscripts of the State Histori-

cal Society; and I enjoyed the friendship of Draper and my colleague, Thwaites at the same time that I was trained in European institutional history by Professor William F. Allen (A.M. Harvard), who taught me ideals of scholarship even if he never made me the exact and critical scholar which he was himself. These two things reacted upon each other in my mind, especially the Medieval History and the manuscripts of Western History. I saw American history somewhat differently than it was presented in the books I read.

Far from being confused over the mixture of medieval and Western American history, Turner was stimulated to reexamine the traditional approaches used by historians writing in the 1880s. The result was a fresh and critical approach to American history; traditional points of view on such matters as English tyranny, the slavery controversy, nationalism, or the rise of democracy seemed to Turner in need of revision.

Allen's letters to Turner reveal his wide range of interests, in the medieval and ancient world, for instance, and in religion and philosophy. Moreover Allen's book-reviewing activities kept him well-informed on current literature. He was thus ideally suited to act as literary guide for talented young students. The books he recommended to Turner covered a wide range of topics, and in the 1880s Turner read a great deal. Milton, Shakespeare, Swift, Dickens, Horace in the "original Latin," Lucretius, Tacitus (part of Turner's reading resulted from the emphasis on classics in the curriculum of the time), Comte, Herbert Spencer, Darwin, Macaulay, John Richard Green, Benjamin Franklin, Emerson, George Bancroft, Cooper, and Parkman are all on the reading lists in his paste board-bound commonplace notebooks, and quotations from these authors occur in penciled drafts of college orations. Allen not only encouraged Turner to read widely, but he taught him to appreciate the particular merits of each author—the social history of John Richard Green, for instance, or the stylistic finesse of Parkman.

The drafts of Turner's college orations sometimes read like preliminary versions of an essay on the frontier theory, for they dealt with the rise of the common man, freedom, and social evolution. Here for instance are jottings from Turner's commonplace notebook dated June 1883 (Turner Collection, Huntington Library, Vol. II), in which the twenty-two-year-old Fred Turner, as he was called, enthusiastically forecasts a "new religion" and "new theory of society":

When once mankind does fully appreciate the dignity of existence & the depths of this life that we so carelessly pass by,—then will melt away all our narrow creeds and dogmas and the mind of man will widen with his awakening to the dignity of his life—

What Newton did for the mind of man in his age—What Copernicus in his—only in greater degree have Darwin & Spencer done for our own—They have given us a new world—And from this enlarged conception of things must come a new era, broader ideas of religion, govts. etc. Evolution & its accompanying features is now in the intellect, when it reaches the hearts of men, then may we not look for a new age, a renaissance in thought, like the 16th C—

Poets have sung of man & poets have sung of nature. But the new poets will read a lesson from Spencer & Darwin & sing Man & Nature —mind & matter subjective & objective forms of the divine, the unknowable—God—

Using Evolution etc as text I could ring in Imaginativeness of Present—Dignity of Existence etc—Or I might put it Modern Science's Mission—& work in all these things—

The world is on the eve of a new religion. Intellectually it has outgrown the old ideas and a new conception of the universe arises from our modern scientific investigations and doctrines. We see Ethics as sternly taught by the new school as the old, but the teaching appeals only to our understanding. It lacks the emotional personal driving force of the old religions—

. . . .

Comte stepped in the right direction but his religion was not adequate.

. . . .

By far the greatest problem bequeathed this age is the social problem. In the past the lower classes have been so completely in ignorance as well as oppression that their condition did not fully make itself known to them.

. . . .

Our age a turning point. We have a new system of nature. We must now obtain a new theory of society.

Turner's interpretive bent was, as this draft makes clear, well developed at the outset of his career. That Turner was indebted to nineteenth-century social Darwinism is also clear to the reader of these notes; he was not, in fact, as self-pollenizing as we have been led to believe. We can also detect here a concern with social history that foreshadows his later development.

Some of Turner's autobiographical notes were scrawled on odd-sized sheets of paper, others preserved in dog-eared pocket diaries in which he also recorded anniversaries, appointments, birthdates, temperature readings, research notes, and other information. In 1888 he wrote, "I was a graduate student at J[ohns] H[opkins] U[niversity] listening to Woodrow Wilson, who told us of his desire for public life." Departmental papers preserved at Johns Hopkins, where Turner joined the "seminary"* of Herbert Baxter Adams, record discussions led by graduate students and by Wilson (a visiting lecturer), and by some of the other younger faculty members. These included Charles Homer Haskins, the future medievalist; Charles M. Andrews, later a leader in the field of American colonial history; and Albion W. Small, a visiting instructor and a pioneer in the exciting new field of sociology.

Both Haskins and Wilson became Turner's close friends. Wilson introduced Turner to the works of foreign writers like Walter Bagehot, the English economist, and argued with him on historical questions. In a note relating to his famous essay of 1893, Turner wrote: "read it in MS to W[oodrow] W[ilson]." Wilson was helpful to Turner in still other ways: he supported Turner's candidacy for a permanent post at Wisconsin in 1889 and was responsible for Turner's receiving invitations to write for the *Atlantic*

* Or seminar, the group of advanced graduate students engaged in original research work under the direction of Herbert Baxter Adams that held regular meetings to discuss projects by members and current works in historical literature.

*Monthly*. In 1896 he was almost successful in convincing Turner to move from Madison to his own university at Princeton.

Yet it was Herbert Baxter Adams who exercised the decisive influence on Turner's early career. Adams' conviction that the "germs" of American institutions originated in Europe, in the forests of the German barbarians, aroused a perverse spirit in the young man. "H. B. Adams," Turner wrote, "told the seminary . . . that American institutional history had been well done. That we would better turn next to European institutions. The Frontier was pretty much a *reaction* from that due to my indignation." Although Turner turned to the development of his own ideas, he nevertheless paid lip service to Adams' "Germ" theory (on the origins of American institutions) in his doctoral dissertation, and in his later writings stressed the importance of America's European heritage.

Turner claimed that yet another negative "reaction" pushed him into formulating his frontier theory: "The Frontier in Am. history," he wrote in his autobiographical notes, "[was] A react[ion] to the Census report of the end of [the] frontier line." Certainly these reports made him clarify his own position and caused him to examine with great care the statistical data on which they were based. Yet it would be mistaken to suppose that we owe Turner's famous essay purely to such negative stimuli, for other autobiographical notes in his research files point to the economists Achille Loria and Henry George as having provided him with the basic themes for the frontier hypothesis. The difficulty of tracking down the influences on Turner's thought is at least partly the result of the mass and complexity of the records he left behind.

In 1889, soon after his marriage to Caroline Mae Sherwood of Chicago, Turner returned to Madison. Following the death of William F. Allen, Turner had been offered, and had accepted, the acting chairmanship of the history department at Madison. With the aid of Richard T. Ely, his former economics teacher from Johns Hopkins whom he had persuaded to come to Wisconsin, Turner set up an interdisciplinary program of study for students of history. This program, with its emphasis upon economic and social factors, came to be known as the "Wisconsin School" of history. The Turner-Ely correspondence in the early 1890s shows how much effort went into the planning and organization of this program. Turner told Ely in a letter of March 14, 1892, that "quality" and curriculum "specialties" would help Wisconsin compete with the aggressive new University of Chicago.

In spite of the very attractive offers that came to Turner from Chicago and other universities, he chose to remain at Madison for a period of two decades. These were for Turner rich years: his seminars overflowed with students and his essays brought him fame. He became a personal adviser to the President of the University of Wisconsin, Charles Van Hise, and a spokesman for the faculty when occasion demanded. He was, for example, one of those who testified on behalf of Richard T. Ely at an investigating committee hearing held by the university's Board of Regents, when the economics professor was accused of teaching socialism to students. Ely's exoneration in 1894 was regarded as a landmark in academic freedom, and Turner shared the triumph with his friend. As chairman of the faculty committee on athletics a decade later Turner put through reforms that did not increase his popularity with the students, who, according to Max Farrand, visited him *en masse* at his home and then burnt him in effigy.

Despite such incidents, the Turners were among the most popular of the younger faculty families. They often entertained in their drafty house on Frances Street, and in summer Turner played tennis or went fishing with faculty cronies.

Turner's professional and social life, then, was satisfactory enough: yet he was not free of worry during this period. His financial affairs seemed in a constant state of near crisis, though disaster was somehow avoided. He always hoped—in vain—that his holdings of Brazilian mining stock would some day make his fortune. Worse than money troubles was the loss in 1899 of two of his three young children from illness. Turner never quite recovered from this blow. One of his close friends wrote in a letter after his death, "It seemed to me that he never forgot those children and parting with them tinctured the years to the end." (Alice Forbes Perkins Hooper to Max Farrand, April 3, 1932.)

When in November 1909 Turner decided to leave Wisconsin for Harvard, he made his resignation a protest against the tendency of Wisconsin regents to interfere in academic matters. By this time he had tired of the constant struggle against attempts to make the university a kind of glorified professional school for budding engineers or specialists in agriculture. Turner also resented the regents' criticisms of the especially light teaching load which allowed him more time for research.

In 1910 Turner was elected president of the American Historical Association. This was also the year of his move to Harvard. Charles Homer Haskins, his friend and colleague who preceded Turner in moving to Harvard, believed that at Cambridge Turner would have "a larger and more national opportunity for work" and would be freed "from the constant interruptions from which he could never escape at Madison." (Haskins to James A. James, Nov. 19, 1909.) Turner's Harvard correspondence tends to support this conclusion.

At Cambridge Turner plunged into teaching and research with renewed enthusiasm. Albert Bushnell Hart and Edward Channing, colleagues with whom he collaborated in compiling a *Guide to the Study and Reading of American History,* went out of their way to alter the curriculum so that Turner's classes and seminars easily fell within the planned course of study. Turner was later to derive special pleasure from a cooperative course called "The History of Liberty" in which he shared lecture time with his colleagues. Nevertheless Turner's letters reveal that he missed his Madison associates.

Mrs. Alice Forbes Perkins Hooper, a close friend of Turner's who also provided financial backing for his Harvard Commission on Western History, believed that Turner was never completely at home at Harvard. Writing to Max Farrand (April 3, 1932) after Turner's death she said:

I never felt that Harvard appreciated him—or knew enough to appreciate him & I felt that he felt it was quite useless for him to butt his head against the Harvard stone wall! I appreciate all that's best about Harvard but Harvard's smug satisfaction has a stunting effect sometimes & I think F. J. T. saw early in the Harvard life that it was useless for him to try to become one of the annointed & I personally felt that he did not take root as he should have but I know he had devoted friends & I may overdraw the picture a little perhaps!

Turner's correspondence tends to confirm Mrs. Hooper's judgment about his Harvard years. His letters betray no feeling of hostility toward Harvard, yet the warmth which colors his references to the University of Wisconsin seems lacking in his comments on Harvard. Nevertheless, as Mrs. Hooper noted, he made new friends on the Harvard faculty and, as he wrote in his autobiographical notes, he was invited to join the Fishing and Thursday Clubs of Boston and the Shop Club of Cambridge. These were dining clubs that he particularly enjoyed, for they met in members' homes and talk often centered around a congenial historical or literary topic. In addition he was welcomed into the inner circles of the Colonial Society of Massachusetts and the Massachusetts Historical Society, where he served as an officer and appeared on programs as a speaker. Turner's acceptance by many of the Boston elite was at least partly because he was a congenial Harvard professor, although he could also, for those who demanded a pedigree, trace his ancestry back to Puritan times. It was Turner's kindly, understanding manner that left a lasting impression on his contemporaries. Bernard Fäy, the French historian who studied at Harvard, was one of those who felt he owed Turner a special debt of gratitude. "Professor Turner," Fäy wrote (to Mrs. Turner, May 16, 1932):

had been for me a guide, a friend and a model I wanted to be able some day to imitate. His kindness, his generosity, his open mindedness were such that I shall never forget him. When I arrived at Harvard as a foreigner with few friends and no understanding of America, he was one of the first to help me, to understand me, and to give me proper information, that enabled me to understand what I had to do.

Another admirer was Allyn A. Young, the economist who had taught at Wisconsin before coming to Harvard in 1922. Writing to Carl Becker on October 9, 1928, Young said that Turner was more of a "gentleman" than any other person he had known in academic life. "My wife," Young wrote, "who is nearly blind and upon whom voice, therefore, makes a deep impression, has said that Turner has the most pleasantly modulated voice and the most winning manner of speech that she has ever heard."

Turner was of less than medium height and of an athletic build, with a firm step and handclasp. At the beginning of the fall term he was usually trim and tanned from summer woodland hikes (the Turners had a summer home at Hancock Point on the Maine coast) and fishing trips. Turner maintained his youthful, athletic appearance even after his blond hair had turned snow white. One of his graduate students, Edward Everett Dale, who first met Turner in the Harvard Yard when he was advising new students during registration in September 1913, recalled the meeting and gives us this portrait:

> My memory of him is of a man with a strong well-knit figure, bronzed complexion, a close-cropped mustache, and blazing blue eyes. . . . When he shook hands I noticed that his hand was hard as though he had been engaging in manual labor, which he had—if paddling a canoe on the lakes of Maine may be so designated.
>
> One of his colleagues came past while we were talking and stopped to ask how he had spent the vacation period. "Up in the Maine woods," replied Turner, adding a trifle wistfully, "and I wish I were up in the Maine woods now."

During Turner's first years at Harvard he completed his term of office as secretary to the Board of Editors of the *American Historical Review*. It was at this time that Frederic Bancroft, biographer, historian of the South, and member of the American Historical Association's council, launched his attack on the Board of Editors of the *Review*. Bancroft and his "reform" group accused Board members of controlling the Association through the powers that they exercised as members of the Board and of manipulating the Association's funds for their own benefit. Turner, as secretary, naturally bore the brunt of this attack—his correspondence assumed massive proportions during this period. A compromise was finally reached in 1916 which provided that the ownership of the *Review* be taken away from the Board of Editors and placed in the name of members of the Association.

Max Farrand, in a Huntington Library memorandum after Turner's death (March 4, 1933), wrote that Turner "felt very strongly" about the affair and had kept this portion of his correspondence separated from his other letters. Bancroft's claim that Association travel funds had been tampered with by the Board was of course untrue; but Turner and his colleagues on the Board, especially J. Franklin Jameson, were both annoyed and embarrassed by the accusations. Jameson's anger was so great that he resorted to blasphemy in defending the actions of the Board. The Board had in fact behaved correctly, but a man like Bancroft, who did not hesitate to make blatant accusations in letters sent to the press for publication, was not easy to cope with: "We know that we are neither peanut politicians nor petty grafters," Turner wrote Jameson (May 11, 1915; see below, pages 49–51, for the text of this letter).

Turner's lifelong friendship with J. Franklin Jameson, which survived even the ordeal of the American Historical Association reform movement, was based in part upon a common background: both had attended Johns Hopkins—though they did not meet there—and both had studied under Herbert Baxter Adams. Their first meeting took place in 1898, but they had corresponded with one another earlier. Jameson, in writing to Mrs. Turner (March 17, 1932), recalled the event:

> It has been a long and happy friendship. I first met him in 1898, at the New Haven meeting of the American Historical Association. My host there . . . had thoughtfully written to know whom I would like to have as his other guest, and I said "Turner." You know what pleasure I had in his companionship in my Chicago days, and again when we had the good fortune, twice, to have you and him with us in Washington.

Like Woodrow Wilson, another "Hopkins man," Jameson opened many doors in the academic profession for Turner. As editor of the *American Historical Review* he encouraged Turner to publish articles in the *Review* and documentary material in the American Historical Association's reports of the Historical Manuscripts Commission. After the founding of the Carnegie Institution in Washington in 1902, Turner suggested the possibility of setting up a historical research center there; Jameson approved of the idea and was largely responsible for creating the Bureau, later known as the Department of Historical Research, of which he became the director. Turner's service on the editorial board of the *American Historical Review* and his work as a "research associate" in Jameson's department at the Carnegie Institution helped keep the friendship between the two men alive; they wrote to each other frequently during a period of more than twenty-five years.

Turner spent most of the year 1916–17 with Jameson in Washington as research associate at the Carnegie Institution, but he found it almost impossible to concentrate on his investigations. His letters of this period show that he was worrying about his personal contribution to the war effort: "I am beyond military age ... but I may be able to run errands, or do clerical work. If here in Washington, I shall at least be in the *heat* of the fray. But, probably my chance to be useful in a direct way will not come at all. The most patriotic thing a man can do now is to plant potatoes and do his best to keep his wife and children from becoming a charge ..." (to his daughter, April 18, 1917).

Turner did eventually find an outlet for his patriotism. His letters of 1917 and 1918 reveal that he became a member of the National Board for Historical Service, a government agency which set scholars to work filling in the historical background of wartime events. One of Turner's close associates on the Board was Waldo G. Leland, its secretary, who had also served as an administrative officer at the Department of Historical Research of the Carnegie Institution and as secretary of the American Historical Association.

Leland, later executive secretary of the American Council of Learned Societies, together with Jameson and Turner helped plan the *Dictionary of American Biography*. Writing to Turner on

December 15, 1928, Leland recalled the beginnings of the enterprise:

Amid the celebrations and rejoicings over the publication of the first volume of the American Dictionary of Biography, we have not forgotten that you were the first member of the Council of Learned Societies to suggest this undertaking. I remember the scene very vividly—we were seated in the front room on the top floor of the building occupied by the Institute of International Education, and you were on the south side of the room.

Turner retired from Harvard in 1924. After a short period in Madison, he accepted an invitation to become research associate at the Henry E. Huntington Library in Southern California, where he continued his studies and advised on the needs of the library. Here, amid gardens of flowers, fruit trees, cacti, and other succulents and the "rarities" of the library's collections in books and manuscripts, Turner made steady progress on his history of the United States in the era 1830 to 1850. His publishers waited impatiently for the final manuscript, but they were not able to bring out the book until after Turner's death.

Robert Oliver Shad of the Huntington Library staff wrote of pleasant lunch hours spent with Turner. Just before noon, coffee would be prepared in the library basement: "Dr. Turner," Shad reported, "would join us there, as did Dr. Parish, Dr. Lockey, or another local historian working at the Library. Here, over his second cup of coffee, Dr. Turner lighted many cigarettes which he smoked very short, and talked on history, fishing, libraries, or life." Max Farrand, Turner's friend and Director of the Library, sometimes joined the group. "Turner," Farrand wrote, "was a gentle spirit; an angler, indeed fishing was his passion."

At the age of almost seventy Turner entered a Pasadena hospital for surgery, and from that time on his health was poor. In a letter of January 20, 1930, to his publishers, he reports on his difficulties in getting on with his book:

Last spring I underwent a severe operation in the hospital in Pasadena, and, while I was able to return in the summer to my Maine residence, at Hancock Point, I suffered several reverses in my health there, so that, at present, I am only doing part-time work on the book, dictating from my couch for an hour or two in the morning nearly every day.

The end came March 14, 1932. Max Farrand, in a letter of March 18 to Arthur M. Schlesinger of Harvard, described Turner's death.

Although Turner was more or less incapacitated several months ago by a blood clot blocking the artery under the knee, which laid him up and caused him considerable pain, he recovered from that and has been coming to the Library every day for several weeks and has been in unusual health and spirits. He was at the Library Monday morning, and several persons spoke of how well he seemed. In the afternoon he was at home, and when Mrs. Turner came in from a walk, she found him lying down and suffering some discomfort from his heart. She at once called the physician, who gave him some injections and was confident his condition was improving. Turner said, "I know this is the end." Mrs. Turner remonstrated, saying that he had said that too often to cause her any fright. But Turner repeated, "I know this is the end. Tell Max I am sorry that I haven't finished my book." A little later he made some joke with the doctor about his condition, and shortly afterward he was gone. It couldn't have been better: there was some short discomfort, but no prolonged suffering, and while I had hoped that Turner might have enjoyed his work for a longer time I have no regrets on that score."

To this brief account of Turner's life we should add that he was the author of *The Rise of the New West, 1819–1829* (New York, 1906), of a book of essays titled *The Frontier in American History* (New York, 1920), of a further collection of essays, *The Significance of Sections in American History* (New York, 1932), and of *The United States, 1830–1850: The Nation and Its Sections* (New York, 1935). These last two volumes appeared posthumously, and *The Significance of Sections* was awarded a posthumous Pulitzer Prize.

Turner, who believed it to be the historian's duty to make the results of his research available to others, was very much aware of the relative paucity of his own publications. And though his works contain an extended statement of his frontier hypothesis as well as of his later ideas on sections, they alone would hardly account for the remarkable influence that he exerted on American historical scholarship. Possibly the theories expounded in his writings are the less enduring, less significant part of his life work; more important perhaps were his contributions to historical methodology, his insistence on the need for a more precise, more scientific, and less restricted approach to research than that practiced by earlier historians.

Turnerean methods were carried across the country by devoted students, and soon the centers of American historical scholarship were thoroughly Turnerean in their approach to historical study. In time Turner's methods as well as his historical theories became so thoroughly accepted in the world of American historical scholarship that they began to seem almost self-evident; Turner himself, in a letter to Arthur M. Schlesinger (May 5, 1925; see below, pages 163–65), complained that his Harvard students found certain of his original ideas old hat—surely not many pioneers in historical thought have had the fortune or misfortune to find their contributions so thoroughly absorbed into the intellectual fabric of their own time.

It is because Turner's significance is not entirely based upon his published works that his letters merit our attention. In these letters we may perhaps identify the roots of that loyalty and devotion that he aroused in so many pupils, some of whom, like Merle Curti and Carl Becker, became leading members of the profession. Unfortunately some of his less able followers used Turner's ideas in a way that Turner himself would not have approved: they took what were essentially brilliant insights into the nature of American history and applied them with a rigidity that helped to make his theories a target of attack. Yet even such misuses of Turner's ideas have, as it turns out, proved fruitful: the controversies provoked by Turner's ideas in the 1930s and 1940s stimulated, in their turn, the searching analyses of the 1950s and 1960s. Not the least of Turner's virtues as a historian was his ability to involve his fellow historians in fertile debate.

## *Beginnings of a Career*

Turner was a profuse letter writer and a confirmed letter saver as well. Few readers would care to peruse the total output in his preserved correspondence. The letters selected for inclusion in this volume are those of particular interest in connection with his professional and personal life.

The first letter in the group that follows was written in 1888, when Turner was in his late twenties, to William F. Allen, his friend and mentor at the University of Wisconsin. Like Benjamin Franklin a hundred years before, Turner is not altogether happy about the influx of Germans into the farming frontier.

### TO WILLIAM F. ALLEN

Montello, Wis.
July 11, 1888

Dear Prof. Allen—

I sent you some mss. on which back postage must have been paid. I was out of stamps and had to mail at the depot. Enclosed find two stamps.

I am here fishing for a couple of days. I find that this country is becoming Germanized, and have asked Mr. Pease, and the German minister to work up the process. They (the Germans) are dispossessing whole townships of Americans and introducing the customs and farming methods of the fatherland. I send you the Express of this week.

Very truly yours
Fred J. Turner

This second letter was written in December of 1889 (during Turner's first year as assistant professor at Wisconsin) to Herbert Baxter Adams, under whom Turner had studied at Johns Hopkins. It is an account of the death of William F. Allen, Turner's friend and teacher. Allen, who had studied at Berlin and Göttingen, passed on to his student his belief in "scientific inquiry"—a belief that was to shape Turner's whole outlook on the writing of history. His death was a severe blow for the young Turner. Perhaps the emotional loss of Allen was the greater because it came within a month after Turner's marriage.* And

* See Turner's chronology, page xix.

within a few months a decision would have to be made on Allen's replacement in the University of Wisconsin history department. But Turner's thoughts at the moment were not concentrated upon his possible candidacy for that position.

TO HERBERT BAXTER ADAMS

Department of History,
University of Wisconsin,
Madison, Wis.
Dec. 10, 1889

My dear Dr. Adams

You already know by my telegram the sad news of the death of Professor Allen. I can hardly bear to write the words, nor can I make them seem true. It was all so unexpected. For several days he had remained away from classes, owing to a severe cold which threatened to run into pneumonia—but the physicians were called so promptly and gave such favorable reports of the case that the family and all of us were entirely reassured. So much was this the case that after reading a little proof with his son in which Prof. Allen was especially interested, I went home Friday to Portage to attend a reception given to my wife and myself. Prof. Allen seemed to be getting along nicely Saturday and Sunday, but was unable to take the proper amount of nourishment —Sunday evening he suggested some verbal changes in his book to Mrs. Allen, who sent off a postal card with the corrections to his publishers. "Now," he said "it is all ready for advance sheets"—It was the story of Baeda over again.

" 'There is still a chapter wanting,' said the scribe, 'and it is hard for thee to question thyself longer.' 'It is easily done,' said Baeda 'take up thy pen and write quickly.' Through the day they wrote, and when evening fell, 'There is one sentence unwritten, dear master,' said the youth. 'Write it quickly,' said the master. 'It is finished now.' 'Thou sayest truth,' was the reply, 'all is finished now' "—And so he died.

"I did not know I was so tired" he said to Mrs. Allen in the morning—And he turned on his side to rest. As she passed from the room she looked back upon his face. It was the quiet face of a man who had closed forever the book of life.

As I was returning to my work from the depot half an hour later I met a group of professors, and then first heard the news. I have felt stunned ever since.

Mrs. Allen is very brave, and thoughtful of everybody—"Write to Herbert Adams" she asked me when I left her a few moments ago—

The funeral is to occur Thursday at 2 P.M.

And so the gentlest, justest, most scholarly man I ever knew, has gone. You knew him and appreciated his great worth.

Sincerely yours
Frederick J. Turner

The maturity of tone in this letter is striking, coming as it does from a young man. Indeed, the tone of Turner's letters does not alter with the years. His good sense and balanced judgment appear to have been natural gifts rather than the result of time and experience. The firm and judicious guidance of his father during his childhood may have fostered these qualities in Turner.

Good sense and balance were the qualities Turner needed in the difficult weeks following Allen's death. Allen had wanted Turner to succeed him, but Thomas Chrowder Chamberlin, President of the University, was reluctant to appoint a relatively young and inexperienced assistant professor to such a responsible position. There was a chance that an outsider would fill the vacancy. Woodrow Wilson, who was teaching at Wesleyan University in Connecticut, watched the situation with a careful eye, eager to intervene on his friend's behalf. Unfortunately he knew no one at Madison who could smooth his approach to the President, and it was awkward to write to Chamberlin without first being asked. Wilson however was not one to shrink from a difficult task. In a letter of December 26, 1889, to Reuben Gold Thwaites, he described his tactics:

In addressing Dr. Chamberlin I gave this turn to my intervention, after confessing impertinence: "You know Mr. Turner, doubtless, as well as I do; and I take it for granted that there is practically no doubt about his succeeding Prof. Allen, by whom he was so much admired and whose natural successor he would seem to be. . . . I am writing, I am sure, in the interests of historical scholarship in America in thus insisting upon being allowed to speak in his praise.

There seems little question that President Chamberlin was influenced by Wilson. No important changes were made immediately in the history staff at Wisconsin, although the precocious Charles Homer Haskins was given the post of instructor in European history.

The following month Turner wrote to Wilson.

EXTRACT FROM TURNER'S LETTER TO WOODROW WILSON, JANUARY 23, 1890

Mr. Thwaites has informed me of your more than kind letters in regard to the succession to Prof. Allen's chair. I know how to value such an endorsement. The matter has been very perplexing to me. I have sufficient respect for the learning and the personality of Prof. Allen to feel a decided modesty in urging any claims of mine to succeed him. The knowledge that this was his own wish, however, and that such men as yourself, Dr. Adams, and Mr. Thwaites, as well as other "lay" friends think me worthy of this place, is chiefly what permitted me to allow my name to be used. When I came to my present position last year I discovered that Pres. Chamberlin, for some reason other than my work—for of this he could know almost nothing—was very reticent to make any tangible arrangement with me, until practically forced by Prof. Allen's wishes and my decision that I would wait no longer.

When Prof. Allen died, he came to me after a week, to inquire who would make a good successor to him, and particularly what young men had distinguished themselves. I mentioned as the only men who would fully satisfy his requirements, yourself particularly, and Dr. Emerton of Harvard. He consulted me about a number of men of whom I had not before heard, and left me with the impression that he desired to select a new man for the head of the department, and that I was not on his list of candidates. But after his visit to Washington at the meeting of the Am. Hist. Association, he decided to recall Mr. Spencer to take the class I had taken, and to give me Prof. Allen's work for the year. In his conversations with me he has steadily avoided any distinct statement of his plans for next year. Matters are simply in *status quo.* Mr. Spencer's engagement is distinctly for one year. The board of regents at their January meeting have just ratified this situation of affairs.

Thus I am left to await the spring market, and in the meantime to be tested, I suppose. I am not entirely pleased with the arrangement, for Pres. Chamberlin's actions will be entirely impossible of prediction, and in the meantime I am kept like Mohammed's coffin. Still I am trying to possess my soul in patience, spite of the fact that I begin to grow weary of having to keep one eye off my work in order to look out for my "official head."

### *The Princeton Offer*

In 1892 Turner was appointed professor of American history at Wisconsin, a position he held for eighteen years. On November 5, 1896, Woodrow Wilson (who had in 1890 become a professor at Princeton) wrote his friend to find out whether he would be interested in an offer from Princeton. Wilson with characteristic directness came swiftly to the point: "As you may have seen in the papers recently Princeton has just obtained an increase in endowment. . . . it seems reasonably certain that out of what has been left free, a chair of American history will, among other things be added; and I am going to take the liberty of asking you point blank, whether you would consider a call to such a chair here, for a salary of (say) $3400." The final decision rested with the trustees, who would make proper financial arrangements if Turner should be interested. In closing, Wilson added a sentence that must certainly have caught Turner's attention: "There is no place in the country where a man is more freely allowed to do his own work in his own way than at Princeton; the spirit of American history dwells here from of old." The offer was enticing and Wilson was persistent. Turner was, to use Wilson's words a few years later, "the coming man in American history."

Turner's reactions, in his letter to Wilson on November 8, 1896 (printed here in its entirety), are typical of the man: open, forthright, taking into consideration all factors that might bear on his decision, and delaying that decision until he had fully considered the matter. In the few weeks that elapsed before his second letter (a long extract from which is included here), Turner had clearly considered the proposal more carefully, had received an answer to his first letter to Wilson, and had finally succeeded in narrowing down the factors that would influence his choice. Equally clearly, his decision tended toward Wisconsin. His Wisconsin library and his love of the Midwest meant more to him than the professional and cultural advantages of a career at Princeton. Although Turner was not entirely pleased by the policies of Charles Kendall Adams, successor in 1892 to Chamberlin as president of the University of Wisconsin, he got on well with the members of his department—with, among others, Charles Homer Haskins and Victor Coffin in European history and with his former student, Orin Grant Libby, an instructor in American history. Moreover Turner was concerned about school facilities at Princeton for his three small children, Dorothy, Mae Sherwood, and Jackson Allen (of whom only Dorothy survived childhood illnesses).

Turner's soul-searching proved in the end to have been unnecessary, as we see in the third of the letters which follow. Yet because he made important decisions only after a careful assessment of the situation, he never had occasion to waste his energy in useless regrets. Turner was to receive a number of attractive offers from other universities, so that his judiciousness stood him in good stead.

TO WOODROW WILSON

629 Frances St.
Madison Wisconsin
Nov. 8, 1896

My dear Wilson:

Nothing could have come to me as a greater surprise than your enquiry. I will not deny that it gave me very great pleasure to receive this evidence of your interest and confidence in me. Princeton is a college that any man might be proud to be connected with, and to have you as a colleague would give me even more personal satisfaction. What my reply would be in case of official overtures, would depend upon the outcome of some more or less opposing considerations, and since you have given me your confidence in the matter, I shall ask you to consider some of these questions with me and aid me by your advice. I want to be entirely frank with you and so I shall risk fatiguing you with a pretty full statement of my own state of mind.

I have been reasonably successful in my work here. When I came from Johns Hopkins the work was conducted by Professor Allen and myself, and the elective classes did not number more than 50 students. Of course the kind of teaching that Allen did was of a grade of scholarship beyond anything that we have been able to reach. But since then our teaching force has increased so that we have now: Haskins, Professor of Institutional History; Coffin, Asst. Professor of Modern European History; Libby, Instructor; and a teaching fellow. The aggregate attendance on our history classes—including some large freshmen required work—is about 600. I have about 175 elective students myself, including eight or ten graduate students. Of course I do not mistake "bigness for greatness," but knowing as I do that my work is regarded as far from being "a snap," I cannot do other than regard this as one test of success here. My salary is $2500, which I increase to $2800 by teaching in the Summer School here for six weeks. I have a library—State Historical—which, in its newspapers and periodicals, government documents, local history, and documentary material on the Mississippi Valley, ranks with the four or five best in the country. This library is about to go into a fire proof and impressive building on the University grounds in two or three years, the foundation is now up. We shall have three historical seminary rooms there, in which all our classes will meet, with free access to books & papers, and with abundant apparatus for lecturing.

I have made for myself a field of study in western history, and if nothing unforeseen happens, I ought to grow more influential in this field as I grow older. There is an abundant opportunity for investigation here, and my library and myself have become in a way adjusted to this problem. There are so few students in this field that it would be a matter for regret to have them diminished even by one.—

Madison is beautiful. I have a home by the lake recently built, and very pleasant. Of course it could be disposed of, without loss, but it is pleasant, and I should dislike to pull up stakes without pretty definite knowledge of the future home.

Haskins is a colleague after my own heart; I should leave him with real regret. My parents live some forty miles away, and are growing old. My wife's people live in Chicago, but as my wife's sister is about to move to Holyoke, Mass., they might be near us by frequent visits— Finally, I have lived most of my life in the West and I like it—

These are the considerations that constitute the cake of custom, and the conservative tendencies in my problem—

On the other hand, Princeton is a noble old University, with evidences that her vigor is augmenting rather than declining. I should doubtless gain by the contact with Eastern men and ideals, and a new sort of students. I should be near to the centers of literary activity in the East. My wife has close friends in New York City, and I should rejoice in companionship with you, and your friends. I think I could find opportunity for reconstructive work on the Middle region and the back country of the South, quite equal to my Western field; and I should like to infiltrate some of my Western interpretation of our national development into an American history course in the East.

Of the library facilities at Princeton, in American history, I know nothing; and I must ask you for more information upon opportunities for investigation there. Where do you do your American history work? Are the students in earnest in their work? What chances are there for graduate development? How many hours of teaching would be expected? Is any religious test applied to professors? Of course I am no radical, or propagandist, but my sympathies are in the Unitarian direction; I have never been accused of lack of sympathy with the other religious movements in my historical work, however.—

What is the winter climate of Princeton? Here I am rendered unhappy for weeks at a time in the winter, by colds of a catarrhal character, and my physician tells me that unless I have a change of climate, I am likely to become "hard of hearing" as a result, in the course of time. Such a possibility as this has often made me declare that if I ever got a call to the seaboard I should accept it; but I might get out of the frying pan into the fire.—Baltimore freed me from any such trouble; but that was farther south. My wife, also, has hayfever, and I wish she might be within reach of the Maine coast, or the Eastern mountains, for the summer. Here we are so far that travelling is an impossibility on our salary.—

What the relative financial gain at Princeton would be I do not know. Madison is not a cheap place to live in, as rents are high; but I suppose provisions and so on are far higher at Princeton, and desirable homes not easy to get. Can you assist me with information on this financial question? My family is not an *in*expensive joy, for the three little children need a nurse, and altogether I have found it almost impossible to make both ends meet here. Would there be likelihood of increase of salary there? What are the normal salaries?

What would be my official relationship to other historical professors? Is there any such system of gradation as in Chicago?

What about schools for the children? Is society there so organized that there is exclusiveness. We are not dependent on our social relations; in fact, my wife and myself do not care much for a great deal of that life; but here we have most pleasant associations in that respect; and I know that in some Eastern cities the "old comers" and the "new comers" are still at odds as they were in the primitive days—Now, I should not have asked so many questions, nor made so tiresome a recital of my situation here, if I were not giving the matter very serious consideration, and if I were not anxious to decide wisely for us all.—

I may add that I am not entirely contented with the policy of President Adams here. I do not look for much progress while he and some of the Regents pursue their present policy. He is not likely to press any vigorous educational ideals; and there are not the most cordial relations existing between the faculty and him—

Mrs. Turner joins with me in kindest regards. I wish we could talk the whole situation over with you, for I rely very much on your good judgement. Confidentially, I may tell you, also, that I have received intimations similar to, though not so definite as yours, from members of the faculty of four other prominent Universities within the past year, so the problem of my remaining here is one that I may have to settle before long, even if your enquiry proves to be another evidence of your friendship and does not result in an official call.

In any case, let me tell you again how much I value your friendship.

Yours cordially
Frederick J. Turner

### EXTRACT FROM TURNER'S LETTER TO WOODROW WILSON, NOVEMBER 27, 1896

What you say regarding rent and provisions leads me to believe that, everything considered, there is no financial gain involved—at least not any very considerable advantage of that nature.—

My library here is certainly a very important element in the problem, and I am increasingly reluctant to relinquish it without very clear reason—I know how difficult it is to do systematic investigation when the library is an hour or two away and involves a daily expense to reach it. And while it would be a pleasure to build up a library on my own ideals, yet you know that Americana, & public documents of the states, are not easily gotten, even with abundance of means. The relative inferiority of the Chicago libraries, (in spite of their rich endowments) in American history has impressed this upon me.—

So it comes to pretty nearly this: ought I to exchange my library advantage here, for the greater dignity of a professorship at Princeton, for the stimulus of new and undoubtedly more inspiring contact with the intellectual activity of the seaboard with its many centers of culture within short distances, and for companionship with yourself—for to me that is a very considerable factor. Over against these advantages lie also the removal from my people and my wife's people, now growing old, the element of uncertainty in building up new work, and the separation from Haskins and my other friends in Madison. Here my work is shaping itself easily and naturally and I can look forward to increasing means, reputation and power in this University as it develops—not to consider the question of other calls.

There is the atmosphere of creative activity in the West, and now that it has laid the economic foundations, I look for the West to turn its youthful and vigorous enthusiasm and initiative into University lines. The men who rise with this uplift will have an influential and important place in American educational life. This may be dreamful; but it is a persistent thought with me, none the less. Wisconsin University is fitted by nature for a commanding place in this development of culture, and it is growing with the growth of the West; for American history it has remarkable advantages in our library.

The last of Woodrow Wilson's letters to Turner concerning the Princeton chair in American history is dated March 31, 1896, and was written following a meeting of the trustees. Wilson's plans to bring Turner to Princeton had come to a frustrating end because of a lack of funds. Wilson seems not to recognize Turner's obvious reluctance to leave Wisconsin; he finds it painful to have to impart such bad news, and puts the blame on the trustees. "My disappointment is more keen than I can say," he writes. The "mortification" of having so "elaborately" disturbed his Wisconsin friend is difficult, even for Wilson, to put into words. "But no more," he adds, "I must write a line to Haskins; my left hand* flags; and I am sick at heart."

* I am indebted to Wilson's youngest daughter, the late Mrs. Eleanor Wilson McAdoo, of Santa Barbara, for information clarifying this reference to Wilson's left hand. During his early years at Princeton her father had developed writer's cramp in his right hand through excessive use, and had trained himself both to write and to type with his left hand in order to relieve the strain. He later recovered completely from this disability.

Turner's reply is kind and tactful, designed to lessen Wilson's feelings of embarrassment at the negative outcome of his undertaking. The reference in the final paragraph is to an article by Turner, "Dominant Forces in Western Life," which had appeared in the April 1897 issue of the *Atlantic Monthly*. Wilson had originally recommended Turner to editors of the *Atlantic* and therefore read Turner's articles in the magazine with considerable interest.

TO WOODROW WILSON

University of Wisconsin.
American History.
Madison,
3 April 1897

Dear Wilson:

Don't be disturbed over the outcome of our migration correspondence. While I gave the serious consideration to your letters that they were entitled to, I never pressed your enquiries beyond the cautious statement that you gave them, and so I have not built improperly on this foundation. Not having before me at any time the Wisconsin alternative to your proposition, I did not even come to full face with the question of the change. As between the prospect you offered, and my present position, your suggestion was attractive, and the prospect of having you for a colleague might have broken my roots here in any case; but it would have been a choice difficult to make, for my library and our lakes are pretty strong grappling hooks here—Perhaps it was after all a ladylike act in the fates to settle it for me! and I value the incident as a proof of your regard.

I shall not willingly let Haskins go, as I told you before. Of course I like him so much that I could not wish him to suffer disadvantages by remaining with us; but if you secure him it will be President Adams' fault, not mine. The truth is, that barring salaries and the distance from the fellow workmen of our craft, Madison has some exceptional advantages for historical work, and I confess I do not know many places where I could be as well content—so long as no upturning of our University traditions is effected. So I am not likely to make any pilgrimage that I can foresee.—

Mrs. Turner, I know, would have found a delightful friend in Mrs.

Wilson—at least they both have certain common traits, I imagine, for my Penelope is also just now engaged in administering nursery and sewing girl—We both hope to welcome you and your wife here some time, and show you some of the reasons why we could find it difficult even to look forward to answering the query you proposed.

I am glad you did not disapprove of the *Atlantic* article. I am arriving at the conviction that the magazine is not my proper platform.

With cordial regard
Yours
Frederick J. Turner

## *The Year in Europe*

In August, 1900, Turner and his family left Wisconsin for a year in Europe—Turner had been granted a leave of absence from the University. Two of the Turner children—Jackson Allen (aged seven) and Mae Sherwood (aged five)—had died of childhood illnesses in the previous year, and Mrs. Turner's health had suffered badly. She felt obliged, Turner wrote to Wilson on March 12, 1900, to take "a rest cure to build up her strength in Chicago." Wilson responded with great warmth:

### EXTRACTS FROM WILSON'S LETTER TO TURNER, APRIL 4, 1900

My dear Turner,

Your letter has been a part of my thoughts ever since it came. Your sorrow was so much deeper than I had heard,—*both* your dear little ones gone, and Mrs. Turner's health temporarily broken. . . . I assure you, my dear fellow, that my feeling for you is not the ordinary kind: separation does not seem in the least to lessen or weaken the sense of comradeship and the genuine affection you have excited in me since I first learned to know you. It is, as you know, one of the abiding disappointments of my life that we cannot be colleagues; and, now that you are in trouble, I feel more keenly than ever the pain of not being able to take you every day by the hand and help you with sympathy at least, if with nothing more. There are not many men to whom I am led to say such things, for all I am an outspoken southerner; but with you it seems inevitable.

The following letter to Charles Van Hise, Wisconsin geology professor (who succeeded Charles K. Adams as President of the university in 1903), was written in mid-Atlantic at the beginning of the trip to Europe that was to help Turner, his wife, and ten-year-old Dorothy recover from the blows of the previous year. The Van Hises were old friends and neighbors of the Turners. These two families, along with Charles S. Slichter and Moses S. Slaughter and their respective families, often went on picnics or on woodland trips together.

TO CHARLES R. VAN HISE

*S. S. Mesaba*
Aug. 22, 1900
Lat 42.35
Long 45.22

Dear Van:

I was glad enough to have your letter before leaving. Next best to being in mid Atlantic—five days out—is to be on the north shore of Superior.

We had a pleasant journey East and found Haskins at New York to see us off.—The journey up to date has been pleasant—almost "mill pond" conditions—and we have not had much sickness. The *Mesaba* is an extraordinarily steady boat, and has almost no roll owing to her bilge keels—The cattle remind us of the farm by their odors at times; but they compensate by ensuring us a steady boat.

We have seen the usual complement of whales, flying fish (by schools that made beautiful flights over the trough of the sea) etc. The southern route was taken to avoid ice. It has been fairly warm much of the time—indeed, but for our daily rain we should have been uncomfortable in the gulf stream; but now we are leaving it and expect colder conditions. We make about 330–345 miles a day and expect now to get in Tuesday night; but of course one cannot tell.

Mrs. Turner's hay fever seems gradually to wear away but it still clings to her. Dorothy has found a crowd of youngsters to play with and has kept about very comfortably most of the time.

We have the usual varied crowd. Missionary families en route to Persia, India, and Constantinople; horse men from Texas; concert hall singers and salt trust magnates. There are seven "Reverends" aboard—but we had no services last Sunday. The missionary corner, however, makes up by keeping up hourly devotions, while the festive youths play poker in the smoking room. One of the star performers in the latter game is a young man from Janesville whose wife is a sister of Brewer the athlete. They sit opposite to us at table and we quite astonished each other by our discovery. I am glad to say that he is sustaining the reputation of Wisconsin in the game.

I have found one man worth close acquaintance—a former Cleveland man on his way to live in London. He is a most unusual fellow with all kinds of interest, from medicine to butterflies, with book collecting on the side.

The sea hasn't yet properly overwhelmed me by its vastness. I can reason out the size of it by recalling that yesterday and the days before I saw the same circle of horizon; but the circle is *limited*. I fail to realize its depths, too. The surface is so palpable and apparently substantial. The most beautiful part of it, is the silvery chasing of the wonderful blue of the waves. That is worth the voyage to see. I presume we may get a storm before arrival, but as yet the majesty of the Ocean lacks a touch which I am quite willing to omit, so far as comfort goes.—

I find it is a good thing to eat every time I get a chance. The stomach needs some food, just to keep it from brooding over the fact that it *is* a stomach—to modify our friend Harum.

I shall miss you and my other friends very much this year; and I wish for some reasons I were to be away at another time; but Mrs. Turner is already showing signs of returning spirits and it is for the best, I think.

Remember me kindly to the Slichters and other friends when you return, and be sure that we are your warm admirers and friends wherever you are—

Dorothy will be writing to Hilda soon. We all send love to your family.

Yours
Frederick J. Turner

During the next half year the Turners toured Europe, spending most of their time in Switzerland and Italy. Sightseeing, hiking, and foreign-language study (French and Italian—Dorothy had special tutors) occupied almost all their time. Writing to his father on September 17, 1900, Turner reported: "Mae and Dorothy are well and thriving on this mountain air." Indeed, as Turner wrote his mother (October 22, 1900), he was also thriving in Switzerland, a country that was "*cheap* & beautiful and healthful." On November 18, 1900, he wrote his mother: "I find it so easy to loaf that I dread to stop it."

A year later, however, Turner was back at his desk in Madison. Here he found a group of eager young men anxious to confer with him about their dissertations. The companionship of these advanced students meant a great deal to Turner: "I love to know that they wish to talk with me," he wrote his temporarily absent wife in a letter of April 24, 1901.

### *The Stanford Offer*

Turner's year in Europe did not diminish his stature among his students or fellow historians. In 1905 Max Farrand wrote to Turner offering him a position at Stanford. Although Turner would have liked very much to have had Farrand as a colleague, and although he was attracted by "certain advantages in California," he had serious reservations about leaving Madison for Stanford. He was particularly concerned about the limitations of Stanford's library and the negative effects that this might have on his research. But he had not, in this letter of June 23, 1905, arrived at a final decision.

#### EXTRACT FROM TURNER'S LETTER TO MAX FARRAND, JUNE 23, 1905

At present, and for some years to come, probably, you cannot hope to supply library facilities comparable to those here, and which are probably essential conditions to my progress in scholarship and productivity in history. Two years would make plainer what Stanford can and will do in this important matter of the library. The expenditure of large sums in history library is essential whether you have a colleague or not.

The library defect would be mitigated somewhat by leave of absence for a month at each end of the academic year, though the *daily* contact with the books &c is what counts. But this leave-of-absence plan raises difficulties of its own. It makes a nomadic life for us all, for I don't wish to leave my family regularly. Moreover it plans for me to use the summer in eastern libraries. But it is one of the advantages of California that my wife can be free from hay fever there in August & September.

Again the plan increases cost of living owing to expense of travel, boarding etc.

The salary of $5000 is, all things considered, probably not equal to my present salary and its accompaniments—My salary is now $4,000, with the regular summer session provision, which allows me to teach six weeks for two summers, and thus secure absence on full pay for one semester.

Moreover my length of service—about twenty years—gives me reason, based on previous practice, to expect generous treatment by this University in case I were incapacitated. Previous practice has produced a sort of informal pension system by election to *professor emeritus* on partial salary and by liberality in case of prolonged illness. I do not expect to avail myself of this practice, for I hope to be independent of any such support in my old age, by my own exertions; but as a financial factor it is to be reckoned in considering a change.

I have a stenographer to the value of $300 per year furnished by the University and available for my personal as well as official use.

Considering the cost of *removing,* the cost of *living,* the cost of *travel,* and the importance of it, in my case, these factors give a distinct financial advantage to me at Madison. I have no doubt that I can reduce my *hours* here to any number that another University accepts, if I make a point of this here. My library here is of course greatly superior to anything that can be gotten together at Stanford for some years at best. My old associations are here and I am deeply rooted. Since my father's death my mother's comfort must also be peculiarly considered, and she might not like California. At present she expects to visit my sister in Oakland this summer.

On the other hand, the fascination of California is still strong. I am not sure but that I have done my work for Wisconsin. The University is now in possession of an assured future by action of the legislature this session. It might be well for me to have the inspiration of a new environment. If I could be free from financial problems and could feel that my family's health were better assured by going to California, I should be willing to be at some inconvenience for a few years in the matter of travelling to use libraries. It is essential, however, for me to consider the financial side of it. I have reached middle life, with the responsibility of a family, and the need of providing in case of their or my illness,—and yet I am several thousand dollars in debt with only my life insurance as collateral. (my house is fully mortgaged) Whatever I do therefore will be influenced by this situation. A man owes something to his family as well as to scholarship, and when he has gotten as deeply on to the wrong side of the ledger, on a total reckoning, as I have, he must face the facts, whatever his wishes.

It is possible that a semester arrangement for a term of years might be made on a sufficiently liberal scale to enable me to live while clearing up my publication, and thus enable me (when the library was ready) to give all my time to California, with the money question eased up.

But these are simply vagrant thoughts running through my mind and out of the end of my pen. The substance is that I am gald to contemplate the *possibility* of life in California—That I do not wish to say *no,* but that I cannot feel ready to give a decisive *yes* to your letter.

Is a decision, after all, necessary at present?

Mrs. Turner has been in bed for a few days after the strain of the past fortnight, but is now better.

We all hope that the woods are doing you good—Blessed be the forest and the streams and the pure air of God's wilderness!

The earthquake of 1906 finally settled the question of whether Turner should accept or reject a position at Stanford. So many Stanford buildings were destroyed that the University was forced to withdraw its offer.

Turner's financial problems were as pressing as ever, forcing him to accept advances from publishers for textbooks he intended to write, but never managed to finish. As late as May 6, 1918, he was still juggling with his inadequate resources (Turner to Edward N. Bristol of Henry Holt and Company): "One other thing. I owe Holt & Co. five hundred dollars, advanced on royalties to be earned by the History. I can either pay this by selling a (coupon —*un*registered) Liberty Bond and sending the cash; or by sending the firm the bond ($500—3½%) and receiving credit for its market value, and paying the balance by check. Which would be preferred?"

## *Intercollegiate Athletics*

As chairman of a faculty committee opposing professionalism in intercollegiate football, Turner inevitably became involved in campus politics. He carried on a voluminous correspondence in 1905–06 with faculty at other Midwestern universities where the disease was particularly virulent. His correspondents included the University of Chicago sociologist, Albion W. Small; a former student teaching at Northwestern University, James A. James; and a professor of Greek at the University of Michigan, Albert Henderson Pattengill, who unsuccessfully attempted to mobilize the Michigan academic senate behind a resolution demanding reform. In the following letter* to Pattengill, Turner considered various ways of removing football coaches Amos Alonzo Stagg, Fielding Harris Yost, and Henry L. Williams from the university scene.

TO ALBERT HENDERSON PATTENGILL

Jan 26 '06

My dear Professor Pattengill:

We cannot settle the coach clause satisfactorily while Chicago retains Stagg and Michigan, Yost. There will be no trouble about King. We will not take him on.

Various solutions are possible

1. The one I wrote of yesterday—i.e. Michigan to take the lead in a truce, either indefinite, or for two years, with meeting a year from now to consider possibility of reopening; or even a one year truce,

—or—

2. Simultaneous abandonment of Stagg by Chicago, Yost by Michigan, and Williams by Minnesota.

Contracts could be preserved by paying the sum stipulated. *It would be cheap.* Or they would naturally fall if we suspended the game. Michigan's contract cannot have pledged to Yost a continuance of football—certainly not any particular kind of football. In any case the State University is bound by a higher contract, its duty to the State.

—or—

3. The poorest solution would be a one year arrangement, giving Stagg leave of absence, and compromising Yost's contract by part payment on condition that he looks after his coal mines. This would avoid the difficulty for a time.

I enclose Small's letter to me responding to a similar telegram to the first one I sent you. I called him up by phone in Chicago. He says the papers are up to their old game, and that he has been misrepresented.

* The manuscript of this letter in Turner's papers appears to be a draft and not a final copy.

He said that when I reached Madison and read the letter (as I had not then) I could send it to you, if I thought best.

If Michigan, Chicago, & Wisconsin and Northwestern act together it will settle the case. It is our duty to do some *real* thing to clear the air.

Wisconsin will be in no hurry to act at once. We shall try to see calmly the whole situation and we shall aim to steer our course for the harbor regardless of storms.

Yours truly
Frederick J. Turner (over)

Barton of Ill. writes of their dissatisfaction with the faculty coach clause. Pres Van Hise whom I consulted about King is unalterably opposed to putting King or any professional coach into our faculty. The only practicable solution which he sees under the principles of the conference is to put all coaching for special purpose on a non-paid basis.

I think this is the best plan if we are to continue the game. The more the "faculty-coach" for intercollegiate contests is considered, the worse it appears.

Would Michigan arrange to get on without Yost, if Chicago withdrew Stagg?

Pattengill brought a missionary zeal to the fight against an "enemy" who glorified coaches and argued that contracts could not be broken. But Turner had had enough. His announcement that he intended to drop the whole affair provoked an anguished reply from Pattengill: "I don't see how you can drop the work now. Very likely you don't know *Why* but I do. You can't be so sick of it as I am—" (to Turner, Feb. 9, 1906).

The few modest reforms which were eventually brought about were largely the result of Turner's efforts. Writing to James A. James late in 1906, Turner reports on the situation at Wisconsin.

TO JAMES ALTON JAMES

Dec. 5, 1906

Prof. J. A. James
Northwestern University, Col. of Letters,
Evanston, Ill.

My dear James,

I am glad to have your letter in which you tell me of the athletic situation at Northwestern. Like the poor, I expect that we shall always have the problem of athletics with us. Personally, I should be glad to be able to give less attention to the matter than I find that I am obliged to give. We got through the season very comfortably with not such an undue frenzy of excitement as past seasons have shown, and yet with a good healthy interest in the subject. On the whole I expect, however, that we shall have to fight to hold things in this satisfactory shape. Naturally the students are already anxious to get into the schedule of games with Chicago, Michigan, etc. If we could keep things quiet long enough to have athletics more thoroughly domesticated, things would be much more satisfactory in the long run.

Cordially yours,*

## *A Trip through the Wilderness*

In spite of university politics, the controversy over professionalism in football, and troubled finances, Turner managed to escape into the wilderness for the kind of vacation he really enjoyed. Here is his high-spirited account of a canoeing holiday in 1908 on the Nipigon River in the forest lands of Ontario bordering the northern shores of Lake Superior.

### TO MAX FARRAND

629 Frances St
Madison Wisconsin
September 27 1908

Dear Farrand:

I wish you had been with us on our trip; it would have suited you— We were gone over a month, paddled in all nearly 400 miles, slept in a bed only once during the time, cut our own trails for part of the route, saw no one but our own party of ten for nearly three weeks, saw lots of moose and bear, (Janet Van Hise spanked one swimming bear with her paddle!) caught pike, pickerel and bass on our first route till we filed the barbs off our hooks to keep from getting too many to eat, (I caught a 20 pound pickerel on a light rod) took a few land locked salmon (it was too early for them) and in general had a bully taste of the real wilderness—Day after day of paddling through unspoiled lakes, running some rapids, camping when we listed by waterfalls and among fine trees, and not delayed a day by rain, though we had

* This letter is a copy and, like others in his papers, contains no signature.

showers enough to keep comfortably moist at times. Our men were real bullies of the northern woods—but gentlemen just the same—a picked crowd whom Van Hise borrowed from the force of the Oliver mining company which let us pay them and use them in a dull season. Erick the head guide was a canny Swede who has lived in the woods some thirty years and can do anything. He is a man of resources, judgement, and brains. Dow was a Canadian Scotch man—a true sport. I had to fight it out with him at every rapid to keep him from running them with my women—We had a joy of a canoe, an Old Town—guide special—18 ft., and Dow just ached to show it off. McCabe was a fine Irish man, strong as the propeller of an ocean liner at the stern paddle, and then there was the cook, a French Canadian, with the gasconade of his people, but clever with the frying pan and able to make better bread than we usually can get at home—not to speak of pies! His only fault was that he carried the cheese for safe keeping wrapped in his clothes in his private-pack sack! Our only real hardship was when we ran out of tobacco and McCabe deprived of that and with no green tea, found consolation only in going quietly out in the woods and cursing his gods volubly—I found him one day just ripping up the elements.

We had some pretty hard work, pushing our way at times against head winds in pretty high seas; at other times pulling our canoes up a narrow creek for half a day, a creek so deep you couldn't pole, and so overgrown with bay bushes and alders that we had to fight each inch of the way. We had a little taste of the old Dawson route from Fort William to the Rainy river, a section of it lying on our course—The old portages cut out for teams and with corduroy road in places made a contrast with the Indian portages we had been following & those which came later. But in spite of the fact that underbrush had largely grown up on the right of way, we found the easy portage not altogether to our taste, for it looked like civilization—

On the Nipigon we made a sensation. The community all protested against our party going up with light canoes and no Indians. The superintendent of the river made formal objection, on the ground we were certain to be drowned. I had heard Judge Bunn say that to use a light canvas canoe on this river was suicidal. Result a council of war. Van & the men all said they could do it. Our order had been: Janet Van Hise had bow & her father stern in one 15 ft. canvas; Hilda and the head guide (who couldn't swim by the way) had a similar canoe;

Dow held stern paddle while I took bow with Mae & Dorothy in my 18 ft canvas—making the largest number of passengers in my canoe, and myself not skilled or muscular. The cook & Mike had been in a fourth little canoe. We had about 1000 lbs. of grub with hardware, tents &c.

Result I mutinied, and determined that my family must have a Nipigon canoe and one Indian who knew the river and the fishing. This greatly disgusted Van Hise who hates Indians, and didn't approve of the 20-ft. dory-like Peterborough they use on the river. However I insisted and then Dow kicked and would not paddle with an Indian! I sympathized with him. He was a true sport; but I had made up my mind that it would be reckless to tackle the river as we had been tackling the other route. So we got our canoe; took Mike in place of Dow, and with a stern wind toiled up to Camp Alexander where the outfitter promised to send me an expert Indian. It was Sunday when we started and the piety of the red brethren prevented any of them going on that day—Dorothy & I both paddled on the up journey at bow, and it was a struggle to push the Lusitania as Mae dubbed her up the current, but we did it and kept in sight of the little canoes all the way up. When our guide turned up at Alexander he proved to be a clever young bluffer, a white lad who had never been up beyond Alexander as we learned later! No Indian could be gotten to work with whites!

Well, we found that it would have been entirely feasible to have gone without the Lusitania or the extra man, as the case turned out. But we missed some good fishing, I think, by not having an expert Indian who could take us into one or two places where prior knowledge was requisite. We ran all the rapids that are permissible to white men, however, and with the aid of the fire ranger didn't get mixed up in any wrong currents—We camped at Robinson's pool (Bunn's old camp) and there I did my best fishing—The only event worth writing about being my capture of a 1-½ and a ¾ pounder on the same leader at one cast—But I got no big ones. They wouldn't come up.—I lost a heavy fellow who took the fly while *under* water, not being able to strike him effectively. We always had trout for the camp, and we used nothing but flies—Erick smuggled a phantom minnow into camp and caught the big trout, but we didn't skin him for our own collection! We saw only one other sport on the river—a Mr Bristol of New York, as we learned, who seems to have been the only other man that kept the faith—We didn't meet him, but he sent his compliments through one of our guides and the guide said that he spent a good ten minutes d—ning the crowd of pot hunters who were taking out big trout with worms. It *was* hard. I had a pretty catch at Virgin Falls—head of the river—one day. The next day when I went back I found 4 *fisher*men *seated* at the pool I had fished. Smoking and watching the fate of the worms they were navigating—It was crool! We camped after leaving Robinsons at Virgin Falls, and we made an excursion to Lake Nipigon—a glorious sheet of water—Returning we found the railroad to Port A[rthur] out of commission owing to a fire, and so we took (chartered) a tug that happened to be there and went by lake. We had a glorious moonlight night. I slept a while in my blankets on deck—but mostly I talked with the captain and helped him find the lights!

On the whole I think the richest experience on the Nipigon was meeting two Buffaloes who said they didn't give a d—n for fishing, but had come expecting to shoot ducks. How any man should have gotten into that forest reserve where fire arms are excluded, and where no one ever saw a duck, under the innocent delusion of these men, I can't see. Fortunately they had a 75 year old man with them whom they called the "kid," and who was a good fly fisherman, as we heard from our guides later. When we met them they were waiting for "the kid" to overtake them at Alexander pool—

On the whole the fishing was a disappointment at the Nipigon—I at least (Van also) couldn't make the big ones rise—nor did I get so many as I should have thought—But we always had trout for the camp and they were the best conditioned beauties I ever saw or expect to see—

On the way from Port Arthur to Duluth we passed almost the whole time along burning shores—The forest fires were very destructive in that region—Our steamer kept her fog horn going constantly.

Well here we are, back at the old stand! And the university about to open up once more—I am 20 pounds lighter & much more muscular. I know the enthusiasm with which you will take hold at Yale. Especially after your Colorado . . . experience with big trout, of which Adams wrote me. Good luck to you—The family all send their warm regards. Dorothy enters the University this week.

Yours

Turner

### *The Move to Harvard*

This account of Turner's canoeing trip reached Max Farrand at Yale, the next station in his career after leaving Stanford. Farrand's impressions of Yale at this time were mixed. He told Turner that he found his colleagues "an extremely likeable set of men," but the library was "badly organized" and "the obstinacy of the Yale tradition" made him uneasy. "But," he added, "I have not yet butted my head into a stone wall—I expect to run around a corner and directly into it almost any time."

Turner, still at Wisconsin, suspected that the time had come for him to move on elsewhere. During 1908 and 1909 it became increasingly clear that the regents were unhappy about the conditions of Turner's employment—conditions which made it possible for him to carry on his research. They were impatient of the arrangement whereby Turner accepted a half-year leave annually in lieu of higher salary. They had little sympathy with Turner's devotion to research, and suggested that such activity indicated a lack of interest in students. On June 19, 1908, at the request of President Van Hise, Turner drafted a report on the students who had worked under him and had won the Justin Winsor Prize, awarded annually by the American Historical Association for the best unpublished monograph in American history. This report was to help the president fight the regents' attack on research in general and, more particularly, on Turner's own scholarly activities. Turner's draft of the report is an extremely detailed document containing an impressive listing of the outstanding scholars who had passed through his seminars at Wisconsin. Here are two portions:

EXTRACTS FROM TURNER'S DRAFT TO PRESIDENT VAN HISE, JUNE 19, 1908

Of course the productive scholars who have worked with me are much more numerous than those in the above list of those who have won the Winsor prize. On the other hand, I would by no means leave you to think that I am conceited enough to believe that the success of these students is exclusively due to their work with me. Other men helped shape their careers, and they had native ability. But I am bold enough to believe that they are products of Wisconsin's emphasis upon research and our excellent library facilities in American history; and that our point of view (sometimes called the "Wisconsin School") of the importance of economic and social factors in American history, and our interest in Western history helped appreciably to shape their monographs.

. . . .

You may be interested in knowing that Professor [George P.] Garrison, head of the history department at Texas University, and author of several books on Western history, wrote in the copy of his "Westward Extension" in the American Nation Series which he sent me, this sentence: "To the master of Western history" &c.

When I regret that I have not published more books, I take some heart from these words, and those of many others, especially of former students of mine who are now pushing forward investigations in American history, and who assure me that my work has been helpful to them. Some of these men, at least, were not aware of my "lack of interest in my students." If I had less interest I should have published more books.

During the same year Turner, at the request of President Van Hise, prepared a progress report on his research. One might suppose that in driving a scholar of Turner's stature thus to defend his academic activities the regents had done their worst. Yet on October 19, 1909, we find him writing the following heartfelt complaint to Farrand: "This year has been a kind of night-mare to me. The thing is likely to clear up soon, I hope and believe; but we have had regents and legislature on our hands in an effort to make over the University on the model of the kind of things each particular tinkerer believed in, and the story is too long to tell now."

Turner's experiences in his last years at Wisconsin seem to have left in him no traces of bitterness, and his subsequent references to Wisconsin are generally marked by pride and affection. In 1909–10 he at last made a decisive break with Wisconsin by accepting a post at Harvard, after declining (as he points out in a memo attached to his own copy of the 1908 report on research projects) an offer from the University of California carrying the unusually high salary of $5,000. In a letter to Farrand of October 28, 1909, Turner described the events leading up to his decision.

EXTRACT FROM TURNER'S LETTER TO MAX FARRAND, OCTOBER 28, 1909

I had been on the edge of accepting a call to U. of California;—in fact, had practically decided to accept, but had not committed myself, when I was asked by Harvard people to delay my decision—The Harvard matter was a surprise to me—I decided that California meant more exploring in new fields and constructing historical clearings and cabins, and that I really ought to settle long enough to raise a crop. For the present, with my long residence and relations to Wisconsin, I did not see how I could do this here; and I felt that I could do the University my best service by accepting a call elsewhere. Not that I could not have continued my semester of research, and even have had a higher salary perhaps, if I would take it. But my own case seemed to be part of a general problem. Some one will find here a great opportunity to use the richest and most workable library of general American history with which I am acquainted for student use; and after I leave, I am sure the regents will be glad to be particularly hospitable to my successor—for they will have learned that too many cooks spoil some broths, anyway.

Turner did not wish his friends to think that he was cutting his connections with the West. As he wrote Carl Becker on January 15, 1910: "Please do not think of me . . . as really dead and buried to the West (sometimes as I have read my mail, I have felt like a ghost caught indecently in pillaging his bodily representative's obituary's notices)." Turner was confident that other capable scholars would carry on the search into America's past: he expresses his belief in the coming generation of historians in a letter to James A. James.

EXTRACT FROM TURNER'S LETTER TO JAMES A. JAMES, JUNE 24, 1910

Indeed, one of the satisfactions I have in changing my residence is that I am not leaving a historical field devoid of explorers—Already you and the group of men about the Middle West are proving the richness of the field and your capacity to deal with it. That I also have been connected with this movement of historical colonization in this fine land, will always be a joy to me, and I think of myself not as having cut myself off from this field, but as getting an objectivity with regard to it, by changing my point of observation, and also as finding an opportunity to report what I see to students who are not so much a part of the movement. These are my consolations for leaving Wisconsin.

Arriving in Cambridge after a brief vacation in the Rangeley Lakes area of Maine, Turner settled down in a luxurious house rented from his Harvard colleague, the historian Roger Bigelow Merriman. In a letter written soon after his arrival to his old friend (and fellow member of Madison's T. and G., or Town and Gown Club), Joseph Jastrow, Wisconsin professor of psychology, Turner gives some of his initial impressions of Harvard. The letter contains a number of references to other close friends in Madison: John William Cunliffe, professor of English; Moses S. Slaughter, professor of Latin; Charles S. Slichter, professor of mathematics; Charles R. Van Hise, president of the University of Wisconsin and author of *The Conservation of Natural Resources in the United States* (New York, 1910); and John Bradley Winslow, chief justice of the Supreme Court of Wisconsin.

TO JOSEPH JASTROW

175 Brattle St
Cambridge, Mass.,
October 5, 1910

Dear Jastrow:

I was heartily glad to get your letter with its report of a fruitful summer and the promise of future crops as well.

We had a delightful three weeks of outing in the Maine woods, as Cunliffe can tell you when he reports to the club how he and I formed the valiant rearguard in attacks upon toll roads and mountain trails north of the Rangeley Lakes. But Cunliffe can't tell you of the fun of troutfishing, and since he will be the reporter, I dare not venture my own stories when I shall not be there to look pained at the remarks of Winslow, who has fished,—in a prosaic way,—himself, and who consequently has judicial doubts on all fishermen's tales.

We only got in three weeks of real outing, for I had to finish a paper in Cambridge during the first part of my escape from summer session and packing before going to the log cabin life.

We are lodged in an old colonial mansion surrounded by the evidences of luxury that my fortunate colleague who rents me his home for a year has been able to gather about him. It gives us time to pick out the quiet spot where we can install such fragments of our own furniture as survived the journey, and it will make a pleasant background for the future of that kind of plain living and healthy pessimism which characterize the lot of the average of us here.

My work begins pleasantly—with a lecture course of about eighty, *net* (i.e. men) and a seminary of ten. The lecture course is largely attended by New England boys, with names that spell eastern conservativism; they are engaging young rascals, and I foresee that I shall have an interesting experience in attempting to guide them over western trails. But there are many western fellows in the class also,—from sons of Seattle sewer contractors to those of railroad magnates and bank presidents.

My immediate task is the writing of the Presidential address for the Indianapolis meeting of the American Historical Association; and I shall be too busy for some months to let the pangs of homesickness get hold of me.

However we find ourselves reading with pride the news of Western "insurgency's" spread into the east, and with apprehension the accounts of La Follette's operation; and with a home feeling the letters that are most welcome from Madison friends.

I attended my first faculty meeting yesterday. It was introduced by *tea* in the president's antechambers. Everybody sat when speaking, and the discussions were conversational and *brief,* though we canvassed such questions as high schools and entrance examinations—a problem of making the way to Harvard more direct (referred to committee); —Radcliffe petitions for college courses; salary payments more frequently than once a quarter; and other topics dear to the professor's heart! Haskins looked very well, high in the ranks of the deans who flanked the president. I rejoiced in the opportunity to keep quiet, no matter what the deans and president wanted. It is a great relief to feel that one's tired right leg can rest with good conscience, even when the overseers and their ideas are mentioned! Just now I feel that I don't want to do anything but learn and teach and do my little stint of writing and read Van Hise's well-muscled book on Conservation which is a mine of good stuff well organized.

I like the men and the place exceedingly in spite of feeling like a visitor and a looker-on for the present.

We have been having a really sultry two or three days, but bright and enjoyable, nevertheless. I got very fit in the woods, and hope to keep my belt at its present hole by walks about the house which is as big as all out doors.

Give my best regards to all the fellows and turn down an empty glass for me—or get Slaughter and Slichter to turn down several till they (the glasses) be empty.

I hope Mrs Jastrow is recovered and I wish you would remember Mrs Turner and myself warmly to her. My wife is unusually well after our summer, and Dorothy is equally in good trim.

Yours cordially
Frederick J. Turner

I attended dinner of the Examiner Club the other day—of which Professor Allen was a charter member.—It was strikingly like the T. and G. in its program. But I think the latter would not suffer when present membership of the two is compared.

### *The American Historical Association Reform Movement*

There was little gaiety or humor in Turner's correspondence of 1915–16 with J. Franklin Jameson concerning the accusations made by Frederic Bancroft and his fellow "reformers" in the American Historical Association. As secretary of the Board of Editors of the *American Historical Review,* Turner could not escape being drawn into the controversy. The following letter argues against an "elaborate refutation" of Bancroft's accusations.

TO J. FRANKLIN JAMESON

Cambridge, Mass.
May 11, 1915

Prof. J. F. Jameson,
1140 Woodward Bldg.,
Washington, D.C.

My dear Jameson:

Replying to your letter of the 10th, I was not made a member of the Board of Editors, as the letter says, in December, 1899, but in December, 1909. This, of course, was a misprint of the typewriter, but conceivably it might make you trouble if left so in your file. I was offered a professorship in Harvard at the time of the inauguration of Mr. Lowell as president, which was in October of 1909; the election by the Corporation was on the 11th of October, 1909, and the matter was publicly announced in the Harvard Bulletin of November 17, 1909; thus the announcement was made prior to the December meeting in New York. Just when my nomination for membership in the Board was arranged I have no means of knowing, nor have I ever had any information on that subject.

I have some doubt to the wisdom of any detailed chronological or other refutation of Mr. Bancroft's proposed theory as to the way in which the board of editors of the Review has been constituted. I cannot see that any possible amount of detailed argumentation will convince those who are not convinced by the character of the men who have been placed on the board. It seems to me that a dignified and civil denial of such animus will be much more effective than an attempted refutation in detail. Of course I do not know anything about what went on in the board in this matter prior to my becoming a member of it, but certainly, so far as I know, the whole association might have been present at our meetings or personal consultations since that time without any reason for taking Mr. Bancroft's point of view. In a word, the only defense that will be effective in my judgment is the character of the men and the universities involved in his charges. The more the charge is given dignity by elaborate refutation, the more weight it may have with the average members of the association. It involves in its essentials an attribution to some of the most devoted scholars of the country of very petty motives for their services to the Association and the Review. If any large number of members of the Association are ready to take this view of ourselves and our colleagues, I shall be surprised. We know that we are neither peanut politicians nor petty grafters. If we proceed to argue it out minutely, we shall not help our cause.

Mr. Bancroft is writing to many people, however, I judge from the fact that I have run across indications of this sort several times in this region. You will find, I think, that he is working on the idea which I heard after the Charleston meeting, that you are the dictator and political boss of the Association and the Review, using the power of patronage through the Review and the Carnegie Institution to weld together an obedient following in shaping the policies of the Association. I am astonished to find that some men whom I had supposed to be better informed and balanced take stock in this report. I do not believe it can have any real influence among those who really know you or who know the men who are under these charges, and particularly I should not suppose that it could be supported by men who have watched the business of the Council, but when a man once gets that kind of small conception of the motives and characters of his associates, you never can tell what construction he may place upon the actions of a body in which he sits. I certainly find it difficult to recognize in either myself or my colleagues the portrait which Mr. Bancroft draws of a group of men seeking to get to the association meetings for nothing, and, at the same time, to profess that their services are for honor rather than for free transportation. Nor have I discovered that we were engaged in Tammany politics. On the whole, it seems to me rather a revelation of the contents of the minds of those who look upon it in this way than a picture of what actually exists; but I repeat, for I think it is important, that if our characters and services on the board and in the council do not convince the Association that these charges are untrue, no amount of elaborate argument will do it.

At present it looks as though I may be able to change my engagement so as to spend Saturday and Sunday, or at any rate Sunday and Monday in Washington at the time of the meeting of the board, but I have important classes on Tuesday morning, so that I must get back in time for a nine o'clock engagement if possible, and absolutely I must be back in time to lecture at noon on Tuesday, the 1st of June. If you would be good enough, if it is possible, to put me up at the Cosmos Club, I should appreciate it. I am leaving here for Wisconsin on the 4th of June and for California from Chicago on the 11th.

Cordially yours,

## *In a Lighter Vein*

The next two letters also stem from Turner's Harvard period. They show that over the years Turner lost none of his modest good humor and certainly none of his good judgment. The first of these letters contains a reference to "Mrs. Max," the former Beatrice Cadwallader Jones, a talented landscape architect whom Farrand married on December 17, 1913.

TO MAX FARRAND

7 Phillips Place
Cambridge, Mass.,
October 29, 1915

Dear Max:

If you expect me in these critical times to miss any opportunity to ingratiate myself with the rising generation, you are mistaken. I am sending you, either by insured parcel post, or by Adams Express prep'd, —I don't know which yet—the largest size photograph in the family gallery. Neither my wife nor Dorothy approve of it. The former cherishes one of the vintage of the nineties, while Dorothy took one with a coldly cynical look, as of one who had just broken a leader on a five pound t—t. This remains, along with one with eyeglasses. If you don't approve of it, send it back, and I will try the eyeglasses on you; or I'll send you a pensive one taken in 1910; or I'll try an old age sitting.

I am well aware that somewhere, in one of your bachelor waste paperbaskets, perhaps,—there is already a neglected Turner; but I forgive you.

With my kindest regards to Mrs. Max, am I

Yours sincerely
Frederick J. Turner

P.S. The possibility that you are collecting a rogues' gallery doesn't scare me, for I have grown older since this was taken in 1913 or 14; and I shall escape—My pack man from Tuolumne meadows to Yosemite told Slaughter on his return to camp that "the old man" got to the top of Clouds' Rest on his own legs—so I *know* the truth.
To Professor Max Farrand
Collector

Edmond S. Meany, the recipient of the following letter, had studied under Turner. Now a professor at the University of Washington in Seattle, Meany had written to Turner about *The Education of Henry Adams,* suggesting that perhaps Turner might have some illuminating insights into the book and its author. Here is Turner's answer.

TO EDMOND S. MEANY

7 Phillips Place
Cambridge, Massachusetts
January 11, 1919

Dear Meany

I have no "master word" on Henry Adams, except that he was an Adams. Once I heard old Professor Adams Hill at a club telling of how he had entered a smoking car and heard someone using violent profanity. "As I went forward" he said, "It was such picturesque profanity that I knew it must come from an Adams, and when I got nearer I recognized that the cusser was not even swearing at a mark; just swearing by and large, and then I knew it was Brooks Adams."

If you read C. F. Adams' *Autobiography* you will see that pessimism is a family trait of all three brothers; and after reading J. Q. Adams' *Memoirs* you will also suspect that it came down from their grandfather, of whom Emerson wrote in his Journal (1843) "He is no literary old gentleman, but a bruiser and loves the melee . . . an old roue who cannot live on slops, but must have sulphuric acid in his tea." Of course, J. Q.'s swearing was probably not literal but an attitude of mind.

It's a New England attitude of mind also, tho' the Adamses raised it to a high power. "The same *healthy spirit of pessimism* in the yard," which a returning alumnus found at Harvard. There is a love of the whimsical, of the clever thrust, the ironic and cynical, in your unadulterated Bostonian Yankee. He must be original and speak from a higher altitude toward his fellows: idiosyncrasy is an essential element of distinction here.

At the same time this elite Yankee shouldn't be taken too seriously, for he doesn't take himself so seriously as you are taking Henry Adams in his comments. Charles Francis Adams once read to a group of historians a letter from Henry (then in France) after Wilson's first election, in which he declared: "The Country has gone to Hell and it will never come back," and C. F. A. chuckled with delight; but both only half believed it, of course.

Henry Adams, nevertheless, (while a prickly, hedgehoggy* outside protected him from people he didn't care to bother with), was a

* [Turner's asterick and note:] The "Porcupinus Angelicus" of John Hay.

lovable personality to those to whom he extended the hospitality of his home and his mind. I have had two or three delightful visits there. But he was intellectually dyspeptic, and somewhat disappointed.

Don't take his account of Harvard as a historically accurate portrait: it is rather a cartoon by a brilliant critic of Harvard's imperfections, and, in that respect truthful and helpful. Later (when it is printed) I will send you some appreciations of his work as history teacher by men who were his pupils. He left a profound impression upon able men who have since become among the leaders in history and politics—men like Taylor (Medieval Mind), Channing, Emerton, Lodge,—and Roosevelt, if I recall rightly.

His attitude helped save history teaching from being pedagogic, uninspiring, unrelated to the criticism of life.

*N.B.* This letter is just kindling for the "friendship fire"—don't print it!

Henry Adams was the leader of American historians in his day. His Education is a literary classic, an illumination and a tonic stimulant—but not normally American.

Cordially yours—and dogmatically!
Frederick J. Turner

### *An Autobiographical Letter*

One of the most interesting of Turner's letters as far as autobiographical material is concerned was written to the New York writer, Constance Lindsay Skinner, who on February 25, 1922, had asked Turner's permission to reprint portions of his 1893 essay in an anthology of "frontier material" she was preparing for juveniles. Turner gave his approval on March 6, and she responded with another request on March 15: "Will you very kindly send me a brief biography of yourself chiefly relating your connection with frontier and Backwoods literature & history in both books and college. I want to use it in my introductory note to your selection with which I plan, at present any way, to open the volume."

Turner, flattered by the enthusiastic reviews she was giving his *The Frontier in American History* in literary magazines and New York newspapers, was pleased to comply. The following letter, a twenty-three-page handwritten manuscript, is given in full. It was published with omissions and errors in the *Wisconsin Magazine of History, 19* (September 1935), 91–103.

The *Wisconsin Magazine of History* version of the letter leaves out (without indicating a deletion) Turner's references to two foreign publications that briefly summarize his work and its significance. Ernst Daenell, of the University of Kiel, in his article "The Literature of the United States" in (*Germanische-Romanische Monatsschrift,* Vol. IV [Heidelberg, 1912]) included a brief but favorable account of Turner's work, describing him as a "pioneer" in Western history. Turner also suggested that Miss Skinner consult a book by the Dutch historian Johan Huizinga, *Mensch en Menigte in Amerika, Vier Essays over moderne Beschavingsgeschiedenis* (Haarlem, 1918), which described him as a leading contemporary historian of America. Turner was particularly pleased at the recognition foreigners were giving to his work, and when Huizinga sent him an autographed copy of the above work (Huntington Library Rare Book, 126360), he wrote in the flyleaf: "An interesting indication of method & attempt of a foreigner to comprehend Am. at present by its origins—spiritual as well as material."

TO CONSTANCE LINDSAY SKINNER

Frederick J. Turner
7 Phillips Place
Cambridge 38 Mass.
March 15, 1922.

My dear Miss Skinner:

I'm afraid I'm not equal to a brief *biography* of myself and my connection with Western history. You will probably find what you need —and a lot more—in these references:—

"Who's Who," preferably the edition for 1922 to appear this spring.

General comments. National Cyclopedia of American Biography

Harvard Bulletin XII. No. 7. Nov. 17, 1909.

World's Work, July 1902, p. 2326.

Encyclopedia Americana, 19th edition, s.v.
"History" pp. 248, 249, 253 (col. 1), 256 (col. 1)
Pol. Science Quarterly, Dec. 1921, xxxvi, 574, 584.
Daenell in Germanische–Romanische Monatsschrift, 1912, p. 348 (Kiel)
Huizinga, Mensch en Menigte in America, 144

*Bibliographies* have been published in the Johns Hopkins University list of publications by their Ph.D's, edited by J. M. Vincent—not up to date. The list is rather too long for your use. Perhaps my "Frontier in Am. Hist." "New West" and the reference to indexes of Am. Hist. "Review" and Am. Hist. Association for collected docts & articles would do for the western end of it. But there is a western interpretation also in my article on U.S. since 1865, in the Encyclopedia Britannica, (1911), and in my part of the Guide to Am. History, 1912, by Channing, Hart, and Turner. I did the revision of western data, and the period since 1865. Also my articles on "Frontier," "Sectionalism" and "Western Politics" in McLaughlin & Hart's *Cyclopedia of Government,* embody western studies. My List of References in the History of the West (revised edition, Harvard University Press) might be mentioned. It indicates a scheme of study, with books, etc. In the Am. Antiquarian Society *Proceedings,* Oct. 1919, XXIX, I published an article on "Greater New England in the Middle of the Nineteenth Century"—devoted to an estimate of the amount of the Yankee element in the West about 1850, and the reactive effects in New Engl.

I have given much attention to Western history, but rather as a process in American development in general, than as a region in itself. My early training was in medieval history, and the aspects of social and economic developments and expansions in that formative age, I probably carried over into my conceptions of how American history should be viewed—older society developing in or adjacent to the wilderness. A thesis in my junior year in the University of Wisconsin on the Fur Trade in Wisconsin which was substantially like my doctoral dissertation in the Johns Hopkins University (Studies vol. IX 1891) indicates an interest in the frontier as a factor in American history and in the social and economic background, or foundations. The address on the "Significance of the Frontier" was preceded by a paper 1892 on Problems in American History, (cited in my book p. 1). But I had already published a little pamphlet of a few pages, "Outline Studies in the History of the Northwest" (Charles H. Kerr & Co. Chicago) in 1888.

This was a slight syllabus for club studies. In the Chicago "Dial," I reviewed the first volumes of Roosevelt's Winning of the West, in August 1889, and suggested a different point of view for approaching the subject, and the need of a history of the continuous progress of civilization across the continent. The Frontier paper was a programme, and in some degree a protest against eastern neglect, at the time, of institutional study of the West, and against western antiquarian spirit in dealing with their own history.

The paper was regarded as a "curious" view by Edward Everett Hale, and some other correspondents; but John Fiske wrote me on February 6, 1894 (see his Old Virginia, 1897, II Chap XV, p 270 for the influence) that he was working toward the same perspective, and called the essay "admirable," so I "had faith in Massachusetts!"—remembering also Parkman and Winsor and Roosevelt, all of Harvard training, —though I wasn't a disciple of Harvard at the time, by any means.

The Frontier paper made an appeal, oddly perhaps, to the editor of the International Socialist Review, of Chicago, which republished it shortly after (vol. VI, 321), and to the "educators," especially to the Herbart Society, which republished it, with some additional matter by me, in the Fifth Year Book of the National Herbart Society; and to the economists (republished in Bullock's "Readings in Economics," and in Marshall's (Univ. of Chicago) volume of similar selections, etc.

In the form of the "Problems of the West," restating many of the Frontier paper's interpretations, it was refused by Mr. Horace Scudder, of the Atlantic, but in 1896 at the request for an article by the late Walter Page, then the editor, I adjusted the paper to the Bryan campaign and he accepted it.

Meantime out of a course on "The Economic and Social History of the U.S." (treating different periods, in different years) I evolved the course in the History of the West, the first, I think, in the country. It seemed to "take"; and now something like half the states have such a college course, and many of the leading universities, east and west, include it in their curriculum. A considerable portion of the instructors were trained in my seminary.

In studying our social and economic development, and the frontier advance, I saw at once, that the frontier passed into successive and varied regions, and that new sections evolved in the relations between these geographic regions, and the kinds of people and society which entered them and adjusted to the environment; and that these sections interplayed with each other and reacted on the old East and on the nation, in economic life, political forms and legislation, and in social results and ideals as expressed in education, literature, religion, etc. In short, the national spirit,—Uncle Sam's psychology,—was a complex, due to a federation of Sections. Behind the apparent state and nation type of federation lay the federation of sections, explaining manifestations of so-called State sovereignty, which are, more deeply, manifestations of sectional differences. This I had suggested in the paper on "Problems *in Am. History,*" already referred to, and in the Herbart Society version of my "Frontier."

I have kept at work on this companion piece to my Frontier in various regional or sectional studies, and quite a literature has resulted. See A. W. Small (Univ. of Chicago) *General Sociology,* 282–3 note. C. A. Beard, *Economic Interpretation of the Constitution,* F. J. Turner, "Sectionalism in the United States," in McLaughlin and Hart's Cyclopedia of Am. Government, and ibid, Geographic Influences in American Political History, abstract, in Bulletin of the Am. Geographical Society XLVI, 591. See also Barnes (Clark Univ) in Encyclopedia Americana (19th ed.) s.v. "History" 256, and especially his article in Journal of Geography, May, 1921, vol. XX, p. 199, and p. 330 (Dec. 1921).

The importance of regional geography in Am. History is also emphasized in my *Rise of the New West,* and in my forthcoming book on the *U. S. and its Sections* 1830–50; and I have quite a mass of yet unpublished material on the subject, besides the chapters dealing with sections in my *Frontier* book.

I am emphasizing it, because along with my *Frontier* interpretation, I should wish to be thought of in connection with investigations into *Sections,* as a means of understanding America. Not merely North and South, and East and West, but the many inter- and intra-state sections. From another angle, my frontier studies emphasized the amount of unworked material on the influence of the frontier upon *foreign relations.* I found it necessary to go behind the diplomat and the treaties of annexation to the frontier forces and sectional interests. Such studies as my articles in the American Historical Review on French Policy (AHR. X, 249) and Atlantic, XCIII, 676, 807, illustrate this interest. I have published a lot of documentary material on foreign relations, (with introductions and editorial work), from archives in this country, France, England and Spain, on the period of the administrations of Washington and Adams. These can be reached by the index volumes to *Amer. Hist. Review,* and Am. Hist. Assoc. *Reports,* including the Reports for 1896, 1897 and 1903, II.—See H. J. Ford, in *Chronicles.* Similarly the evolution of *Government* on the Frontier interested me, and my papers in Am. Hist. Review, I on "State-Making in the West in the Rev. Era" are illustrations of this kind of study.

So far my interest in *agriculture* and rural life has been more in evidence through the work of students like Taylor, Hibbard, Colter, Trimble, Stine and Nils Olsen and others (who also reflect the influence of my colleague, Dr. Ely). My interest in *Lands* likewise has rather stimulated studies by R. G. Wellington (Political and Sectional Influence of the Public Lands 1828–1842. Boston (1914); Geo. M. Stephenson (Political History of the Public Lands, 1840–1862 (Boston 1917); Miss A. C. Ford, Colonial Precedents of our National Land System (Madison 1910) and (in part) John Ise, Forest Policy, and other students than printed in my own publication. These, except Ise's, were theses under my direction, suggested and worked out in my seminary.

My interest in the *Indian,* helped (along with Dr. Thwaites' influence) to produce Miss Helen Blair's *Indian Tribes of the Upper Miss. Valley* (Cleveland, 1911) which she dedicated to me.

The theme of discovery and the conception of the "Old West," influenced C. W. Alvord and Lee Bidgood in writing their *First Alleghany Explorations;* and Archibald Henderson, *Conquest of the Southwest.* The conception of persistence of meaning, in American life, of the frontier ideals influenced Guy Emerson in his *New Frontier.* With the exception of the last named the books in this paragraph were also dedicated to me, as was also the volume, *Essays in American History dedicated to Frederick Jackson Turner* (N.Y. 1910). They help explain how the life of the teacher of graduate students checks his own historical output, but furnishes compensations. The above are rather illustrative *types,* (and especially those related to my frontier interests), than complete statements of this side of my work. Since coming to Massachusetts the material available has tended to turn my seminary candidates for the doctorate rather to Mass. political history, but with emphasis upon economic and social *interpretations* of politics.

This is an outrageous kind of answer to your letter. But if you live through it, you will see that there is not the desire to exploit myself, but to give you a point of view in connection with my work—and a *point* can be reduced to the size of your pencil tip.

I was, as an undergraduate in Madison, given the freedom of the

Draper Collection (with limitations! I had only a third of one year in Am. History) and the other western manuscripts of the State Historical Society; and I enjoyed the friendship of Draper and my colleague, Thwaites at the same time that I was trained in European institutional history by Professor William F. Allen (A.M. Harvard), who taught me ideals of scholarship even if he never made me the exact and critical scholar which he was himself. These two things reacted upon each other in my mind, especially the Medieval History and the manuscripts of Western History. I saw American history somewhat differently than it was presented in the books I read. I was for a year a graduate student in Johns Hopkins, where Herbert Adams and R. T. Ely had an inspiring influence upon ambitious students, and where Woodrow Wilson gave a special lecture course. (See Dodd's *Wilson,* p. 20 (but I was not a fellow student, only a member of W's courses in Government)—and see *pp. 27–28 especially;* also Wilson's comments on my "West as a Field for Historical Study" (Am. Hist. Asso. Report, 1896, I). Wilson emphasized the neglect of the sympathetic study of the South, and I that of the West, in our conversations.

When I came back to Wisconsin I started a formal seminary in the library of the State Historical Society of Wisconsin, and began to study, by periods, the social foundations of American history. The Frontier and the Section were aspects of these interests. I recognized them as *parts* of Am. history—*only* parts, but very important ones. However, I have not conceived of myself as the student of a region, or of any particularly exclusive "key" to American history. I have tried to make some changes in the perspective, and as a pioneer, with others, I have found it necessary to talk a good deal upon these aspects. But it is in *American processes* I have been interested.

I began my publication when Roosevelt and Winsor were active, and my colleague, Thwaites soon took up his editorial work. Roosevelt, though with a breadth of interests, was more concerned with *men* than with *institutions,* and especially with the strenuous life, and more particularly, the fighting of the frontier. Winsor approached the West as a cartographer and librarian. Thwaites' instincts were toward the romantic side, and toward editorial publication.

The West appealed to me as *a factor* in interpreting American history and the life, ideals and problems of the present. And the West meant also various *sections* with their reactions. While the *great shadow* of the slavery struggle still cast itself over history-writing, even in the works of Rhodes and Von Holst, and while the epic period of the West fascinated Roosevelt, Winsor and Thwaites, I was trying to see it as a whole,—on its institutional, social, economic, and political side, its effects upon the nation as a whole, and I saw that there was a persistent pervasive influence in American life, which did not get its full attention from those who thought in terms of North and South, as well as from those who approached the West as fighting ground, or ground for exploration history. This was my opportunity. I was interested in economics, as well as in institutional history, and I soon (though an instructor) went into the Geological course (physiography) of Professor Van Hise, and tried to get a scientific geographical foundation.

I spent my youth in a newspaper office in contact with practical politics, and in a little town at "The Portage," Wis. over which Marquette had passed. There were still Indian (Winnebago) tepees where I hunted and fished, and Indians came in to the stores to buy paints and trinkets and sell furs. Their Indian ponies and dogs were familiar street scenes. The town was a mixture of raftsmen from the "pineries" —(the "Pinery road" ran by my door), of Irish (in the "bloody first" ward), Pomeranian immigrants (we stoned each other), in old country garbs, driving their cows to their own "Common"; of Scotch, with "Caledonia" near by; of Welsh (with "Cambria" adjacent); with Germans, some of them university-trained (the Bierhalle of Carl Haertel was the town club house); of Yankees from Vermont and Maine and Conn. chiefly, of "New York-Yankees," of southerners (a few relatively); a few negroes; many Norwegians and Swiss, some Englishmen, and one or two Italians. As the local editor and leader of his party, my father reported the community life, the problems of the farmer, the local news, (which I helped to "set up"), went as delegate to state and national Republican conventions, assigned the candidates of his party to the varied nativities and towns of the county, as chairman of the Board of Supervisors, harmonized the rival tongues and interests of the various towns of the county, and helped to shepherd a very composite flock. My school fellows were from all these varied classes and nationalities, and we all "got on together" in this forming society. Occasionally some fortunate youth went out to

Montana or Colorado and returned to tell of mines and ranches. I rode on the first railroad into the pine forests of northern Wisconsin and fished along rivers and lakes in the virgin pine woods, where French names made real the earlier frontier, and followed Indian trails.

Is it strange that I saw the frontier as a real thing and experienced its changes? My people were pioneers from the beginning of the seventeenth century—though they did not go back to Scotch or Irish moors and highlands! One of my ancestors was the Rev. Thomas Hanford who early went to the frontier town of Norwalk, Conn. His parishioners complained that he called them "Indian Devils"—a horrid thing to the Puritan pioneer. But Cotton Mather tells us that what he really said was that "Every *Individual* is in danger of Hell fire," and having defective teeth, he had been misunderstood. My people on both sides moved at least every generation, and built new communities—from Conn. to central and western Mass., to Vermont, to the Adirondacks, to the Dela Valley in N. Y. and to western N.Y. to Mich. and Wisconsin, and others of the family to Nebraska and to Alaska. My father was named Andrew Jackson Turner at his birth in 1832 by my Democratic grandfather, and I still rise and go to bed to the striking of the old clock that was brought into the house the day that he was born, at the edge of the Adirondack forest. My mother's ancestors were preachers! *Is it* strange that I preached of the frontier?

Very sincerely and apologetically yours,
Frederick J. Turner

P.S. Of course this is for your personal information and not for publication. Don't smile, please—

## *The Huntington Library Years*

Three years after his retirement from Harvard in 1924 Turner accepted an invitation from his friend, Max Farrand, to become a research associate of the Huntington Library in Southern California. The last two letters in this group were written to Farrand in 1927 at the start of this final and very happy period of Turner's life. The friend referred to in the first letter, Carl C. Thomas, was an engineer and former Wisconsin faculty member. Robert A. Millikan, to whom Turner reports being introduced, was a Nobel Prize–winning physicist.

TO MAX FARRAND

1111 Harvard Avenue
Claremont, California
March 1 1927

Dear Max:

I had just written my postal of rejoicing over the Huntington announcement in the Los Angeles Times when in came your letter, giving the inside facts.

I am truly happy over it all. We came west via Los Angeles, San Antonio, Tucson, and Pasadena, stopping a week or so at each place en route. Otherwise I might have had the fun of seeing you at the Huntington Library or the Tech. We visited old friends of ours, the Carl C. Thomases, in Pasadena, over week end, and he took us out to these centers, where I met Mr. Millikan, a delightful man as well as a great man. I had only time to see the setting of the Library and to do an airplane (*qua si*) inspection of its contents. I could see the truth of what you had said and now say about the need of developing it into a well rounded institution for researchers whose interests are not primarily in the collection of Americana, but you can do this, and you will have a career as the organizer and leader of a new center for scholars in this wonderful land that has already produced such notable results in science and will in art, as well as the humanities in general. You could have no wiser and keener critical and sympathetic advisers among the Harvard group than those you consulted.

Even if you can at first only gather for part of the year the men who wish to carry on research in the splendid field you have chosen; with opportunity to supplement Huntington resources by a travelling fund to gather from the resources of other libraries, you will make it one of the notable centers of the nation for scholarly research in contrast with machine production of masses of students—often reluctant material! What Gilman did for Johns Hopkins you have the opportunity to do for this center.

There is vitality, vigor, initiative in the men out here, and already I have profited in my own health and spirits by the sojourn which my medical advisors thought helpful, though not necessary, for me. I shall take my way back to our bungalow at the close of this month with a real elation over the way I expect to see this land and its people affect the United States. Even the fierce beauty and solemnity of the desert fascinated my wife as well as myself, as it had done two years ago in Utah.

We have fallen into a delightful *casita* and charming garden, which Mrs. Watkins has evolved from the rocky soil here and which Mrs. Farrand ought to see as an example of what a loving amateur can do. Perhaps she would not find it "right," but at any rate she would love the orange trees, the palms, the humming birds and mocking birds, the balmy air and Old Baldy and his footmen showing snowy tops across these vales and cañons. But I shall get cacophonic if I don't stop!

Thank you for telling me of the solution, and let a mere nomad welcome you back to California and wish you the best of good fortune. We return by U.P. to renew our acquaintance with our inter mountain friends—Lots of good stuff among these men and women too, awaiting only leadership and a chance!

We change in a week or two to some other location but will leave forwarding order, and, anyway, if you are too busy to do more than drop my *paean* in the waste basket, I shall hope to shake hands with you and your wife next summer in Maine—a land of charm too! Life is good to us in offering these delectable pieces of nature's handiwork.

Mae joins me in a vote of confidence and warmest good wishes to both of you.

Yours as ever
Frederick J. Turner

After getting better acquainted with the resources of the Huntington Library, Turner wrote again to Farrand, who was in the East terminating his work as director of the Commonwealth Fund of New York. Turner mentioned his talks with President James A. Blaisdell and Dean Ernest James Jaqua of Pomona College, and the possibility of a temporary or permanent post at Pomona. He had also met George Ellery Hale, astronomer and Huntington Library trustee, and the founder of the library, Henry Edwards Huntington.

TO MAX FARRAND

*Unofficial!*

408 South Orange Grove Avenue
Pasadena, California
March 19, 1927

Dear Max,

I have been here now nearly a week getting generally acquainted with the Library. Monday, the 21st, we move to a bungalow, Suite 5,

"Court of the Oak," 1067 San Pasqual Ave., Pasadena, to be within more possible reach of the Library. I shall not impose my impressions upon you in your present Commonwealth rush, except to say that I have read your admirable Report, and agree with it. The more I sample the Library, the more I am astonished and delighted at its riches in many fields—

When I wrote my letter regarding the financial aspects, I talked out louder than was perhaps wise in view of the distances that separated us. I had had conversations with intermediate persons, including some purely tentative enquiries from President Blaisdell and Dean Jaqua of Pomona (Claremont) College regarding *possible* future temporary or continuous location in this delectable land; and I suppose that the combination of climate, recuperation, possible alternatives, cost of living, &c, got so jumbled up in my letter that you must have been in doubt about what it all meant!

I have at your invitation, received and accepted an appointment by the Trustees at $500 for a month as Research Associate. The future is left unsettled, of course. The financial ruminations reflected my impressions as to probable *total* income needed for living in Pasadena, including the retiring allowance from the Carnegie Foundation. This would go on. I have little other income, unlike professors "on leave."

Next winter would better be settled after I have more fully discovered how far my own special work is consistent with being in residence at the Huntington; what *kind of* service would be expected of me as Associate, what I find with regard to the feasibility of housing, transportation etc. within reach of the Library, without an automobile (which I neither own nor drive!). When we meet in Maine we can better take this side of the matter up, *if such a delay is not incompatible with your plans*. If it is, be perfectly frank and let me know. You have a free hand. I do not feel now that I know just what is expected of me if I became an Associate next winter. If I should be expected to spend the winter chiefly in exploring the Library, or in laying aside my existing work—(to complete which I am under obligation)—in order to do definite research in some other field in some one of the many rich collections in the Huntington, I should doubt the wisdom of my undertaking the appointment. On the other hand I have no desire to use Huntington funds for my own advantage and thereby to limit their usefulness by application to other appointees who might better fit—all this in spite of the fact that I need both California and income! and that I rate companionship with you even more highly than you do with me. So I wish to know as concretely as possible before settling matters, just "what I am here for," in the words of the . . . ,* and what would be expected in the matter of service in the Library; hours, &c. Also I ought to test out my fitness in the matter of health, both for your sake and mine, before a final decision is made by either of us as to next year. I am much more fit here, but not yet what I would wish.

I have the feeling that the wealth of mediaeval and early modern English material, of which the MS. part is at present unorganized and really unknown in any detail, would make it highly important, both for the Library and for information of American scholars and even for those of Europe to have Haskins here long enough to form impressions of it, and for the Library to have a sufficient force to protect it against the ravages of time, or loss.

In the matter of American material I am coming to the opinion that the most serious gap is in the Congressional Public Docs—The problem of running from the Huntington to Los Angeles, and to remoter centers, to get such things is a matter that needs conference if the goal of your report is ever ultimately to be reached, and if the modern conceptions of what American history should be, are to be worked at *in loco;* for your *fields* all run together in a history of Anglo-American civilization.

At worst, the Library and its allied art collections, grounds, etc. constitute a new and wonderful center of civilization in this country. Treasures of the Old World in books & pictures and mss. are set here in an inspiring landscape, and no American scholar of real quality will know what his country offers without visiting the Huntington Library, even as it stands.

How your project as set forth in your Report can be made possible in view of physical conditions regarding residence, transportation, the widening of the collections into less noble but essential books, is one of your problems—involving questions of funds, of *possibility* of acquisition of needed sets, of new building to meet expansion, &c

I have met Mr. Huntington in his home, very pleasantly, and Dr. Hale is an inspiration whenever I see and hear him.

Regards

Yours sincerely
Frederick J Turner

* Illegible name.

# 3

# Turner's Educational Concerns

## *Introduction*

Carl Becker, in an essay on Turner as teacher, writes of Turner's "unusual ability to look on the wide world in a humane friendly way, in a fresh and strictly independent way, with a vision unobscured by academic inhibitions."* The open-eyed unprejudiced quality of Turner's judgments, his lively concern for the people around him, help explain why so many of his students and associates placed such a high value on his advice.

Turner's active interest in education is evident in letters written during his time as a student at Johns Hopkins. Weighing the advantages and disadvantages of the methods used at Johns Hopkins and at the University of Wisconsin, he comes to the conclusion that the Wisconsin method of assigning topics for study was especially appropriate for advanced students, whereas the lecture-textbook approach used at Johns Hopkins was more suitable for less mature, less independent students.

Late in Turner's life the same concern for education and the same quality of unblinkered rationality illuminate his letters. Thus he welcomed Harvard's decision not to require the M.A. as a prerequisite for the doctor's degree. For while no one was more vigilant in protecting university standards than Turner, he cared little for regulations that placed useless obstacles in the way of doctoral candidates. With obvious pleasure Turner tells Farrand that Wisconsin was ahead of Harvard in adopting a similar ruling (Turner to Farrand, Jan. 8, 1931).

Turner's lifelong interest in education was not limited to the training of practitioners in his own field, nor was his interest sim-

* "Frederick Jackson Turner," in *American Masters of Social Science,* ed. by Howard W. Odum (New York, 1927), p. 295.

ply passive. The letters that follow show him, from the beginning of his career on into his later years, working to improve the cultural level of both the community and the country.

Other letters show Turner's great concern with the quality of university education: for instance, he wanted his students to study from original rather than secondary materials and to have rigorous training in foreign languages. Turner vigorously opposed attempts to lower university standards for the convenience of the professional schools. His battle for official recognition of the need for time and facilities for research has been referred to in the first portion of this book. He was particularly disturbed by the regents' interference in academic affairs. In a letter to Max Farrand of June 21, 1908, he comments: "We have had to fight here for keeping the College of Letters & Science the central thing in the University. Some of the regents wanted to push research in Engineering and Agriculture, but wished to back water on this tendency in L&S. Van Hise defeated the move for the present at least, and he thinks, permanently."

Turner's letters of 1908–10 show that he had grave doubts about the possibility of upholding standards of excellence in a state university. He was alarmed by the tendency to push practical at the expense of theoretical disciplines. A narrow, vocationally oriented educational policy would inhibit a faculty, already overloaded with classes, from carrying on what Turner saw as the first responsibility of the scholar—research.

An intriguing portion of Turner's correspondence deals with his views on the relative importance of research and teaching. He was, of course, convinced of the importance of an educated populace, and particularly of a populace well-informed about its own past. But what really fascinated Turner was historical scholarship carried along scientific lines: his own studies were to add to the foundations of this new kind of history, and he was interested in training others to be competent, reliable scientific workers, capable of continuing the work of historical research. Thus in one of his early letters (Oct. 31, 1888, to Professor Allen) we see that it is the advanced seminars that catch his enthusiasm, ones that produce "new and valuable contributions to science." The particular skills which a historian must have in order to make such contributions are discussed by Turner in a letter of 1921 to his student Arthur H. Buffinton. In the letter to Farrand of June 21, 1908, he expresses great interest in the idea of a university for advanced students: "What do you think of Jordan's* plan for a University that shall eliminate the junior college? Can it become a center of graduate students? The proposition for such a university is very interesting, and is in line with what I have long believed desirable. I think it was helpful to J[ohns] H[opkins] U[niversity] on the higher side of education."

Turner's reaction, on the other hand, to a suggested résumé of American history for public school children was, for him, unusually abrupt. Such a course would not encourage the "historical mindedness" that comes from "fuller contact with historical problems, processes and *methods of study*" (Turner to Arthur M. Schlesinger, Oct. 22, 1922). The general public, Turner believed, would benefit from university extension lectures if the speakers were recruited from an "intellectual clearing house" such as Johns Hopkins. In a letter of January 18, 1892, Turner reported to Herbert Adams on the heavy schedule of extension work he was carrying in addition to his regular Wisconsin classes and seminars: "I am fairly well satisfied with the success of my extension work, for I shall have given seven courses of six lectures each in as many places, before the close of the season. In one little community of six hundred inhabitants—farmers, etc.—I have an audience of over two hundred people."

Thus Turner's concern with education at the most advanced levels—the training of doctoral candidates and the self-education of mature scholars—did not prevent him from concerning himself with education at all levels. He went so far as to urge one of his former students, James A. James, in a letter of January 21, 1894, seriously to consider accepting the presidency of a new normal

* David Starr Jordan, President of Stanford.

school. He believed that a connection should be established between the university and the normal schools, which might result in a "more inspiring and scientific body of teachers":

the main thing was to get a man who possessed not only Normal School training, and knowledge of pedagogic ideals, but also a man who would add University breadth of culture, and the inspiration of University ideals—The Normal Schools have been in the past prone to a mechanical view of the teacher's art. They must in the future partake more and more of University spirit, by the infusion of University men and methods into them. They have an academic as well as a normal school function. They ought to be feeders to the University, and the transition should be natural and harmonious. If we could thus affiliate our normal schools to the University, and assist in supplying their teachers, there would be a gain in the community, to the school, and to the University and the State. Above all a more inspiring and scientific body of teachers would be produced.

Some years later, in 1921, when his teaching career was near its end, we find Turner writing to Farrand (the letter is included in this group) in evident excitement, drawing the attention of his old friend to an article in the *Atlantic Monthly* concerning the need to educate people for leisure in an industrial society.

Turner's view of his profession and of his own obligations as a professional historian gradually led him to a degree of disenchantment over the possibilities of working effectively within the confines of the university. The "American practice," he wrote Merle Curti on October 12, 1921, "doesn't recognize the usefulness of leisure in the production of scholars." Committee work, administrative duties, classroom lectures, and student conferences were among the "wildcats" that lapped up the limited supply of energy possessed by the average instructor. Little vitality remained for what Turner called "productive scholarship."

Turner, writing to Woodrow Wilson in December of 1896, was pessimistic about the ability of American universities to provide the nation with the leadership it required: "the prospect of most of them is not bright . . . ." Turner's comments on his colleagues were usually generous, so that the critical note here is surprising. However the leadership potential of students and colleagues was something Turner usually ignored. For the most part he was concerned with their professional capacities, and favorable judgments on their professional competence did not preclude doubts in a wider context.

Occasionally in Turner's letters we find the suggestion that there may be better places for the scholar than the university. In a letter to Max Farrand of February 13, 1919 (a portion of which appears in this group of letters), Turner calls attention to the foundation of new organizations outside the universities that may be of interest to the academician. Almost a decade later he comes back to the same point (Turner to Farrand, March 8, 1927): "Merk or (and?) Schlesinger of Harvard have great promise as researchers and interpreters.—Oh, a lot of men, if they could be furnished means to break away for at least part of the time from college and university routine. Sometimes I think that the Universities are sapping the energies of such men and that private foundations offer the real hope of scholarly productiveness." Viewed in the light of these remarks, Turner's moves from Wisconsin to Harvard and to the Huntington Library evidence a certain pattern: far from being merely progressive steps in a successful career, Turner's progress may be interpreted as a movement from a university hostile to research in his field to one sympathetic, and from there to his final position in an institution set up for that very purpose.

Turner's beliefs about the central position of research in the historical heavens also helps us to understand his almost religious attitude towards university libraries. They were the very lifeblood of his profession, indispensable for the research that he believed to be the most important function of historical scholarship. Without excellent library facilities there could be no genuine professional training for future workers in the field. Turner felt that the exploration of the past need not be haphazard, subjective; through an intelligent use of original sources, historical reconstruction could be given an authority that the more subjective, narrative history prevalent up until Turner's time had perhaps lacked. Modern historical research must be based upon research in a well-equipped library, rich in areas such as economics and geography as well as history.

Turner's letters tell us that he was also attracted to libraries with abundant source materials. He was excited by discovering "treasures" or "unique material" at the Wisconsin State Historical Society, the Library of Congress, or, in later years, at the Huntington Library. While at Harvard he urged that the library install a photocopying machine so that copies of rare materials would be available for research purposes (Turner to Archibald C. Coolidge, March 26, 1914). Yet it was not only rarities that Turner prized. A good reference library had to include standard books and journals in the humanities and the social sciences. Turner also depended heavily upon published documents. Institutions otherwise attractive sometimes failed to meet Turner's high standards on these points. A cursory examination of the Huntington Library in the spring of 1927, for instance, left Turner uncertain as to whether it would be adequate for his own investigations or for those of other scholars (Turner to Farrand, March 8, 1927): "I could probably work profitably at the completion of my MS. 1830–1850 for one winter, tho' my impression to date . . . is that I should be handicapped by lack of congressional documents, state docs. &c news paper files, etc. which have hitherto been available to me." Turner therefore suggested that provision be made for Huntington Library scholars to visit other libraries: "I can see that trustees, & Mr. Huntington might be sensitive to such a proposal . . . . We both see that history is no longer the narrative collection by placer-mining, but involves the use of wide agencies more like the chemical laboratories . . . quartz crushers, etc. The library extended into economic, social, literary, political, religious resources, becomes necessary to the modern type of historian of the evolution of civilization. This is our sun and stars and planets." The standards set by Turner for university and research libraries were very high indeed. Little wonder that Turner carefully inquired into the library facilities of the universities from which he received offers of positions.

A good library, then, is an essential tool of the professional historian. Turner also regarded libraries as immensely important for the education of the wider public; they were, therefore, essential to the healthy development of democracy itself. Writing to Herbert B. Adams on September 27, 1890 (the letter is included in this group), Turner urged his former teacher to stress in a forthcoming talk before members of the Wisconsin State Historical Society the high purpose served by the Society's library in the training of teachers: "The thing that is needed is a utilization of the resources of the State Hist. Library to *fertilize* and *spiritualize* the system." These were lofty aims. But Turner was convinced that the historical library had an essential part to play in the intellectual life of the state.

Therefore libraries—especially large regional American libraries, strategically located for use of scholars and advanced students, which he had come to appreciate through his experience of the excellent one at Wisconsin—were a matter of continuing interest to Turner. Moreover he was expert in appraising the qualities of libraries in his own field—he knew what ought to be in a library, and he was aware of difficulties likely to be encountered in getting it. Both his estimate of the difficulties of assembling a reference library and his ideas about overcoming the obstacles were realistic; he was a professional in his field who took into consideration present conditions and future likelihoods before coming forward with suggestions.

Here then are letters and parts of letters covering the years 1888–1931, in which Turner comments on a number of matters pertaining to education and libraries in the United States.

### *Turner at Johns Hopkins*

In the first letter of this group, written from Johns Hopkins in 1888 to William F. Allen, Turner reports on educational developments. The Chautauqua, referred to in this letter, were "assemblies" held in the state of New York, a uniquely American attempt at combining mass education and entertainment.

EXTRACT FROM TURNER'S LETTER TO WILLIAM F. ALLEN, OCTOBER 8, 1888

I have just returned from an interview with Dr. Adams. On consultation with him I find that it may be possible for me to take my Ph.D. degree with only this year's residence here, provided I can get up reading French and German at sight at the end of the year following, and thus receive the degree in 1890. Indeed, Dr. Adams thought I could take the degree this year before he knew that I could not read French and German at sight.

He has also in contemplation a plan for annexing Chautauqua to the Johns Hopkins University—but this is as yet a secret. I think I may explain to you, however, that the plan embraces the University Extension idea—J.H.U. is to be the "intellectual clearing-house" for supplying speakers to the Chautauqua circles that may desire historical instruction by lectures, and these speakers are to be drawn from the graduate students of the various universities.

The idea of a *correspondence university* is also involved in it—the plan being to furnish instruction in the field of general history (so far as Adams is concerned;—There are various departments) He wishes me to arrange a syllabus of Keary's Dawn of History—the topical idea, as you use it in your classes. This is to be read in a month—and examinations given upon it. Coupled with this month's work is the plan of having an essay upon some subject like Primitive Religion—or The The Family etc—; to aid the student in preparing this a bibliography is contemplated, of the best works on that line of subjects—Next month Oriental history is to be considered. But one *essay* is to be required in the year and this may be given on whichever month's work the student may choose to write on at the close of the year—He wishes me to attend to this department, for a compensation. I think I shall try it.

The seminary met last night for the first time. I need not describe it to you, for you are doubtless familiar with the workings of it here—The paper read was by a fellow—Blackmar, formerly instructor in the University of California, who takes his degree this year. The subject was the history of State Aid to Higher Education—particularly in the

United States. It involves a treatment of the aid furnished by the federal government, and by each state legislature, all research being in the original authorities—a most excellent and laborious summer's work —I judge from the extracts—There was not very much discussion. The main points made by Dr. Adams during the evening were the desirability of working up the history of Education in the various States; and the importance of the University-Extension movement. He looks upon his having "stumbled across" this work of Arnold Toynbee* as "the best thing that ever happened to him"—as he says, he is "crazy" on the subject. I expect that the graduate students of J.H.U. will before long evolve into a veritable school of peripatetic historians—Dr. Ely has the "Chautauqua idea" as thoroughly as has Dr. Adams the University-Extension scheme, and he persuaded Adams to go to Chautauqua this summer—Adams found in the Chautauqua school an evolution from the camp-meeting, which in turn came from the hunters outdoor life, and he insists that the Chautauqua Assembly is only another form of the Folk-Moot. When he found as the germ of this Chautauqua school the Folk-Moot, and as one of its *possibilities,* the University Extension movement widely applied, he championed the cause of the CSSC and "bagged" the movement for J.H.U.—

In another long letter to Allen, Turner described classes and seminars at Johns Hopkins. Richard T. Ely placed great emphasis on the writings of John Stuart Mill. "The method," Turner wrote, "is (1st) to understand Mill; then to compare him with Walker and others." For Herbert Baxter Adams' classes, Turner had been studying the writings of the German historian Arnold H. L. Heeren, and Edward Everett Hale's two-volume *Franklin in France,* which appeared in 1887–88.

### EXTRACT FROM TURNER'S LETTER TO WILLIAM F. ALLEN, OCTOBER 31, 1888

I have limited my work with Dr. Adams to his graduate work (taken by all the graduate students): Roman Constitution—upon which I shall do only what reading I find necessary—and Nineteenth Century where I shall do a good deal of reading; and consisted of a

* Arnold Toynbee, 1852–83, English social philosopher and economist.

study, by lectures & topics, of international relations in Antiquity based largely on Heeren, and recent Monographs—Later we use a text book and study certain treaties—from originals—by topics.

I have ceased attending the lectures on Church—and am doing more reading and work on American history—shall go to Washington soon and look over the material for work on the Indian department with especial reference to its bearing on the development of the west. I am just now reviewing Hale's Franklin in France II.

Your letter shows me that I must have failed to describe the undergraduate work by topics properly.

As you see from what I have already said—the institution does aim to bring the student into close connection with original sources. This is effected in two ways: (1) by bringing original sources into class, and passing them around with advice to read,—and with questions introduced in the periodical *quiz,* that disclose whether such reading has been done. *Quellenstudium* is a favorite word with Dr. Adams. In church history for example, the basis of work is Genesis (so far) and the article on Israel in Ency. Brit. There are classes which read Livy & Tacitus from the historical point of view, in the original—and Herodotus & Thucydides in translation—(2) Dr. Adams and Dr. Ely both use topics—*but not daily*—

If I were to characterize the difference between the two methods used here & at home, I would say that here lectures and a text book were made prominent for undergraduates, and especially for freshmen; while at home the topic is made prominent and the text book incidental —The advantage of the former is in the steady guidance given to the crude material, and in the increased interest awakened in the class by substituting the comments, or the lecture of the teacher, for the necessarily less attractive and the imperfect presentation of the facts by the *student lecturer*—and finally by the alertness of the whole class, —individuals expecting to be called on daily—

The advantages of the . . . [latter method] lie in the greater frequency of topics for each student,—in the self-dependence awakened, —in the stronger emphasis placed on the *subject* as compared with the *book*.

On the whole I am inclined to believe that the method here might be followed to a greater degree as regards freshmen, and profitably— and that the method used here would derive gain from an increased adoption of the topical method with upper classmen—as used at Madison—

I am inclined to think that the institution here needs also a little more cautious scholarship in the historical line—But the power of getting men interested and at work, is certainly remarkable—One very good feature is the close connection of library and recitation rooms—But about this you already know—

I enclose you a copy of the course at Boston—which Adams calls "the best planned course in the United States,"—and also one of the circulars of this institution—

The difference which I note in the plans regarding American history both here, at Boston, and at Harvard, as compared with Wisconsin, is the closer connection of the studies in English Constitution, American History, and American *Constitution*. Here the subject is all taught as one course—and the Constitution is expounded in the same class and during the same term that the history of the United States since 1789 is studied. It is in short, the development of the American nation *politically* that is emphasized—The great lack of it all is in getting any proper conception of the Great West. Not a man here that I know of is either studying, or hardly aware of the country beyond the Alleghanies—except two. One is a California man who is working on the Spanish missions of that State—and the other is a fellow who was casting about for a thesis for his degree, to whom I recommended a study of the land companies of the "Back Lands" and who will quite likely take this field—

I am very glad to hear of the success of the clubs—I miss them a good deal—but our graduate-student talks about the seminary table partly fill the place—

Yes, surely Dr. Chamberlin overestimates what may be done with seminary among undergraduates. And such solid work as you propose in regard to *prices* is only suited to advanced students such as you mention. To get a seminary of Juniors—or lower—the subject must be on a lower plane—I have thought that perhaps a seminary in Northwest History, from the sources, might attract students, and be feasible for the undergraduates—But your work on Rogers is the *real* seminary work, which produces new and valuable contributions to science—Such contributions are not to be expected from others than the few best Seniors—at the best. Work such as I suggest above could only be made useful by setting students at work, and having the instructor perhaps sift and use the best materials brought up—where so much rough work of assorting must be done, as in the West, this work could be utilized—

On March 14, 1889, Turner wrote again to William F. Allen, making a more detailed comparison of the teaching methods used at Johns Hopkins University and at Wisconsin. Turner was by this time also corresponding with President Thomas C. Chamberlin of Wisconsin about a teaching post at Wisconsin to start in the fall, and he wanted to clarify his views on what a university teacher could reasonably be expected to do in the way of classroom teaching. He felt certain of one thing—teaching is not made more effective by increasing the number of hours spent by the teacher in the classroom.

In the last of these five extracts Turner discusses Johns Hopkins from the student's point of view, commenting on the extreme difficulty of passing foreign language reading examinations, and on the enjoyable lectures given by a young man staying at his boarding house: Woodrow Wilson.

### EXTRACTS FROM TURNER'S LETTER TO WILLIAM F. ALLEN, MARCH 14, 1889

I am impressed with the importance of allowing a man time to prepare, and a sufficient condensation of his work so that he can come to his class with some freshness and vigor, rather than teach a variety of subjects many hours. It is merely a question of relative gain by the University. When I talk about the "15 hour" arrangement to the men here, they are surprised. It is a system that belongs to the earlier growth of the institution. There is always the danger in presenting this view of seeming to shirk work—but I am sure that this is not my intention. I wish to do what will be the best thing for the institution and I am convinced that the value of teaching in History certainly does not increase with the number of hours per week spent in the class room—

. . . .

Course I (Dynastic) has always been a problem to me—and I am going to offer some suggestions upon that, with the diffidence that one feels in advising on a subject which he understands less than the one with whom he talks—

The fundamental ideas of the course, namely: general history, based rather on dynastic divisions than on the "life of the people," taught by making the student go to original sources or to standard authors, as far as practicable, are, it seems to me, undoubtedly sound—

But I have become convinced that as I taught it last year, the *Freshmen* found the subject less stimulating than it should be. The trouble is that while the Freshman does learn, (after some hard knocks and failures), to find his own material and to study at a particular topic—he finds the natural difficulty in *telling* what he knows to the class—and tho' the discipline of doing this is good for *him,* it is discouraging to the class. The teacher himself is withdrawn at the very time in the student's career when he is most needed. It is true that the teacher co-ordinates the topics; but if his work is effective he must also go over the topic himself, disentangling the meshes of detail into which the Freshman has snarled himself and emphasizing vital points. Now all this to students at this stage is not quite what is needed. They are perforce confused by the two presentations, and the subject is not appreciated in its true bearings—At this stage of their mental growth I imagine that what results is this:

1. The student looks upon his own as the most important topic of the term—the one on which his work has been placed. This impression on the Freshman mind can not be entirely overcome by the remarks of the teacher.

2. In the same way other topics leave an impression on his mind, derived not from their intrinsic importance, but proportioned to the clearness and force with which they were delivered.

3. The student is not a successful lecturer—particularly the Freshman, and although the golden rule of bearing with others as you would be borne with is a good moral discipline, it is not helpful to an *interest in history*—What is needed at this period, if I correctly apprehend it, is:—

I A love for history, derived from the stimulus of an earnest teacher, who gives a liberal amount of guidance.

II A knowledge of how to find books and use them. Here I fear I did not give enough help in the past—The amount of aid that will enable intelligent *self* help, however, is all that should be given—

The topical system is particularly strong on this point.

III A body of knowledge, and a historical *spirit* should be acquired —and discipline should be given—

Dr. Adams makes his undergraduates do a good deal of outside reading. For example—before graduation Motley or Gibbon must have been read through—His plan is—to use his words—to "keep their noses on the grindstone"! at this period.

*How shall these ends be attained?*

Probably the topical system at the University of Wisconsin would do it under some teachers, but I must confess that I did not succeed so well with it with *Freshmen* as I wish to succeed. And I would like to suggest as an experiment for one year this plan:

Text book—Myers' two volumes, and Labberton's Atlas without text if possible, with Ploetz strongly advised for reference (this will serve them throughout their course and life!)*

Method—Discussion by the teacher on the basis of Allen's Topics, with daily lessons in the text book and perhaps some assigned readings—

*Topics* should be assigned as heretofore, subject to be called up, instead of the teacher's remarks, and the pupil always expected to hand in a syllabus, and statement of reading done on the topic, but the entire class held responsible for the discussion in Myers and notes on the remarks of the teacher.

*Maps* and *Charts* as before—

. . . .

I submit this for what it is worth, and more as an experiment than anything else. The strictly topical system might be pursued in upper division if divisions were made on lines of Juniors and Freshmen—Of course you will not hesitate to ignore the suggestions if they are not of value, as I confess I am not sure—

. . . .

It may interest you to know that Dr. Adams told me today that both he and Dr. Ely thought I could take my degree this year. I was obliged however to confess too much ignorance of French and German to pass the rigorous requirements of the reading-at-sight examinations required of non-Hopkins men, as yet—I am hoping to hear from Dr.

* Turner probably refers to Philip Van Ness Myers (who wrote a number of textbooks on ancient and medieval history); Robert H. Labberton, *New Historical Atlas and General History* (New York, 1886); and Carl Ploetz, *Epitome of Ancient, Mediaeval and Modern History* (Boston, 1884).

Chamberlin soon as to what I shall be expected to teach. Another $1500 position in Brooklin went begging around the table this morning—

Please remember me to my friends in the faculty, and pardon this long letter.

Very truly yours
Frederick J. Turner

P. S.

I am taking Woodrow Wilson's lectures on Administration this term, and am very much impressed with their value. His text book on this subject will be out in the fall, embracing Central Administration, Local Self Government etc., including the United States. He rooms at my boarding place and I have heard him read several of his chapters —It would be pleasanter to teach this subject than Political Economy; even I am becoming deeply interested in it.

### *Turner at Wisconsin*

After leaving Johns Hopkins, Turner continued to keep in touch with Herbert B. Adams. Adams shared with his former student an intense interest in general education and a remarkable breadth of vision (Adams' classroom lectures on political institutions ranged over ancient Israel, Greece, and Rome, and traced the passage of political "germs" from Germany and England to America). And Adams passed on his preoccupation with the university extension system to Turner, who in his early years traveled all over Wisconsin giving "extension" lectures. In the first of three letters written in 1890–91, Turner explains some of the fine points of Wisconsin's educational system and comments on the importance of the library of the State Historical Society. The letter provides background information for Adams, who had been invited to speak in Wisconsin by Reuben Gold Thwaites, superintendent of the State Historical Society.

TO HERBERT B. ADAMS

Department of History,
University of Wisconsin,
Madison, Wis.
September 27, 1890.

Dear Dr. Adams:

Mr. Thwaites tells me that he has invited you to deliver the address before the State Historical Society this year. I am more than glad that he has done so, for I think that you are pre-eminently the man who has a message for us. This meeting occurs at the time of the biennial session of the legislature which makes it especially important. As you perhaps know, the Historical Library is supported by the state and is managed by the State Historical Society as the trustee of the State. In this respect it is almost unique, so far as I know. It is also out of the usual line of historical societies of its class in that it does not devote its time to collecting information as to the first white child and that sort of thing; but rather to accumulating what is already one of the best libraries on Americana in the country—particularly in respect to Western history and local history.

As you know, we have developed a spontaneous and peculiar form of University-Extension in Wisconsin in our Agricultural Institutes and School Institutes, under the guidance of the State University. They are steadily growing into a natural *inter*-relation. The district school is being brought into a healthy connection with both; and preparation is being made to open a way for district schools to send students directly to a primary agricultural course in the University. It is hoped that this may act as a feeder to the supply of district school teachers, now sadly deficient in point of educational fitness as well as in capacity for bringing their teaching into connection with the life and work of the community in which they live.

The thing that is needed is a utilization of the resources of the State Hist. library to *fertilize* and *spiritualize* the system. Wisconsin is not so thoroughly Philistine as some other States, but there is decidedly a need of some such a movement as this. I do not wish to make any suggestions as to a subject but I desire to say that you as the representative of the idea of University Extension, and the use of *libraries* in this end, have here a field in which to do a missionary work, and help on a movement of great significance, and direct it into the higher path. I sincerely hope that you will embrace this opportunity to see our West and help on that process of cross-fertilization which you and your institution has been so instrumental in promoting. The West needs Eastern ideas; I think the West, too, has a word for the East.

It is a delicate task to bring home to our legislators the utility of the higher education and the practical value of an institution like the Historical Society. Heretofore the state has supported it nobly and it has escaped attack—partly perhaps, because it has not made itself over prominent; but the time has come, I think, when it ought to be more of a force in the movement of higher education of the people. Of course it stands in a peculiar relation to the commonwealth. The library cannot be utilized as at Buffalo because Madison is not a great city. Its importance lies as a fertilizer of students and teachers of the state. *A word from you on this subject would not be amiss.* But at any rate I earnestly ask you to accept the invitation and come to see us. It would do our historical department good—but that is incidental. *The main point is the opportunity to present University extension in its higher aspects to a State ready for the seed by its spontaneous acts in the same direction.*

Very truly yours,
Frederick J. Turner

Two months later Turner sent Herbert B. Adams a more detailed description of the Wisconsin extension program, outlining the industrial side and explaining the need for a corresponding program in history. Part of Turner's letter describes the work of Charles David Marx, Wisconsin professor of civil engineering, who in 1890–91 unsuccessfully attempted to develop mechanics institutes.

TO HERBERT B. ADAMS

Department of History,
University of Wisconsin,
Madison, Wis.
December 8, 1890.

Dear Dr. Adams:

The report from Mr. Thoms on the relation of Agricultural Institutes to the district schools I have been unable to get owing to his pressing official duties. It is not essential, however. The idea is simply that this bringing the farmers together in connection with University lectures and so on, stimulates the district school so that a better interest is taken in it, and the teachers are awakened to better work. The report of Prof. Marx is also delayed owing to the fact that his work is not yet fully formulated. He goes to various cities and studies the local conditions relative to industrial matters. Then a course of graded lectures is arranged by him. He calls in the aid of expert mechanics in the city and a local club is organized. Professor Marx may lecture, for example, upon *materials* in mechanics relative to some special industry of the city one week and the next a practical mechanic will give a practical demonstration of the principles developed by Prof. Marx. He will also give instruction to these local bodies in draughting, leaving the immediate charge of the work to local experts. Special lectures will be added by local talent and by others. The local manufacturers are brought into the work. This may grow into a system of manual training schools in connection with the public schools. Prof. Marx hopes to see it develop into a system of Gewerbe Schulen, but Pres. Chamberlin does not lay any stress on this,—indeed he wished that it should not be mentioned in print. A particular aim of the work is to prevent the students of public schools from rushing to the shops at the age of fourteen, or younger, as they do in our manufacturing towns.

This gives the industrial side of University Extension here a combination of Agricultural Institutes and Mechanics Institutes. The "Culture side" of the work has not yet been developed to a great extent. The faculty have now under consideration a plan for bringing all departments into relation to the work but it is yet too undeveloped for public notice. *The President regards the industrial side of the work as only a part of it, however.* He has asked me for a report on historical extension and says that he finds a particular demand for this work. He suggests the question of whether the demand can be filled without taking too much of the time of a member of the faculty and whether we might not *appoint* certain workers in the historical field throughout the State as adjuncts to the faculty for this purpose, after the fashion of the Agricultural and Mechanics system. I would be glad to have any printed material that you can lend me for a few days, if you feel at liberty to do missionary work in this direction. I am to report next Monday so that if I make use of any suggestions or material it should be here before then. We are counting on your lecture with much interest. Pres. Chamberlin is to speak on University Extension at the teachers' convention which meets here in the holidays.

Very truly yours,
Frederick J. Turner

Can I be of any further service to you in the way of Wisconsin matter? I find there is a "Travel Class" at Columbus where I am lecturing.

In 1891 Turner wrote to Adams about the possibility of publishing a volume of printed source materials, possibly as a cooperative venture with other Hopkins graduates (J. Franklin Jameson, Woodrow Wilson, Frank W. Blackmar, Charles M. Andrews, and Albion W. Small) who could use it in their classes.

TO HERBERT B. ADAMS

University of Wisconsin,
Madison, Wisconsin,
May 17, 1891.

Dear Dr. Adams:

I have it in mind to prepare a syllabus of my work in American History. My particular effort this year has been to get the students to working on the original authorities. Taking for my motto that all history is comment on a text, I have aimed to indicate to the class such texts as would best serve as the material for discussion. My first thought has been to get up an outline something like Professor Hart's except that the references would be chiefly or entirely to the original authorities, rather than to secondary authorities. It strikes me that a better plan, however, would be to *print a collection of texts.* In libraries there are seldom sufficient duplicates to permit the class if it be large to use the documentary material as the sole basis of work. Why could not something like *Stubb's Select Charters* be gotten out to illustrate, or rather to furnish the basis of, a course in American Constitutional and Economic history? Preston's Documents are too meagre. My idea would be to print a good sized volume or perhaps two, containing significant speeches, Presidential messages, selections from debates, treaties, Supreme court decisions, laws (Alien and Sedition, e.g.), Reports, like Hamilton's, Walker's, Gallatin's, etc., etc.

I have not fully thought the matter out, though I have been for some time collecting references to original authorities in this line. I am not prepared to get the book up purely as a personal venture, though if it was judiciously compiled I think it would be used in a large number of colleges. Would it be possible to get the book issued as an extra volume of the Studies and secure co-operation in the compilation from some of your graduate students, and particularly from Hopkins graduates who could use the book in their classes? For instance if Professors Jameson, Wilson, Blackmar, Andrews, Small, and others could be interested, the work would be made easier, *better* and more certain of paying for itself. I would gladly become one of such a co-operative company, under your editorship. Please let me know what you think of the scheme.

Yours truly,
Frederick J. Turner

Adams' letters to Turner in the early 1890s are full of good advice. He advised his pupil to stay away from textbook writing but to "continue publication of individual studies on important chapters of American history." The best of these might later be used for textbook purposes. To some extent Turner kept to his plan. He did at any rate republish his essays in book form, and his books might almost be considered textbooks for other historians.

Meanwhile in the 1890s, with Adams' encouragement, Turner prepared a series of syllabi (printed outlines of lectures together with suggested readings). These were useful in helping participants in university extension courses to prepare for attending lectures, and Adams seems to have approved of Turner's efforts in this direction.

Adams counseled Turner on other matters as well, for instance on the development of the history department at Wisconsin. Immediately after the death of William F. Allen in 1889, he urged Turner to consider the recruitment of able new faculty members: "A great responsibility now rests upon you to sustain the Historical Department at the University of Wisconsin."

Turner took this advice seriously, building up at Wisconsin a new "school" of history, political science, and economics. A key figure in the development of the program was his former teacher at Johns Hopkins University, Richard T. Ely, whom Turner perusaded to move to Wisconsin in 1892. In the following extract of a letter to Ely he discusses the manner in which the Wisconsin program of study must be developed if it is, in the future, to bear comparison with the University of Chicago, with its ample resources and excellent faculty, including the German-born historian, Hermann Von Holst.

EXTRACT FROM TURNER'S LETTER TO RICHARD T. ELY, MARCH 14, 1892

Our strong card here must be our *State* connection. Chicago's faculty will be so well equipped financially that we cannot expect to cover all the ground they will cover with so much detail. We must have *specialties*. Your own way of treating Economics is so different —and superior—to their economists that we have a specialty in that field. Our state historical library gives us a chance to do special work in American history which need not be overawed by the neighborhood of Von Holst. Dr. Haskins is a very strong teacher in Institutional and Classical history, and has a strong critical ability. We must be careful not to let some other institution get him—they are looking his way already in one or two cases, I know. Then we need a man for Administration. He must be a man who is chosen because he has had a peculiarly strong training, and is naturally in love with the subject. Not because he would like some place to teach. If we can develope in a well minded way, some of these specialties we shall have no reaction. But no matter how much money we get, we cannot compete with Chicago if our *history* is all undergraduate, and if our *civics* is not excellent in quality as well as quantity. Otherwise a reaction will come, however good the Economics may be.

During the late 1890s teaching and research absorbed most of Turner's time, but a recurring subject in his letters is the history textbook for college students that he planned to write. Here he sets forth his ideas about the kind of book it was to be.

### EXTRACT FROM TURNER'S LETTER TO EDWARD N. BRISTOL OF HENRY HOLT AND COMPANY, JUNE 11, 1897

Next year I propose to concentrate my teaching almost entirely upon the colonial and revolutionary period, and I shall organize my material in text-book form. My idea is that such a text book should give a clear elucidation of the more important lines of development of economic life, political institutions, and social ideals. It should show how these came from European conditions; it should mark out clearly the effect of the new surroundings, and should treat the subject in such a way as to lay a foundation for the next period. If I am not wrong, it is in this idea of unity and grasp of the essential phases of development, that most of our text-books are defective. If I have seemed dilatory to you, it is because I have so clearly realized what I thought ought to be done, that I have not been ready to do it. Now I can see my way clearer to doing it in portions as suggested. If the ideas I have can be carried out, the work should lay a foundation for the use of economists, in dealing with the industrial history of the United

States, and for the student of government. It is my belief that high school economics can be best taught through United States history, and that "United States Civil Government" should be intimately related to the same subject. Such a book as I have in mind could be useful in high school libraries as well as in college classes.

Turner's history textbook was to serve as an introduction to the study of government and economics. Turner was of course equally interested in broadening the scope of graduate training in history. In the following letter of 1904 to Carl Becker, he outlined the interdisciplinary program of study required of doctoral candidates at the University of Wisconsin, a program largely designed by Turner himself. Becker at this time was an assistant professor of history at the University of Kansas.

TO CARL BECKER

University of Wisconsin
Madison
School of History
Jan 9 1904

My dear Becker:

I am much pleased that you are considering taking your degree here.

We have been accustomed to require two minors, one of which should be history. The *second minor,* however, involves only one full study for the year—say 1/3 of a year's work, and I believe you must have had economics, political science, sociology, or some such course, to this amount. We usually accept the *class record* for this without further examination.

European history may be a major, or minor, and American history a major or minor, for the rest. That is, History for major and 1st minor.

We examine (by written examination) the candidate on the *general field* in each subject, but do not expect minute knowledge on this general test. We also give a written examination on *a particular field* or *period* of each major & 1st minor, chosen by the candidate with our approval. We also have an *oral examination* of an hour and one half or two hours, covering the above fields. We think, on the whole, the candidate's real status comes out better by these various tests than by a single oral.

Our thesis requirement exacts publication within the year, but this time limit has not always been enforced, particularly when the candidate has published portions of it sufficient to warrant us in permitting him to come up. I would support a request for more time in your case, and believe our committee is ripe for it. But they may decide to defer the degree till publication. I should accept a *portion* of your whole work, if you are willing to publish a portion first and would be glad to have it in our Bulletin. You could republish in a volume, with completed work later.

We require a *reading* knowledge of *French and German* at the beginning of the year in which the student comes up for the degree. The certificate of the Columbia or Kansas men would be accepted;—or for that matter—the certificate of the men with whom you took these languages here. But, as a rule, they exact an examination, using historical material & giving the candidate a fair chance to look over his assignment before calling upon him to read at sight.

I know of nothing to prevent your coming up for the degree, and should be glad to have you do so.

Cordially yours
Frederick J Turner

Professor Carl Becker
University of Kansas

If you wish, I will present specific requests to the Committee for you.

It took Becker four more years to complete his doctorate, during which time he was assistant professor at the University of Kansas. The following letter to Becker, written in 1908, begins with a brief reference to Becker's doctoral dissertation (*The History of Political Parties in the Province of New York: 1760–1776,* Madison, 1909) which was about to be published.

TO CARL BECKER

University of Wisconsin
Madison
Department of History
February 24 1908

Dear Professor Becker:

I have no report yet from the editor; but I *hope* we can manage it in one number—

Regarding our courses, I think they are satisfactory. They provide for certain fundamentals and leave the rest free, except for the major, and for technical courses. I think a *basal requirement* such as we have, and a *major* present distinct advantages over a free elective system, which is anarchy, on the one side, and a specified course (other than technical) which is apt to be educational graft, on the other.

We require no more languages than is usually done in the best universities, I think, considering our *entrance* requirements and theirs.

The course gives opportunity for men to enter from schools which are behind in their linguistic training. In such cases, however, the student is held to the *extra* language work provided in the course, for two reasons: (1) otherwise the bars would be let down for those schools which give language training not because they prefer to but partly because the University requires it for entrance, and as a matter of response to educational fashion set by the University's standards. Such schools would be apt to yield to popular economic arguments, and our whole requirements would in practice drop to a lower level; (2) because the languages afford such essential tools for the student who means to go really into his work, and such *windows* into other literatures etc. A liberal language training is perhaps the striking difference between provincialism and real culture. The *earlier* a man gets it the better, but he must get this training or lose much. So at least it seems to me—Possibly some relaxation would be possible without harm, but certainly not very much.

Yours

Frederick J Turner

## *The University Library*

Many of Turner's letters in the early 1900s dealt with libraries, especially in connection with research and graduate study. In the following extract from a letter to Dean Edward A. Birge of the College of Letters and Science, Turner points out that a new School of History would result in fuller use of the excellent library resources at Wisconsin. The attractive offer Turner had received from Chicago was, it would seem, to be used to win concessions from Wisconsin.

### EXTRACT FROM TURNER'S LETTER TO DEAN EDWARD BIRGE, APRIL 14, 1900

I am reluctant to leave Wisconsin, however. Aside from the gratitude I have to this University and the pride in its growth, I realize that the library of the State Historical Society is one of the great treasures of the country, not to say of the University; that it is in effect the most valuable single educational asset of the state, the product of its bounty and of the wise and devoted administration of the men who founded and conducted it. As a Wisconsin man and an alumnus of the University I have a strong desire to aid in the full utilization of this splendid library, and to continue to make use of it in my investigation and instruction.

It has seemed to me that if President Adams' proposal of the creation of a School of History were embodied in detail so as to make it a real and vigorous institution, the history department would be enabled to make such use of this library as its importance demands. Adequate utilization of the library and effective organization of a School of History seem to me to require such provisions for increase of the staff and equipment in history as will make more effective the instruction of undergraduates in history and afford larger opportunity for investigation, publication, and advanced instruction on the part of professor Haskins and myself. In Chicago the work required of us would be limited to graduate instruction, and but two courses, amounting to eight hours or less per week, would be expected of us.

In his correspondence with Max Farrand in 1904, Turner set down his conception of the principles which should govern the setting up of a library in the field of American history at Stanford. Turner, it will be recalled, was at this time considering the possibility of leaving Wisconsin and moving to Stanford.

TO MAX FARRAND

October 4, 1904.

Professor Max Farrand,
Stanford University, California.

My dear Farrand:

Replying to your letter of the 28th, I am unable to answer some of your questions as specifically as I should like.

In the first place, I do not know what the scope of the Sutro Library is, except in the most general way. I suppose it to be a good working library in Modern European history, however.

I have not seen the Bancroft Library, and only know its contents in such a general way as comes from looking over the bibliography at the end of Bancroft's volumes. The question of how large a proportion of that library is devoted to the early Indian and Spanish materials, would naturally affect one's judgment as to its importance as a university library.

In general, it seems to me that the Pacific Coast particularly needs, in each of its large universities, an extensive and well-chosen historical library. The largest appropriations should naturally be made for American history, but not omitting in the other historical fields good working libraries, leaving to the future the fuller development of those libraries. For some time to come, advanced students on the Pacific Coast, in ancient, Medieval, and Modern history, are likely to go East or to Europe for their more special researches. Nevertheless, it is important, as I have already indicated, that there should be a substantial working library in European history. This is needed even from the point of view of American history, which can only develop on broad and enduring lines when in contact with efficient work in European history. In American history, the libraries ought to possess, first of all, those large collections of documents, such as the colonial archives, congressional records, works of American statesmen, general histories and biographies, sets of periodicals, et cetera. It would be unwise to build up very special collections without a broad foundation of general American historical material. If you will permit me to illustrate on the basis of our own resources, I will say that, roughly speaking, there are in the combined historical libraries of the University of Wisconsin and the State Historical Society, between 200,000 and 300,000 titles, including pamphlets. The University library furnishes a good working collection on the lines just indicated, for American history. The State Historical Library, besides duplicating the more common collections, goes farther and adds its great collection of American newspapers, reaching back to the beginnings of the press in America and covering all sections of the country. It has also an exceptionally large collection of local history, biography, and genealogy, covering also the entire country. Special collections, such as material for the history of the Civil War and the slavery struggle, are included. But the library is strongest in the manuscript and printed material for the study of the region between the Alleghanies and the Mississippi. While it furnishes a library which, in some respects, compares well with the seaboard libraries in material for the Atlantic Coast, it is built up on the theory that its special position is to furnish the documentary material for understanding the growth of the region between the Alleghanies and the Mississippi. Any student, living in this region, who would study in detail its history, must come to this library to do his work.

In my judgment, a similar state of affairs should be created on the Pacific Coast. There should be this broad general foundation, and there should be a special collection which should do for the Rocky Mountain States and the Pacific Coast, what the State Historical Library of Wisconsin does for the interior of the country. I do not suppose it would be possible to secure a collection for this purpose that would rival the Bancroft collection, but, upon this point, I am not sufficiently informed. If the $200,000 or so that is supposed to be asked for the Bancroft library is to be expended chiefly on early Indian and Spanish records, I should feel less confident of the wisdom of expending that amount of money, if the documentary material for the American period of the history of the Rocky Mountains and the Pacific Coast can be obtained elsewhere. To obtain this latter material, I presume would be a task of many years, and possibly the collection in the Bancroft library could not be rivalled. Our own experience in regard to the collections of pamphlets, documents, and manuscripts which Dr. Draper made for the Middle West, leads me to believe that the first collector has an advantage that can never be repeated for later gleaners.

The possession of a special library for the study of the history of the Rocky Mountains and of the Pacific Coast, would make possible the addition of more recent material, by sending out agents at a comparatively small salary, to locate and collect the scattered material, and, if such collections could be used to supplement the Bancroft library, it would give to the vast area of the mountains and the coast an adequate supply of material for understanding their development. When one looks at the map and sees what a great stretch of country is covered by these regions, and when one reflects that they lack a library for the study of their development, or, at least, one open to the public, it is a matter of surprise and regret. I have already expressed similar sentiments to the history people at the University of California. It seems to me the duty of every man interested in the continental study of American history to preach this gospel. Why should not the Pacific Coast do for its sphere of influence, what New England has done for its, and what is done here for the Mississippi Valley?

If I had a half million dollars to expend, therefore, I should expend it on the lines already indicated. I believe that librarians estimate that books now in print cost about $1.50 per volume, taking them in general. On this basis, two or three hundred thousand dollars expended for a general working library, with the emphasis on American history, would lay a sufficient foundation. The remainder might be devoted to the acquisition of the Sutro and the Bancroft libraries. I certainly should not advise the expenditure of the whole half million for the two collections. If the Sutro library is a good general collection of European history, the acquisition of it would doubtless serve part of the foundational purposes which I have emphasized, and its cost might be included in the appropriation for the general library.

There are, as you very well know, great masses of material which are impossible to estimate in money, because they are practically unique. I suppose that a million dollars would not enable us to duplicate the library of the State Historical Society. When I consider facts like these, I am tempted to say that the proper policy would be to expend the entire $500,000, without regard to a special library, and to make a campaign for some wealthy donor, who should furnish the special resources necessary for work on the history of the Rocky Mountains and the Pacific Coast. It ought to be borne in mind, moreover, that there is a large area in which American history, economics, politics, and literature, overlap so that books for the one serve also as books for the others. Thus a good deal of this expenditure would be serving the needs of these other lines as well as those of history. But, at any rate, it is the duty of every section to collect the necessary data for understanding its own past.

I have carried out your wishes in regard to your letter, and I perfectly understand the fact that these inquiries are not based upon any very immediate prospect of a free hand.

Mrs. Turner writes me of the very pleasant visit she made to Stanford, under your kind guidance. She was more than enthusiastic over the magnitude and beauty of the buildings. We are hoping to have her back here Friday night.

Cordially yours,

## *The University and the State*

During this period, when Turner was corresponding with Max Farrand about West Coast libraries and the possibility of moving to Stanford, the University of Wisconsin was under criticism from the Board of Regents and the state legislature. Turner wrote in a memorandum, preserved among his letters, that he had become a focal point of attack when the regents attempted "to overturn" his "arrangement of half-year leave annually for research." This concession had been made by the regents because Turner had been invited to consider "a like arrangement in Stanford Univ." Turner also noted that certain regents were hostile towards him because of his support of Charles Van Hise for the presidency of the university after the resignation of Charles Kendall Adams in 1901 (Turner's memorandum on his draft of a letter to President Van Hise, Oct. 12, 1908).

The situation became more complicated by the intervention of the state legislature in 1906 when an investigative committee began probing the management of the university, especially research costs which President Van Hise emphasized in budget requests. The committee soon began investigating professorial "outside activities" and complaints about the tendency of full professors to leave the teaching of "lower classes" to assistants. Turner, who saw himself quoted inaccurately in a newspaper account about the issues involved, particularly textbook writing, took it upon himself to compose a letter to Senator George Wylie, Chairman of the legislative investigative committee. Here are extracts from his long letter to Senator Wylie in which he pinpoints basic educational concerns of the scholar-teacher in the state university.

### EXTRACTS FROM TURNER'S LETTER TO GEORGE WYLIE, FEBRUARY 22, 1906

For a number of years, I have had contracts with a publisher to prepare a high-school history and a college history of the United States. The fulfilment of these contracts has been postponed, because I have not found the time to carry them out without sacrificing some of the *un*remunerative investigations in which I was interested. The publishers, who insist that there is both a real educational need and a financial reward for these books, have become impatient, and this year I consented to use my second semester, to work on the book, and I shall receive an advance royalty. I have leave of absence this second semester, secured by teaching without pay for two summer sessions, according to the regular university system.

May I also take advantage of this opportunity to say that in my opinion the writing of a text-book has a distinct advantage of an educational nature to the University. The author is forced to consider more intimately pedagogical questions, such as mode of presentation, selection, arrangement, and emphasis of material, perspective, etc. This is directly helpful to his teaching. A good text-book for schools by a scholar, incorporating the latest knowledge, is also useful to the public, by keeping learning fresh and vital.

In general, with regard to remuneration for books, may I be permitted to say this?

An able and ambitious man can hardly be expected to serve universities if he is limited in his income to salaries usually paid. I have myself refused at least two publishers a year every year for the past ten years, when they have suggested remunerative royalties which were expected to aggregate more annually than my present salary. I have also refused overtures to abandon university work in order to accept an arrangement (suggested by two publishers) by which I should receive a regular income advanced on royalties much in excess of my present salary. Up to the present time, I have preferred to investigate and lecture in a university; and it seems to me that a university ought to have room, and be able to make provision, for a man with these desires, such that he can continue. As a matter of fact, however, up to the present, with one or two exceptions, all of the really important historical *writing* in this country has been done by men *not connected with universities*. In other words, to be a productive scholar in history, and to produce *a large work*, it has been necessary *not* to be connected with a university. This ought not to be the case. It also tends to limit the historians to men of private fortune.

The result of my own policy has been to leave me badly in debt. I have never been able to live on my salary, and this has not been due to an extravagant life.

I have refused to go to some of the most important universities of the country at a higher salary than I receive here, because I preferred to work at Wisconsin.

. . . .

There are certain men in every great university who, after years of service, have developed their science to such a point that they are more useful in training juniors and seniors and graduates than in dealing with elementary students. It is an old adage that it is poor policy to use a razor to cut grindstones. To use the man who by training has brought his chisel to the point where he can do delicate, artistic and creative work, in the rough-hammered stonework of foundations, is poor economy. On the other hand, he may well give some work to elementary students for inspiration and suggestion rather than in the way of regular training.

Moreover, however useful the highly-trained scholar might be for elementary work, he could not be gotten to give the larger part of his time to that work.

If he *could,* it would be too expensive to fill the positions with as many men of this type as would be necessary in order to bring students and instructors into close relations in small groups.

It is therefore necessary to recognize the fact that a university needs two types of men in its faculty: the investigator, who meets undergraduates in his classes, but whose main service is in investigation; and the teacher, who keeps his teaching vital by some investigation, but whose main work is with undergraduates. In each department, these types should be represented.

To recommend that investigators should teach more classes, have longer consultation hours, etc., would endanger their usefulness to the university, if, indeed, it did not result in losing their services. They would then be replaced by men of less reputation—by men, indeed, of the type of those *now* occupying the less highly paid positions in universities. Where would be the gain to the university?

When the prestige of the university was diminished by the loss of scholars of national reputation, the men who were called to the university would be less ready to accept a moderate salary than they would in a university whose reputation was great. A better man can be gotten for the same salary to fill a chair in an institution which has a reputation for scholarship, and an honorable standing in the educational world, than to fill a chair in an institution of inferior honor. The presence of scholars gives this reputation to a university.

Higher salaries would undoubtedly attract to undergraduate teaching a higher grade of ability. There is at present a real danger that the instruction in universities will deteriorate because the able and ambitious young men find little to tempt them in a teacher's career.

. . . .

Unless universities meet these conditions by some mode of attracting better men, the teaching will decline by dry rot. There must be greater prizes at the top of the profession, and greater immediate rewards to those who enter the career.

If universities do not wish instructors to have any "outside" interests, higher salaries must be paid. But outside interests have one advantage. They keep the man from being a closet scholar; and, by bringing him into contact with life, they enhance his usefulness. Perhaps the main difference between the traditional college professor, supposed to be impractical, visionary, and out of touch with the world about him, and the professor of the present time, lies in just this tendency of the modern professor to mix up with the life of his fellowmen and to do his share of the work of the world while he does his teaching and research. In those departments where remuneration can be secured for some outside work, it may be wiser to allow this freely, rather than correspondingly to increase salaries and prevent outside activity. In certain departments, however, investigation, etc., which is unremunerative, though profitable to the commonwealth, should be regarded as a necessary part of university work and be paid for by the university.

Turner's letter to Senator Wylie may well have had a moderating influence upon the legislative committee reporting on the University. The lawmakers praised the scholarly reputation of the institution in their conciliatory report, but they did raise questions about research that might interfere with undergraduate teaching.

The Turner-Farrand correspondence meanwhile survived the earthquake of 1906 (which put a sudden end to Turner's negotiations with Stanford) and Farrand's move to Yale. On March 18, 1909, Farrand wrote to thank Turner for an offprint of the essay on "The Old West": "As I was going to my office this morning I took from the Post-Office the copy of 'The Old West,' which you were good enough to send me. Instead of blessing you for it, however, I very nearly cursed you, for I immediately became so absorbed in it that I did not notice the passing of minutes and got to my lecture room barely in time to keep the class from bolting."

Turner replied three days later in a letter which opens "What a pity it wasn't interesting enough to have given the class their bolt!" The following extract from this letter reveals Turner's continued uneasiness at the (often well-meant) interference of the regents and the state government in university affairs.

EXTRACT FROM TURNER'S LETTER TO MAX FARRAND, MARCH 21, 1909

I shall soon send you, I hope, Becker's PhD thesis (Bull. U. W.) in which he develops the relation of democratization, party alignment &c, in relation to the Revolution in New York. He thinks the social reorganization as important in many ways as the fight for local self government, and I guess he is right. But his thesis is too full of detail I fear for the public. Jameson has always laid stress on the social transformations of the Revolution. I think that when such studies are related to those on the settlement of the interior, with its related subjects, we shall have to do over the colonial history of the 18th century. The new line of work for the future is the history of the development of American *society,* ideals, &c.

Your flattering, tho' totally unjustified comments on my work always do me good. I don't take any stock in that polite respect for age and infirmity which you show in awarding me my seat at the historical dinner table; but I like the attention. And here in Wis. where all our best students are engaged in saving the state and nation by studying political science, law, and economics,—or are helping *on* the Wisconsin crusade for educating all the people, any time, any where, any how, as Lincoln Steffens has recently pointed out, I feel the need of encouragement. Our regents are determined that our pork, poultry and cows shall have a great moral uplift, and as a loyal exponent of the economic interpretation of social development, I have every reason to rejoice. The University is the "instrument of the State," and the state at large is busily using it—There are thirty bills in the present legislature regulating us, from antisegregation, anti vivisection, University extension &c to allowing every student under discipline to have an attorney and to suffer no testimony except under rules of law &c &c. I'm glad I'm not dean. It really looks as though instead of sending the state of Wisconsin to school, as Steffens called it, we are sending the University to school to the legislature, and to the crossroads philosopher. Perhaps we shall learn something.

Turner was indeed weary of the persistent demands to make the University of Wisconsin the "instrument of the state." At Harvard, where he moved in the next year, he found relief from such pressures.

### *Turner at Harvard*

Writing in 1910 to his future colleague Edward Channing, Turner outlined his plan for a graduate "seminary" and explained how he hoped to work together with his other Harvard colleagues, Albert Bushnell Hart and William Bennett Munro.

EXTRACT FROM TURNER'S LETTER TO EDWARD CHANNING, JANUARY 2, 1910

Dear Channing:

The kind of general combination which I had in mind, in my reply to Hart's letter regarding the seminary which he and Munro carry on was quite in line with your idea of a historical conference, with meetings, say monthly, sometimes of a social character, in which instructors, or students, or eminent outsiders might address the gathering, especially upon results of their work. Such informal meetings might, or might not be open to the public; but at first I should think it might be better to have them limited to the advanced students interested. The suggestion that they might well be held in the houses of the instructor seems to me a good one.

As I wrote Hart, there is a kind of graduate course which I have been accustomed to call "seminary," where a single limited field is cooperatively studied by research. Such a course I should wish to give on Van Buren's administration next year.

For direction of advanced students in their particular pieces of work, individual conferences seem a natural device; and students will of course select the instructor on whose guidance they would chiefly (but, I should hope, not exclusively), rely for such direction.

Turner set down his first impressions of Harvard in a letter to August C. Krey, a former Wisconsinite who was beginning his teaching career at the University of Texas.

EXTRACT FROM TURNER'S LETTER TO AUGUST C. KREY, FEBRUARY 6, 1911

You are carrying too many things evidently. The man who does more than his share is the man who gets on, provided he doesn't do it so long that he is taken for granted too much. Can't you persuade them to let you try the Wisconsin scheme of combining lectures and quiz sections?

Harvard is an interesting study—But I have been too busy with my own work with my classes to get very far into its mysteries. It is interesting to see the respectful attitude toward Wisconsin & its work here. The alarm over socialism, leading to a willingness to concede regulation—the fear that regulation is to go farther—&c.

My classes are abundantly stocked with western men, chiefly Ohio Valley &c but running from coast to coast and G Lakes to Gulf, freshmen to graduates. The men of large means—the "Mt. Auburn youth," tried it a day or two; but when I announced that the way of salvation lay through the library, they left in sadness rather than anger. But these men are mighty promising stuff if one could set fire to their purposes. It is too good seed to be mildewing. But the extra-legal activities are too engrossing and the traditions of avoiding the reputation of greasy grinds are in the way of their own interests. They do much better topical reports than examination papers, and I am convinced that practically all of these reports are done by the men themselves. The football team was largely represented, took its medicine like men, and got good grades.

I am buying books in western history on a fund of a thousand a year given by Mrs. [Alice Forbes Perkins] Hooper in memory of her father the late Pres. Perkins of the Burlington R.R. The library is better off than I had supposed in these lines, and I find this fund effective in filling gaps &c—

## *The Harvard Commission on Western History*

Soon after moving to Harvard, Turner began to expand the Harvard Library collections in Western American history. This was made possible by the generosity of the wealthy Mrs. Alice Forbes Perkins Hooper, who provided most of the financial support for Turner's newly created Harvard Commission on Western History. Turner particularly wanted the cooperation of leading historians in the West such as Henry Morse Stephens of the University of California, to whom he sent the following letter.

TO HENRY MORSE STEPHENS

153 Brattle St
Cambridge, Mass.,
April 25, 1912

My dear Stephens:

I am enclosing the circular of the Harvard Commission on Western History—which I obviously am not responsible for, as you will see by its immoderate reference to myself—because I wish to make it clear that we wish to cooperate with yourself and the California group.

Our aim is to build up *in the East* an adequate center for the study of the West as a whole. We realize that we can't ever hope to rival your collections for Pacific slope history, of course. We do not expect material to which your institution has a superior claim, though we ought not to refuse material which might be given to us in case it would not be given to another collection. But we wish to cooperate,—drawing from duplicates and extra material in Western libraries where possible, and adding interstate and interregional material which may legitimately come to us.

I hope to see here before long some travelling fellowships for American history which will enable our best men to work on the Coast and elsewhere on the special collections which we cannot hope to reproduce, even if we had the ambition to do so.

With best wishes,

Yours sincerely
Frederick J Turner

Writing to Archibald C. Coolidge, professor of history at Harvard and director of the University Library, Turner suggests ways in which the library might further the work of the Commission on Western History.

TO ARCHIBALD C. COOLIDGE

March 26, 1914.

Dear Professor Coolidge:

Following your suggestion when I talked with you on the matter, I am putting in writing the substance of my conversation regarding a room in the new Library building* for the purposes of the Commission on Western History.

The correspondence of the Secretary and Archivist is so increasing that some provision is desirable on the administrative side. The advantage which a home of its own would give the Commission in attracting its alumni and other friends, especially in the west, to give material to the Library is also obvious.

If the Commission had a place where photographs and maps illus-

* The Harry Elkins Widener Memorial Library, or "Widener Library."

trative of western development and conditions at different periods could be exhibited, where undergraduates and graduates could come and to which they could send collections, it would cement the bond between Harvard and the country beyond the Alleghanies.

Whether it should be equipped with facilities for storing manuscripts is a question for consideration; probably economy of administration would require all manuscripts to be preserved in a single department.

I know from my own experience with Harvard students that they would be delighted to cooperate in sending photographs of western scenes and data illustrative of conditions that are rapidly passing away. Such cooperation helps to make them effective workers in other directions also. The room would be a visible sign that Harvard had an interest in the west. The various western alumni associations could be interested in contributing to it.

Illustrating the possibilities in this direction, suppose the library [was] to exhibit in such a room photographs or reproductions of drawings etc. illustrating a city like Chicago or Denver or San Francisco or St Paul, from days of Indian treaties, block house forts, early frontier village life and buildings, on by decades to the present. This would have a scientific as well as a value in arousing interest, and it is only a type of many things which are possible now, with little or no expense for collecting if we will only meet our alumni and students half way in the matter.

It does not need a large room—Cabinets (of the vertical filing system) could contain a large mass of material in small compass. But the larger the room possible, the more impressive it could be made. Its walls could be lined with photographs of scenery, Remington prints, etc. etc.

Sometime a similar room could be arranged for the South, and thus the more distant sections be made present, so to speak. Thus also, the Western and the Southern men would feel that they had an intellectual center and a home center for their own section in the Library.

I am enclosing with this, or will send you later copies of letters and reports by Dr. S. J. Buck* (Harvard) of the University of Illinois, which indicate how much more thoroughly and effectively that institution is doing its work of collecting western material than we can do

* Solon J. Buck completed his doctorate at Harvard in 1911 specializing in Western agrarian history.

with our present facilities. Similar evidence could be secured from Wisconsin and other states.

Particularly I would call your attention to the need of a photo-copying machine which could be used to collect manuscripts and newspaper copies from families or libraries when the original cannot be obtained. This machine would be useful to many other departments, of course.

Such a plant as this great library should be treated by the University with the same liberality and business-like considerations of efficiency that are used in providing the apparatus appropriate to a laboratory and a museum. From this point of view, a copying machine is really a matter of relatively small expense.

The Library should also be the home of a University photographer who should be available for operating the copying machine, making lantern slides, and doing similar work. I understand the room is already provided and that the man whom the University faculty members now use for slides etc. (Mr Collyer) would be willing to take a University position of that nature at a moderate salary.

In a word, photographic collections and apparatus are essentials of every large *modern* library. The University of Wisconsin has had such a provision in its Library building for some years, and regards it as indispensable.

I shall be glad to discuss these matters further with you if they interest you.

Yours respectfully,
Frederick J. Turner

(Dictated by Mr. Turner,
but signed in his absence.)

Turner was from the first convinced that the proper development of the Commission on Western History depended on the establishment of cordial relations with rival libraries. He was therefore disturbed to hear from Thomas P. Martin, student and archivist of the Commission, that the Director of the Wisconsin State Historical Society, Milo M. Quaife, considered the Harvard Commission to have been "conceived in iniquity." Turner scrawled this information on the carbon copy of a letter he sent to Quaife.

EXTRACT FROM TURNER'S LETTER TO MILO M. QUAIFE, JANUARY 7, 1915

Mr. T. P. Martin, my assistant, tells me that he learned from you in Washington that you were disposed to think Harvard's Commission on Western History an undesirable activity, on the ground that Harvard was creating a new field of collection and trespassing upon Western preserves. He was giving me his impression rather than quoting you, and he was desirous of avoiding mutual misunderstanding. I tried to avoid any collision of interests between our undertaking and those of Western societies in framing the policy of the Commission at the outset, and I should be sorry to have you misapprehend it. I trust you will understand that what I write, therefore, is in a friendly spirit, not in resentment of what you felt called upon to say at the meeting. I know Harvard can help the cause of Western history by co-operative action, and of course I know that she is acting in the interests of American history in general. I think you would agree if we could talk it out together.

As Turner's subsequent correspondence shows, suspicious "Westerners" like Milo M. Quaife were not easily mollified. Harvard must take special care not to appear greedy, Turner wrote Archibald C. Coolidge.

EXTRACT FROM TURNER'S LETTER TO ARCHIBALD C. COOLIDGE, MARCH 26, 1917

Our desire to foster Western history in Harvard can best be promoted by cooperation rather than by fighting the western agencies for their material. Harvard's general position would be far from advantaged by that kind of a contest. You don't want it, of course, any more than I do.

But we can gain a lot by developing, not the *unique* or spectacular "find," but rather the typical material by gift, exchange, etc., leaving to each state its legitimate exceptional documents and taking from Mass. material, except in our eastern area, where material is as much eastern as western.

We can defend our action when we accept gifts which would not under any likely conditions be made to the state involved by a Harvard man, or friend, and likely to be lost unless preserved by gift to us—But such cases will be exceptional.

So much for the strategy of the situation. Now regarding the value of the material, I should wish to see more of it before passing a final quantitative judgment, but I have seen enough to convince me that it is worth while. Certainly there is a mass of it here.

Turner was never able to win the confidence of all the collectors and libraries in the West. One of his more stubborn critics was Judge Walter B. Douglas of St. Louis who was convinced that Turner was collecting material that should be deposited with the Missouri Historical Society. Besides, the Judge had found that Easterners knew very little about the West. Turner left an undated draft of one of his letters to Douglas (other letters indicate that it was written in the fall of 1919) in which he attempted to win over his opponent: "I am myself a western man engaged in teaching western history at Harvard. I do not find the same amount of ignorance about the West which you found here, though there is room for further understanding. I dare say that every one of the American sections need to know more about the others than it does if we are to avoid misunderstandings. That, I suppose, is one of the reasons I was brought to Harvard."

### *Lectures at Berkeley*

During the summer of 1914 Turner lectured at summer sessions at the Universities of Washington and Oregon and took part in an excursion of a group called "the Mountaineers." The experience was so enjoyable that he accepted an invitation from his friend, Henry Morse Stephens, and his former student, Herbert Eugene Bolton, to lecture in the summer of 1915 at the University of California at Berkeley (where he took part in another outdoor trip under the sponsorship of the Sierra Club). In the letter below he discusses tentative plans for the summer session. It is probable that a revised and condensed version of this letter (the letter is a typed original and is unfolded and unsigned) was sent to Stephens, whose earlier letters to Turner indicate that he planned to publish an announcement of the lectures.

TO HENRY MORSE STEPHENS

The Harvard Commission on Western History
Harvard University Library
Cambridge, Massachusetts
May 14, 1915.

Prof. H. Morse Stephens,
University of California,
Berkeley, California.

Dear Stephens:

In bringing together some of the material to take with me for my lectures in California I find myself not quite clear as to just what is desired by you and Bolton in the matter of the extent of my lectures on the study and sources of the history of the westward movement in America. My difficulty comes partly from my ignorance of what kind of an audience I shall have. If it is, for the most part, a fairly general audience, it would seem to me questionable whether much attention should be given to methodology and bibliography which might seem to be implied in "study and sources"; or if by sources should be meant a general discussion of the original material and of the use of it, as such secondary writers as Parkman, Roosevelt, Winsor, Thwaites, H. H. Bancroft, etc. There would be little room for anything else in six lextures. What do you think of the plan of handling methods of study and sources in the conferences which are proposed for the two afternoons in each week? In that case, would you and Bolton prefer a program that should represent my more fundamental and larger views with reference to the westward movement? Or would you sooner I should take up in some detail, perhaps based upon my class lectures, particular phases of the movement on which I have not yet published much. Concrete illustration of what I have in mind is furnished by the following:

Six lectures on phases of history of the West.

Lecture I: The Frontier and the Section in the Westward Movement.

This lecture would be a summary and restatement of my various essays on the significance of the frontier and the significance of sections. Possibly it might profitably be accompanied by lantern slides. It is a lecture that might interest teachers of geography as well as others, and it may very well be that my audience will not be so familiar with my published papers on this subject as I am!

II. The Beginning of the Westward Movement.

This would be based upon my two papers, "The First Frontier of the Mississippi" and "The Old West," covering chiefly the period from the close of the seventeenth century to the middle of the eighteenth century.

III. The Winning of the Mississippi Valley and the Great Lake Basin (Down to about 1815).

If this lecture stands in its present form, it will be necessary to sketch the trans-Allegheny movement of the Boones, etc., the period of collision with the Indians, the French, the Spaniards, and later the English, during the period of the French and Indian Wars, the Revolution, the diplomatic era of the French Revolution and the Napoleonic wars, ending with the War of 1812, in large strokes with a view of bringing out simply the essential features. The subject is obviously too big for any other treatment, and I am not sure about the wisdom of trying to bring it into a single lecture, yet I do not wish to give all my attention to the earlier period. It might be possible to take only one fragment of this period, suggesting the other topics merely.

IV. The West as a Factor in American Politics (From the close of the War of 1812 to the middle of the century).

This would be in part based upon my "Rise of the New West," except that the period would be extended and the treatment would be more summary; the main point to be brought out is the balance of power held by the West between the leading parties and the leading sections during that period.

V. The Pacific Coast in the Westward Movement.

Here again the problem is one of generalization of the movement with illustrations of some of its fundamental features. The effort is to make a synthesis of the various forces. I have already written papers on the significance of the Ohio Valley and the significance of the Mississippi Valley and the middle West. This would be an attempt to deal with the significance of the Pacific coast in American history.

VI. The Last Phase of the Western Movement.

This would deal chiefly with the region between the Missouri and the Sierra Nevadas. It might be called the significance of the Great Plains, the Rocky Mountains and the deserts in American history. It would include some of the generalization which I printed in various papers in which the effect of the disappearance of the frontier upon American democracy and industrial life has been discussed.

All of these subjects are appallingly large for single lectures. It may be that the treatment will, partly for this reason, seem somewhat shallow, and yet I am not sure that it may not be the most effective mode of dealing with the subject. An alternative program, with which I am not quite satisfied, might be as follows:

Lecture I. The Beginning of the Westward Movement.

II. Crossing the Alleghenies.

III. The influence of the Great Lake Basin of the Mississippi Valley.

IV. The Occupation of Texas and the Pacific Coast.

V. The Occupation of the Great Plains, the Rocky Mountains, and the Desert (to about 1884).

VI. The Close of the Westward Movement and its Influence upon American Society and Politics.

These are tentative suggestions; I may work out quite separate subjects. But I should be obliged to you if, as soon as you can, you would send me a night letter in answer to these questions:

1. Is much stress to be laid upon methodology and bibliography in the lectures? 2. Have you any preference between the first and second sets? 3. Have you any suggestions?

I should not bother you in this way except for the fact that you suggest the words "study and sources," and I want to be sure of your ideas in the matter, and I should like to know more about my probable audience. As I leave here on the 4th of June, it is desirable to get your ideas by night letter at my expense.

It is inexpressibly good of you to look after us in the matter of a location, as I have already written you. I do not suppose that I should be able to avail myself of a card to the Bohemian Club to such an extent as would warrant me in asking it, in view of the probably urgent demands upon you in this matter.

Cordially yours,

### *Editorial Policies*

It will be recalled that in 1915–16 Turner and his colleagues on the editorial board of the *American Historical Review* were accused by the "reform" group of entrenching themselves in power by reelecting themselves to office. In one of his letters to Clarence W. Alvord, editor of *The Mississippi Valley Historical Review* (now *The Journal of American History*) and professor of history at the University of Illinois, Turner discusses the editorial policies of the *American Historical Review*.

#### EXTRACT FROM TURNER'S LETTER TO CLARENCE W. ALVORD, JANUARY 27, 1915

I have before indicated my opinion that our readers needed some doses suited to their tastes, but I don't wish to give the impression that I think any lowering of standards would be for the best interests of American scholarship. It is worth a good deal to hold up a standard that is high. When I go to a meeting of various learned societies to which I belong, I always expect to *submit* to more papers than I enjoy, knowing that science is getting advanced in certain fields that I don't understand, or particularly care about, just as it is in the few articles or papers that I do enjoy. Something of the same principle attaches to a learned *Review*. All the tendencies in America are to "socialize us into an average," and we both agree that education means elevation rather than conformity. But we ought to print more American history articles, I think myself.

When you get leisure to think it out, I should welcome some indications of what you think ought to be the guiding principles in determining, for instance, whether an article dealing with Miss. Valley history, or Southwest history, or Pacific Coast history, &c., should be first submitted to the sectional review, or to the Am. Hist. Review. Is it practicable to work out such a principle to be suggested to contributors and to editors; or will this of necessity be left to work itself out? It seems clear that a logical extreme would lead to promoting a non-national attitude and that sectional treatment not open to one of the existing sectional Reviews, might fall back on the A.H.R., but we shouldn't like this—any of us!

I must add that I haven't any doubt that these sectional reviews serve an indispensable purpose; that they should receive and publish some of the best work done in this country; and that I am in sympathy with them, as you know. But the difficulty appears, for example, in the case of the large body of historical students outside of the particular section who can't afford so many reviews, and who don't have libraries which take them all. Thus except for the AHA, the particularly sectional [journal] which may often exhibit the really significant forces that shaped *national* history, the mass of historical readers remain uninformed. There is a real problem here.

I haven't anything on tap at the present for the M.V.H.R., but before the end of the year, I may find something to submit. If I happened to select a topic that needed election maps in black and white to illustrate it, could you publish them?—say three or four?

Cordially yours
Frederick J Turner

## *The Philanthropic Foundation*

In 1919 Max Farrand left Yale to assume the directorship of the Commonwealth Fund of New York; his temporary leave of absence was to prove permanent. Writing to Turner on February 12, 1919, he briefly described some of the attractive features of his new post.

This is not for publication, but just at this time when I need complete change and to get out of the rut there came a request from New York to take charge of a big new philanthropic fund that has been created. This I declined to do, but I did consent to take a year's leave of absence and try and formulate a plan of work for them. They want me to travel over this country and report on what I think are the best lines open for such a fund to take up. It is a fascinating job, will give me a chance to meet people, and get out of the academic atmosphere for a time, and appeals to me as the best sort of a change that I could get. I am so eager about it that I'd like to drop my work now; but that is of course impossible and I shall not undertake the job until next July, and even then I have specified for two full months off.

Turner responded enthusiastically to Farrand's account of the new foundation.

### EXTRACT FROM TURNER'S LETTER TO MAX FARRAND, FEBRUARY 13, 1919

What you write of your plans interests me very much, both because of yourself and because of the possibilities of such a foundation. The

Farrand family are in the way of constituting an interlocking directorate of some of the best agencies for a better order in America.

It is significant that the pioneer principle of association—"raising," "quilting bee" &c—is being applied to the higher life by great wealth. And that such foundations now tend to be formed *outside* of the Universities, rather than through their agency. Has this a significance in American life and cultural tendencies?

I have an idea that with all the need for such activities as the other agencies are carrying out in promoting medicine, relief of suffering, alleviation of the lot of labor, etc., there is a field of activity in keeping alive and extending among the—shall we say?—*Bourgeoisie,* the best ideals of our pioneer era—and helping to keep a knowledge of the America of the past clear while we adjust it to new conditions. Business men, even of college training, tell me that among themselves there is little real knowledge of American history as we understand it. Any safe construction should be built upon a consciousness of what historically is meant by the Promise of American Life. What could your philanthropist do in this direction? Medicine, Astronomy, Egyptian and Classical archeology, are looked after. What of the *American* background and fore-ground?

Do we really understand as a people what we have to give to the world,—what we have to build on for the future? The Carnegie Institution, except for scientific history, has been of late almost entirely a scientific laboratory—useful and highly important. But a laboratory on American civilization, its processes, and tendencies, the things of the spirit could also find a place.

You have executive gifts. The man who can hold the lever and the steering gear of a machine of several millions $ horsepower may well consider this side of things.

You needn't tell me that it would be easy to waste the energy in idealistic schemes—salaries to visionaries or academic dreamers in easy chairs—I know it. It isn't so easy to apportion funds to really important and useful work in the humanities as it is in Science. The problems are neither so definite nor so concrete as problems of hook worm, chemical dyes, the milk supply, etc. But they are real problems. *The creation of an attitude of mind toward the problems of American society and toward what America means, in its past,* as well as in its present and future, is as important as the problem of applying philanthropic gifts of exceptional individuals directly to *particular* scientific, or even social activities.

Effective building must proceed from the *general consciousness of the American people* as well as from foundations suddenly created out-of-hand by the exceptional man. And this consciousness is, in part at least, *to be created.*

How's this for sermonizing? I grow garrulous in my old age. But it may be a soporific for you.

Yours
Frederick J. Turner

## *Popular Education*

In his correspondence with Farrand, Turner criticized American universities for demanding too many teaching hours of faculty members, with the result that too little time remained for research. But he also recognized the need for good teaching, both in and out of the university; he recognized that the trend toward a shorter working week would place new demands on adult education programs.

### TO MAX FARRAND

7 Phillips Place
Cambridge 38, Mass.
[October, 1921]

Dear Max:

If you haven't read Arthur Pound's "Iron Man," in the October *Atlantic,* by all means do so. It deals with the effect of the automatic machine upon society, and particularly upon education,—education of the masses of producers for *leisure,*—the masses under automatic production being brought to a condition comparable to that of the son of wealthy parents.

Of course his town, (Flint, Mich.) an automobile producing center, is exceptional in that automatic machine production holds a position there which it doesn't in the average manufacturing center. But the exaggeration of conditions aids in analyzing the general situation—I think he hits a fundamental problem—how to educate for leisure.

Yours truly
F.J.T.

The tone as well as the content of the following letter to Arthur M. Schlesinger (then teaching history at the State University of Iowa) made clear Turner's dissatisfaction with the way in which history was taught in American secondary schools.

TO ARTHUR M. SCHLESINGER

Cambridge, Mass.,
October 22, 1922.

My dear Mr. Schlesinger:

I do not feel that I can advise very helpfully about the adaptation of history to secondary education. I have the general apprehension that in the proper recognition of the social studies and of the importance of fitting for the *present,* some short cuts may be taken on the history side which will be disappointing and misleading in their results. "Historical mindedness" is among the most important elements needed in modern civilization. I do not feel that in the past the schools accomplished much in this direction. But I suspect that a rapid résumé of historical factors in a course designed to help the pupil to understand the present will not be a substitute for the *training* that comes from a fuller contact with historical problems, processes and *methods of study*. Droysen's dictum that history is the "self-consciousness of humanity" deeply affected my own thinking and study; and my paper on "Social Forces in American History" still sums up most of what I should try to [express] in an answer to your letter.

Very sincerely yours,
Frederick J. Turner.

Will you kindly communicate this letter to your colleagues—I have taken the liberty to ask the Yale Review to send you a copy of my *Sections and Nation* in the October number.

## *Young Historians*

Arthur H. Buffinton had studied under Turner at Harvard. At the time of his correspondence with Turner he was teaching at Williams College and at the same time working on his doctoral dissertation. In answer to Buffinton's inquiry about his "scope and methods," Turner drew attention to his American Historical Association presidential address and to the views set forth by the historian-sociologist Harry Elmer Barnes, who at this time was writing about the "new history" and its relation to the social sciences.

EXTRACT FROM TURNER'S LETTER TO
ARTHUR H. BUFFINTON, FEBRUARY 26, 1921

Barnes' general point of view I agree with, tho' as you say, he may carry the reaction to an extreme. On my general ideas of the scope and methods, see my Social Forces (Pres. Address)! The man who does general history on these lines must indeed be a genius; but with some equipment in the other social fields and some knowledge of the scientific method and tools he should be able to consult the special works intelligently so as to proceed not too narrowly in the orientation of his subject and the development of it. But this can be done to more advantage in a limited than in an extensive field. And there must be monographic studies which are limited to the older type of history also; even these, restricted in whatever way the decision of the writer selects, will gain something from the consciousness that they *are* really restricted and that it is only a fraction with which the author is dealing. I don't object to rather rigid limitation of a study, if it is done expressly, and with the consciousness of the limitations.

Writing to the youthful Merle Curti at Beloit College in Wisconsin, Turner comments on the heavy demands placed upon the beginning instructor in American colleges and universities.

EXTRACT FROM TURNER'S LETTER TO MERLE CURTI,
OCTOBER 12, 1921

You are learning the lesson that all university or college men have to learn in the earlier, and too often in the later stages, of their experience, that American practice doesn't recognize the usefulness of leisure in the production of scholars. I saw a poor little spring in the Maine woods this summer which was doing its best to fill up, but on my return by the trail a few hours later I found it dry, and the tracks of the wild cat in the mud about it. This seemed to me a fair illustration of the experience of the instructor who seeks the career of productive scholarship—a supply of living waters to give the student, but whose supply is so drawn upon by the demand for constant giving that it has too little time to refill. Nevertheless, we have all been through this stage, and we do manage somehow.

Even after the stage of fewer class hours is reached, it is apt to come when the vitality is somewhat diminished, and there is the committee, administrative duties, and other wild cats to exhaust the supply, and then there are the personal conferences which take more out of the spring than is sometimes realized, for the graduates are expert *drinkers* and they are not satisfied with anything less than *fresh* water. On the other hand there is, to the instructor who reaches this stage, a stimulation and renewal in the suggestions and information,—and even in the errors,—that come to the teacher from the student, while the college instructor also has the inspiration and the challenge of the youth who come to his classes—So there you are!

You will find my old home much changed from the days when I was there; but you will like it, I think, and the men are able and wide awake and interesting instructors and *persons.* The library is a great workshop, especially on the West.

Thank you for your friendly words. It is cheering to know that one's students think he is not "lying down on the job." I took a long rest this summer, and feel just now that I know more about trout, canoes, and *Fords,* than I do about maps. But I am on the front trenches again, and getting limbered up.

I have to thank you for your work and your appreciation more than you have to thank me for anything I may have done.

Turner was full of admiration for his former student Homer C. Hockett, who taught the requisite number of hours at Ohio State University *and* carried on research and wrote books.

EXTRACT FROM TURNER'S LETTER TO HOMER C. HOCKETT, JANUARY 21, 1926

I am much pleased to hear of the success of your history and that this means to you larger opportunity for writing. I have felt that there was too little continuation of research writing on the part of men who have taken their doctor's degree after they became placed and that this was partly due to the exactions of the class room. University authorities, under the pressure of taxpayers, or benefactors in the business world, have felt it wise to insist upon class room hours, rather than upon investigation and the freshness to impress their students when they met them. In my own case this has not been so much a check upon writing as have been the number of graduate students who have needed personal guidance in so many and so different fields that I have had to scatter my research. The thing to do is to be born rich, or to get independent before you to try to write! Seriously, I class hours is reached, it is apt to come when the vitality is somewhat diminished, and there is the committee, administrative duties, and other wild cats to exhaust the supply, and then there are the personal conferences which take more out of the spring than is sometimes realized, for the graduates are expert drinkers and they are not satisfied with anything less than fresh water. On

"... graduates are expert *drinkers* and they are not satisfied with anything less than *fresh* water."

A Portion of Turner's Letter to Merle Curti, October 12, 1921
*Courtesy of the Huntington Library*

have always admired your ability to support a family, win Phi Beta Kappa, and handle classes and write. We need productive scholars.

### *The Huntington Library*

The Henry E. Huntington Library in Southern California, opened to scholars in 1927, was an institution devoted solely to research, and a new center for the study of Anglo-American civilization. In the following letter Turner describes the new institution to Marcus Lee Hansen, a brilliant young student who had studied under Turner at Harvard. By the time Hansen received Turner's tentative proposal about working at the library he had already accepted a fellowship from the American Council of Learned Societies to continue the immigration studies he had started at Harvard.

TO MARCUS LEE HANSEN

Hancock Point, Maine
July 22, 1927

Dear Hansen:

At Pasadena, California (P.O. San Gabriel, Calif.), there has been established a new research institution for the study of Anglo-American civilization historically. Mr. Huntington gave his library—a rare collection, strongest on Eng. & Colonial America—(mss. & rare books, with a good working library in the field to supplement it)—to trustees, with an eight or ten million dollar endowment for historical research and to provide for broadening and enlarging the library. Max Farrand is the newly chosen director. I am to go there in the fall for a half year as "Research Associate." Provision is under consideration for permitting research associates and assistants to visit other libraries in the period before the completion of the Huntington collections. Although a "collector's library," it profited by Mr. Huntington's purchase of whole libraries to get items wanted.

I have urged Farrand to consider immigration as a factor in shaping Anglo-Am. civilization and reactive influence (& I found him already sympathetic) and in you a possible member of the Research group of fellows and associates. He will need to make his trustees see this side of the subject—they are such men as Hale, the astronomer; Millikan, the physicist; Henry Smith Pritchett, of the Carnegie Foundation &c—& the idea is to do for Anglo-Am. history what the group at the Wilson Observatory & California Tech. are doing for science there.

Nothing is settled yet, and may be nothing will come of the immigration side. But he has asked me to get you to send him (Reef Point, Bar Harbor, Maine, his summer home) four to six separates of your *Review* paper on immigration (& other papers on that line if in print) in order to influence his trustees to see this side of Am. history. I don't know your plans but if you wish to write out, and amplify your present studies, I think that here would be a real opportunity, both to push this side of Am. history, to join a new center for research, and to carry on your writing. However, so many fields open before the director that I do not know how far he can be able to go at present in the way of providing researches & research material in that subject. The income of about a half-million is large, but so is the subject of Anglo-Am., the needs of enlarging buildings & library etc. So I should not count on any offer there in making your plans, but, for "the cause," you could advantageously send the separates, if you can, to him as a starter.

Cordially yours
Frederick J. Turner

[P.S.] *Scribners* Mg. for June, or July of this year has an illustrated article by Dr. Hale on the library.

The following report contains a survey of the material in Turner's field that scholars were likely to need but that the Huntington Library did not have.

TO MAX FARRAND

*F J Turner* to Dr *Farrand* Oct 25 '27 *Memo*
Needed in my investigations and not in the H.E.H. Library

Various sets of the works of American statesmen, including J. Q. Adams, Memoirs, and Writings among many others.—Just now I needed to consult G. S. Hillard's . . . [edition] of *Memoir and Correspondence of Jeremiah Mason,* for some Webster correspondence, important in my investigation of the period 1830–1850, and did not find it here. If I took a trolly or automobile and went to Los Angeles, I should probably not find it there. In any case it would mean about a half day away from this Library to look at material which might cover a page only, and yet be vital to my understanding of the subject.

This is, however, merely typical of difficulties of a like nature, especially in the period 1800 to 1860, and after the Civil War in the U. S. I am, I hope you understand, not making a complaint, for I understand how inevitably this condition arose. But for the future development of research here along the lines of your report, and for my immediate needs as Research Associate, I have thought that you should know the difficulties. The highly expensive rarities are here in such abundance as to astonish and delight the scholar, in the English and Colonial fields. But the region between the Alleghanies and the Sierras—so influential upon the form of American development, and the long period between 1800 and 1860, say, need additions of books, not expensive in comparison with Mr. Huntington's purchases, but essential to the student of American history, who must have the printed sources and the work of investigators and writers already published, if he is not to do over work already done, and to miss important suggestions for his independent treatment of these subjects.

A collection of doctoral theses in history would be important in this connection.

Sets of historical periodicals and similar publications not here should be added soon. Newspapers, so essential to the study of our politics and our civilization must for the most part be sought elsewhere, I fear, owing to their rarity, and to the strength of other libraries, in different parts of the country, in this material. This could be remedied in part by setting aside a moderate amount in the budget for traveling expenses of men appointed to research positions here when the policy is developed later; or possibly in the case of some important newspaper files, by the use of the photostat, which would, I suppose, give greater assurance of long life than the pulp paper of these newspapers themselves. Such reproductions have already been furnished by some libraries.

In view of the need of research scholars in the period since 1789, in studies not only of American political and constitutional history, but also of our economic development—industrial, financial, agricultural; —efforts should be made, in my opinion, to acquire a set of public documents of the United States before it is altogether too late. The Supt. of Documents, (Washington, D.C.) should be consulted on this problem. Lowdermilk once had a complete set for sale, but this was some forty years ago when I heard of it. Possibly some college or public library in a smaller town, where they have depositories and would gladly have space thus used for other purposes, in view of the fact that researchers did not frequent the library, might sell the H.E.H. a set as a whole, down, say, to about 1850, when the Los Angeles Public Library, perhaps, contains the continuation. Mr. Waters* just comes in and tells me that the law as now existent forbids "depositories" to sell or give, except to the U.S. But this may, I imagine, not be applicable to libraries which received the earlier volumes not as legally designated "depositories" under the later laws.

Mr. Waters tells me that when he was in Washington the Library of Congress had duplicates of much of the earlier public documents. He doesn't think these have been turned over to the Supt. of Docs. Probably Dr. Putnam, Librarian, would be ready to co-operate, by information on what could be done to bring here these important sources.

* Willard O. Waters, Huntington Library cataloger.

In a factory it would spell bankruptcy, if the workman had to take a railroad trip for a tool or a material immediately needed in his regular operations; but something like this exists here with respect to the men who may be called as research associates or assistants to work in the *national* period of American history. I have no doubt that similar difficulties will confront the student of English history, in his region and period, by the absence here of similar public records which may be obtainable now, but with difficulty and at high cost in a few years.

In American history, (by way of illustration), I do not find, after enquiry, that there is a set of the U.S. Financial Reports,—the reports of the Secretaries of the Treasury, with accompanying documents, —only sporadic numbers (in the Washington, and in the Civil War collections chiefly). But, as you know, and as any *business* man will realize, to attempt to deal with American development without such sources for financial, banking, money, taxation and similar factors, is hopeless. A set of census reports is lacking, (and for the earlier decades of its publication also at Los Angeles). This is serious for the student of social as well as economic history.

To supply such gaps now will be a relatively small expense, particularly when the princely sums paid by Mr. Huntington for the Library's treasures in rarities are considered. The cost of a single book bought by him during the Collector's Library development, would supply much of immediate needs in these tools and materials for its new function of research. But the rapidly increasing demand for such books by libraries and collectors is likely before long to make them obtainable only at prohibitive prices.

May I, from time to time, make note for you, of similar types of gaps which I meet? And may I say that all this implies no failure on my part to recognize, appreciate, and be grateful, for myself and for the profession, of the wonderful riches now in the library. The nuggets are mined; what is needed is the machinery and the material for treating this gold, for minting it, and for acquisitions in the ore fields essential to our work, but where the initial cost is low. I realize the financial problem also; but I realize also that cost and difficulty of purchase increase almost day by day.

So it looks to me. If it seems otherwise to you, no harm is done, any way, by these reflections.

Respectfully yours
Frederick J Turner

In the last letter of this group Turner comments briefly on Stuart A. Rice's *Methods in Social Science,* a case book published by the University of Chicago Press in 1931 which included a description of his own methodology written by Merle Curti. The paragraph on President Abbott Lawrence Lowell's Harvard report shows that Turner's interest in educational problems was as lively as ever in the closing years of his life.

TO MAX FARRAND

January 8, 1931

Dear Max:

The copy of *Methods in Social Science* which I sent you was one that I had myself ordered in advance (some time ago)—which may be the explanation of what you say regarding receipt of the book. With your comment as to its difficulty in "getting anywhere," I think I can agree; and also that it is far from being "light reading." The fundamental difficulty lies, perhaps, in the fact that, as one of my friends used to say, "Sociology includes everything from plumbing to psychology!" They are undoubtedly, however, working toward a better definition.

I am sending you my copy of President Lowell's last Report (which you may not have seen). On pages 5 ff. you will see (what I had long foreseen) that the tutor for the general undergraduate is becoming "an additional teacher in the course." This undoubtedly is a great pity; and the recognition by President Lowell (pp. 7, etc.) that the general undergraduate is not keenly interested in knowledge raises the question whether "the general run of undergraduates" does not include boys who would better never go to college. I note also what he says (on p. 9) of the increase of the normal scale for full professors; but the salary of the professor *emeritus* is based upon the old five-thousand-dollar rate. This does not seem to be quite in keeping with the realization that the cost of living has increased. *Eheu!* What I am interested in particularly, however, is [the] part that bears upon the fact that the Harvard doctorate should no longer be limited to those who have received the master's degree, and that he intimates that the problem is rather the real fitness of the man for receiving the doctor's degree than the number of years or the previous degrees that he has taken. When Dean Slichter was here this fall he told me that in Wisconsin, for the proved exceptional man, they did not even require the bachelor's degree as preliminary to the doctorate. With all of its danger this seems to be a move in the right direction; and Wisconsin seems to have moved earlier in that direction than Harvard.

Yours sincerely,

Dictated but not read.

# 4

# Social History and Politics

## *Introduction*

The two main tasks of the new history, wrote Harry Elmer Barnes in his *A History of Historical Writing* (1937, p. 391) are: "to reconstruct as completely as possible the civilizations of the past and to trace the development of the leading social institutions of today." It is a measure of the modernity of Turner's approach that such a statement serves admirably to describe his concept of the proper concerns of historical scholarship. Turner believed that the historian had an obligation to trace the social changes which paved the way for modern society, and in his 1891 essay on "The Significance of History" he called for historical studies on "society in all its departments."

Turner would have found it difficult to say where history ends and where contemporary affairs begin. As the readers of the letters in this group will discover, he was very much concerned with the relevance of past history to contemporary life, and particularly interested in pursuing those aspects of the past which might cast light on the present. "The value of our studies is not merely historical," he wrote William F. Allen in the first of the letters to follow. "If properly worked up they will be a basis for State legislation—And that is the right kind of historical work."

Such a point of view of course carries with it certain dangers: historians may overestimate the objectivity with which they approach contemporary affairs, forgetting that they cannot escape the pressures of the day. Thus it was that Turner, carried away by his sympathies for England at the time of the First World War, undertook work of a propagandistic nature. In later years he exercised a greater caution, recognizing that knowledge of the past does not necessarily provide the key to the present.

Turner was in any case convinced that "ultimate histories," whether of the past or of the present, could not be written, because there is no such thing as completely truthful and objective history. In "The Significance of History" he wrote that "*each age writes the history of the past anew with reference to the conditions uppermost in its own times*"; in other words, the age we live in dictates to some extent our view of the past. The relativity of historical knowledge was later stressed by both Carl Becker and Charles A. Beard.

Turner, along with Becker, Beard, and James Harvey Robinson, emphasized the importance of a broad, interdisciplinary approach to historical study and the relativity of historical truth. But of these four scholars it was Robinson who argued with the greatest conviction that selective study of the past would bring about improvements in the present. Turner certainly wanted an educated public, and believed that history could and should influence legislation. He believed that a knowledge of history helps us in arriving at wise decisions on future policies. Thus he argued that the frontier had been a safety-valve for Americans seeking a better life. The closing of the frontier introduced a period of dwindling resources, making planning more necessary than it had been in the past. Turner's attention was also focused on the larger—often international—problems. Yet it cannot be said that he regarded history as a means of bringing about *specific* social, political, or economic reforms.

Beard was not altogether satisfied with Turner's handling of the socioeconomic side of American history. In a censorious review of *The Frontier in American History* in the *New Republic* (25 [1920], 349–50), he accused Turner of neglecting the "conflict between the capitalist and organized labor." Turner apparently answered his critic, but all we have is Beard's letter of May 14, 1921: "I fear we must agree to differ about the influence of the West" (given in full in the letters that follow). Beard seems to have regretted attacking Turner in his 1920 review, and later wrote that Turner made important contributions to historical thought in giving stature to economic history and "in putting history on a scientific plane" (to Merle Curti, August 9, 1928). Turner's comments on Beard were few; he sometimes advised students to avoid treating history in Beard's "determinative" manner.

Other letters from Beard among Turner's papers are merely invitations to Turner (from the year 1919) to lecture at the New School for Social Research, organized in New York by Beard, James Harvey Robinson, John Dewey, and others. Robinson also tried to convince Turner to accept a lectureship at the New School.

Robinson and Turner had known each other since the 1890s. In 1911 Robinson wrote to ask Turner whether he would be willing to read David S. Muzzey's "new" American history textbook to see if it "kept within the bounds of well authenticated facts." Turner seems to have declined, for there is no further mention of the matter in his papers.

Turner considered himself a social historian; but neither he nor such competent social historians as Arthur M. Schlesinger and Dixon Ryan Fox ever produced a satisfactory description of this field: how is it related to cultural or intellectual history (to literature, religion, philosophy)? Does it include economics, politics, science, and law? Does it impinge on sociology in dealing with such matters as marriage and the family, class structure, and leisure-time activities?

Turner never attempted to answer these questions, but his preserved writings, correspondence, and notes show that his interests covered practically all of these areas.

Turner "hammered hard" on the frontier theory in his early essays, but he also did much to develop the concept of sectionalism in American history. In a draft on sectionalism preserved among his papers, Turner summarized his findings by stating "that the frontiers entered and crossed geographical provinces or regions which varied from the older colonizing regions; that these older regions themselves were unlike each other, and that in the extension of the older sections, differing men, societies, institutions, and ideals were being carried forward."

Thus Turner's theory of sections emphasizes the diversity and complexity of historical forces. To investigate these complex phenomena, to probe into the origin and development of regional societies, new methods of research were needed: in particular the social sciences had to be drawn into the process of historical investigation. At the same time the sectional concept provided a frame for the vast accumulations of data relating to American social history, data that might be confusing or meaningless without the unifying concept of sectionalism.

Modern society, Turner believed, could best understand itself by comprehending the complexity of historical processes. In his essay on "The Development of American Society" he reaches for a poetic image to describe the movements of history: "To him who looks below the surface of things," he wrote, ". . . society is a human sea,—mobile, ever-changing, restless; a sea in which deep currents run, and over the surface of which sweep winds of popular emotion, a sea that has been ever adjusting itself to new shorelines and new beds . . . ." Turner was indeed a confirmed social evolutionist. He probed the past in order to locate the roots of American character and government.

During the First World War Turner's commitment to the British cause led him to seek a more active role in national life; this he found in his work for the National Board for Historical Service, an organization that seems to have been allied with the Creel Bureau, the official department of government propaganda.

Turner was convinced of the rightness of America's alliance with England against Germany, and disturbed by what he believed to be biased or false arguments by those who opposed America's entry into the war. In a letter to Max Farrand on May 5, 1917, he indicated that he hoped the Board would operate in a purely scholarly fashion. Yet the atmosphere of the times made such hopes illusory. Turner argued in this letter that the Board would counteract "shallow historical argumentation" and "sinister manipulators of public opinion" by presenting authoritative historical arguments. Turner's letter to Farrand however makes clear that the "sinister manipulators" were those who attacked

England's past actions and that the Board's duty was to come to England's defense with historical arguments. Turner regarded his work as a patriotic activity which helped to counteract pacifist ideas. He believed moreover that professional historians were the right people to undertake this job.

Although Turner's connection with such activity may seem to us unfortunate, the belief that led him to it—that history is an extension of the present backward into time—was a healthy and vigorous one, lending excitement to studies that might easily have appeared dry and academic. For instance it seemed to Turner that the internal history of the United States might offer leads in preventing future wars, for the major American sections were not unlike nation states. Turner imagined a federation of European countries in which interest groups would cut across national boundaries and act as a deterrent to international wars. His description of a supranational body with broad powers, especially in the area of international commerce, has a prophetic ring about it, although in 1915 Turner recognized that such a development was at best a remote possibility. As late as August 22, 1925, Turner wrote to his student Edgar Eugene Robinson about the possible development of international political parties which might fight "sham battles" instead of real ones.

In an earlier letter to Robinson, written on August 8, 1911, Turner confessed that he was "fascinated" by "the dramatic quality of contemporary history as seen from the background of western development." His concept of history as a flow made it almost inevitable that the present should be included in his deliberations. But he did not maintain that all history contains lessons for our own day. In his letter to Richard Henry Dana of 1915 we find him rejecting attempts to use ancient history to explain the present. The bond is too tenuous, too many of the basic conditions of life have changed between that time and this.

Turner's modernity as a historian lies not only in his concern with the ties between the past and the present, but also in his many-sided approach to history. Again and again he emphasizes the need to investigate the interplay of social, economic, and geographical factors in order to arrive at a historically valid conclusion. In a letter to Dixon Ryan Fox of Columbia University (March 27, 1919) Turner stressed the psychological factors that influenced voting: prejudices, habits of thinking, or any one of a number of factors that might be more decisive than the material interests of the voter. In a letter of 1922 to Arthur M. Schlesinger, other neglected but possibly fruitful areas of investigation occurred to him—the history of agriculture and the development of the great urban centers.

Finally the letters in this group exhibit what might be called a scientific concern with the reliability of the evidence. The scholar must be expected to provide adequate documentation for his statements. Thus Turner, reading an article by his former student Louise P. Kellogg, dealing with France's policies toward America at the time of the American Revolution, is disturbed by her failure to examine material in French and Spanish archives that might have shed light on the question and made speculation unnecessary. In another letter he warns a colleague against the naïveté of accepting a newspaper's own figures as to its circulation—a minor point, but suggestive of the care, the lawyer-like zeal in sifting the facts, with which Turner surveyed the raw materials of his craft.

The reader of the following pages will be disappointed if he hopes to find treasures of historical thought that never found their way into Turner's books and essays. Turner's professional obligations simply did not leave him time to carry on the sort of correspondence in which historical ideas might be fully explored and developed. Nevertheless we discover here some of the qualities which we admire in his published work: the wide-ranging mind intent on what he calls the "processes" of history rather than on individual men and events; the insistence on a many-sided view of historical development; and the use of highly developed techniques of research designed to reduce to a minimum the unavoidable distortions of time.

*Social Forces in America*

The first letter in this group is to William F. Allen; it was written at Johns Hopkins after Turner had returned from the 1888 meeting of the American Historical Association in Washington, D.C.

The "Dy & Ty" course referred to by Turner was Allen's course on dynasties and tyrannies. Turner suggests that Allen follow it up with a detailed study of a period or country, or perhaps of an ancient and a modern state. Turner also refers to George M. Knight's "The History of Education in the Northwest" (summarized in *Papers* of the American Historical Association [New York, 1889], *3*, 252) and to Simon Nelson Patten's *The Premises of Political Economy* (Philadelphia, 1885). Turner's personal copy of the Patten volume at the Huntington Library (Ref. HB 171 P3) is heavily annotated and dated "JHU Nov. 10, 1888," indicating that the book may have helped him formulate his theories on the westward movement of emigrant peoples.

TO WILLIAM F. ALLEN

909 McCulloh St.
Baltimore, Md.
[Dec. 31, 1888]

Dear Prof Allen—

In spite of the fact that I have just sent you a letter, I wish to take advantage of my few moments of leisure just now to express my interest in the emigration work that is being done by you and Mr. Roeseler—It seems to me a *most important* work, as you know. I am glad that you are working out the fact of the dispossession of one nationality by another. Wisconsin is like a palimpsest. The mound builders wrote their record and passed away. The State was occupied, as I indicate in my fur trade paper, by the most various peoples of Indian race—Then came the French—Then a wave of Northern New York, and Vermont fur traders—those who living near the L. Champlain route or the Great Lakes, caught that fur trading spirit. At nearly this time came the miners from the South. Then the emigration from the *New York parallel* again, to the farm lands. Now begins the state's policy of attracting immigration. And see the effect on the legislative policy of Wisconsin (1) in its land grants to railroads, and (2) in the quick and ruinously cheap sale of its educational lands—(This last point, you remember, Knight's Am. Hist Assoc. paper brings out well) —This is an *early* illustration of what you speak of—the danger of immigration to our public school system. The railroads need careful study in this connection—their land policy is a vital factor in Wisconsin's peculiar development. And you will find that they are in some degree responsible for continually changing the character of the population, by inducing western emigration—

On the reason why a higher type is crushed out by a lower in some places, Dr. [Simon Nelson] Patten (Premises of P[olitical] E[conomy] p. 11) says "The ignorant and inefficient classes displace the skilled and intelligent, because their wants are so limited that they are able to give a greater surplus as rent than the higher classes do, and whatever class can give the greatest surplus gets possession of the field of employment, and thus the survival of other classes is prevented. By these social causes a high price of food can be brought about—" See all [on] p. 11 et passim for the elaboration of this idea. Wisconsin's experience would seem to strikingly confirm this view of Patten's as to the social causes of rent.

The social causes also work to *continue* the movement of dispossession of one type by another, when once begun. If you can get Mr. Pease (Montello) to make a careful study of Marquette county with a view to explaining the "Germanizing" of it, which I have before called your attention to, you will have interesting light on this side of the question. The effect of this movement on the school system there is also very noteworthy and confirmatory of what you have found. Permit me to suggest—(if it has not already occurred to you)—that the State Supt. of Schools, and the county supts. can furnish valuable assistance on this question.

I do not regard the movement as entirely to be feared. I think peasant proprietorship is not being weakened by these German settlers. The quick settlement of lands in small farms has, I judge, prevented the absorption of much territory into great estates. The population is on the whole a physically sturdy one—I remember that the Romans and the English were—if in a less degree—a "colluvio gentium omnium," and that it did not seem to *injuriously* affect them, at the least. I think that the German dispossession of the Irish in Marquette has at any rate increased the economic value of the county, and has substituted Lutherans for Catholics. But the Germans who hold so-called "free thought" ideas, and anarchistic ideas—and there are many along the Lake Shore, I'm told—need a revival of real religion and a vigorous administration of the common schools—The value of our studies is not merely historical. If properly worked up they will be a basis for State legislation—And that is the right kind of historical work.

It is interesting to know of the desire for higher history—It has seemed to me for some time that you were denying some students the best advantages to be gotten from your scholarship in this course in Dy & Ty Hist—and this idea has been emphasized since I came here by noting that Adams turns away his preliminary work, almost wholly to undergraduate instructors—But if I may be pardoned a suggestion I would advise a detailed study of some period or some country, rather than Andrews—For instance, take, as an illustration, Adams' plan of combining Roman history and Prussian history, from an institutional and *political* and administrative standpoint. This would be a year's study—Or other combinations of one ancient and one modern state, exhibiting similar tendencies, could run through a year's course—That, if I judge from my own experience, is what your students would like. They have the bird's eye view from the Ty & Dy course. Now let them have a good thorough study such as you so well can give, of some age, or some one people on other than purely institutional lines. I need only call your attention to Mrs. Sheldon's class to show that such work would not lack in popular appreciation —that it would gain in scientific value—needs no stating—Of course this presupposes the foundation work—

I shall be glad to have any disposal of my Fur trade paper that suits the society—I am becoming more than ever impressed with the fact that the French exploration, occupation and struggle for the Northwest, and the secret of its hold over that region, were not religious, nor chiefly personal, but that primarily they were governed by economic considerations—And I believe that the economic relations of civilized with primitive man is a neglected chapter in history in general—

You will excuse this long letter, and I will be less profuse hereafter—
With regards to your family

I am
Very truly yours
Frederick J Turner

Oh, by the way—Have you seen Bryce's *American Commonwealth?* And do you know that Howard* of Nebraska is writing a work on Local Government in the U.S.,—an institutional and constitutional discussion? And have you read Edward Bellamy's *Looking Backward?*

Turner's 1908 letter to his colleague at Wisconsin, John R. Commons, the economist, is an example of his astonishing ability to grasp—almost instantly it seemed—complex interrelationships between social, political, and economic history. Here he comments on the importance of Horace Greeley's editorials in providing a key to the understanding of many aspects of American development.

TO JOHN COMMONS

November 30, 1908.

Professor John R. Commons,
The University of Wisconsin.

My dear Professor Commons:

I am so much interested in what you showed me recently of your work on the editorials of Greeley that I am urgently desirous that the suggestion you made of the possibility of publishing a volume of his social writings should be made effective. One of the serious gaps in American historical writing is that of accounts of the social thought of the country. We have dealt with political institutions, and with economic life in a rather general way, etc.; but there is, as you especially know, a mass of material on the genesis and progress of movements for social change, conscious attempts to see whither American society was tending and to affect its development in the interest of democracy, which are too little known. I am sure you are making, and will continue to make, valuable contributions to this subject. For the immediate future, I doubt whether any more interesting or generally acceptable contribution could be made than the rescue of these writings of Greeley. He, as editor, was for years the prophet and mouthpiece of that New York–New England stream of settlers which made an intellectual section in the Old Northwest and the North East at the

* George E. Howard's *An Introduction to Local Constitutional History* was published in 1889.

time when this section was exerting a fertilizing influence upon American thought, framing social programmes, and proposing reforms (many of which were afterwards worked out into legislation). To understand the background of the reform policies of Roosevelt, for example, and the labor movement, the land policy of the United States, and in general the trend of American democracy in its social aspect, these editorials of Greeley have a special value. Through his writings the currents of social agitation of many reformers, many leaders and groups are revealed. Such a publication would be very timely in the present revival of interest in such subjects.

I should be very glad to be of any assistance in impressing a publisher with the importance of this undertaking.

Very truly yours,

The Indianapolis meeting of the American Historical Association in 1910 was one of the highlights of Turner's professional life. His presidential address, "Social Forces in American History," was widely praised. Almost equally gratifying was the moment when a handsomely printed volume, *Essays in American History Dedicated to Frederick Jackson Turner* (New York, 1910), was presented to him at a dinner given in his honor by his former students from the University of Wisconsin. In the letter below Turner mentions how much he enjoyed Carl Becker's contribution to the book, "Kansas," an essay which reflected Turner's own interest in the development of the American character.

TO CARL BECKER

Harvard University
Department of History
Cambridge, Massachusetts
January 21 1911

Dear Becker:

Your article on the Indianapolis meeting (I assume that you did it) naturally interests me very much, and I thank you for your kindly treatment of me and my paper. I find that you bring out the central thought of my address rather more clearly than I did.

But I am not content to have you think I am departing from the old faith! My whole attitude toward the relation of the West and the frontier especially is consistent; and I am just as much interested in these topics as ever. But I have always conceived of my work as that of dealing with the processes of American history rather than with a geographic section. The progress of these processes leads naturally, by the pressure of the facts, to the point when the frontier becomes subordinated in influence to general social forces—The West does not thereby cease to be influential, or a subject of deepest interest to the historian; for it happens that its growth and rise to power is coincident with the period of settlement for the nation of the questions of social structure, political institutions and ideals demanded by the closing of the era of free lands. It has a potential voice, and it has its characteristic Western ideals and social traits, at the time when it especially is in the position to arrest tendencies in the industrial life and society of the East, which if continued might result in the European type—So the West, as the heir to the experience of the frontier and of the democratic aspirations of the pioneer period, may be *creative* as well as *obstructive* to tendencies that menace the "promise of American Life,"* as Croly puts it.—

The frontier is and will be just as important a subject as ever for study in the era of its dominant importance. The West which has evolved from the frontier will continue to be fundamentally important, and there is much Western settlement, social and political construction, still to follow. The end of free lands doesn't mean the end of creative activity in the West. It is still in its infancy—But now we are face to face with more complex interrelations and with the restraint upon contending forces involved in the placing of them at closer quarters in a nation no longer flowing into the wilderness, and we must study these interactions.

What a bully essay on Kansas that is, of yours! I have also read with interest your Walpole, and await the more difficult test of your second paper. So far it seems to me you make your case and offer an important illustration of application of seminary methods to an interesting question. I had not seen the article before; but had heard Adams talk of it.

Jameson says of the Essays "You ought to be so proud of a tribute like that that it would be safest for you to carry weights in your pocket for some time"—They are there!

Cordially yours
Frederick J Turner

* A reference to Herbert Croly's book, *The Promise of American Life,* published in 1909.

*Politics and the Progressives*

In writing to yet another of his students, Edgar Eugene Robinson of Stanford, Turner touches on two themes of continuing interest to him: fishing and politics. Robert M. La Follette was at the time representing Wisconsin in the Senate.

EXTRACT FROM TURNER'S LETTER TO
EDGAR EUGENE ROBINSON, AUGUST 8, 1911

I have been working at home (and moving!) all summer, and shall not get away till the end of August—It has been exceptionally hot and I am anxious to get into the woods where I can try to raise a trout—Farrand and I are booked for a few weeks in Maine together in September—Mrs Turner and Dorothy are visiting this fortnight on the shore near Falmouth—We have had a pleasant year; but I am so ingrained a westerner that I rejoice at the newspaper accounts of how La Follette and the Western Insurgents are making new tariff history, even though there is "politics in it" and we shudder at the possibility of closing our woolen and cotten mills and our shoe shops and our bank accounts! The dramatic quality of contemporary history seen from the background of western development is very fascinating to me—

In the following letter Turner comments on the Progressives and on party politics, and makes some predictions about the presidential election of 1912.

EXTRACT FROM TURNER'S LETTER TO
EDGAR EUGENE ROBINSON, DECEMBER 26, 1911

We are well and happy, tho' we miss our Wisconsin friends—always shall, of course—and the snow and keen air,—which may be imaginary for Wellington dropped in yesterday with his waist line cut in two and told of tennis and golf all winter to date in South Dakota—It's wonderful how progressive politics will change the climate and reduce weight.

I find great interest in Wisconsin and La Follette—and more in the progressive movement here about Boston; but I am determined not to get so interested actively that I shall not be able to tell my story without prejudice or the reasonable apprehension of bias on my part by the

TURNER'S PARENTS

"My mother was the village school-ma'am."
*(Turner's autobiographical notes)*

Turner's mother, Mary Hanford Turner

"A man . . . who helped his fellows, and stood for good things."
*(Turner to Max Farrand, Nov. 16, 1908)*

Turner's father, Andrew Jackson Turner

*Courtesy of Dr. and Mrs. James G. Edinger*

Herbert Baxter Adams' "Seminary in History and Politics," Bluntschli Library, The Johns Hopkins University, 1890. Courtesy of the Johns Hopkins University Library.

Left to right: Charles Homer Haskins, James Albert Woodburn, John Hanson McPherson, John Martin Vincent, Herbert Baxter Adams, Andrew Stephenson, Toyokichi Iyenaga. All seminary students in the photograph except Stephenson were awarded the Ph.D. degree in 1890 from Johns Hopkins (including Turner who is marked as absent on a Huntington Library copy of the print). Haskins and Turner taught at the University of Wisconsin and Harvard, Woodburn a Indiana University, McPherson at the University of Georgia, and Vincent at Johns Hopkins Iyenaga lectured at the University of Chicago and Columbia but devoted his career to journalism Stephenson seems to have dropped out of the academic profession without completing hi doctoral work.

In his charming biographical sketch of Herbert B. Adams, John Martin Vincent wrote " 'History is past politics, and politics is present history,' formed the motto . . . painted on th walls of the seminary. Freeman's phrase needed much explanation to make it true, but it was fair description of the activities in those precincts." *American Masters of Social Science*, edite by Howard W. Odum (New York, 1927), p. 111.

"It is . . . one of the abiding disappointments of my life that we cannot be colleagues . . . ." (*Wilson to Turner, April 4, 1900*)

Woodrow Wilson in 1897

*Courtesy of the Library of Congress*

A Wilderness trip:
"Nipigon River Lake to Mouth," 1908

"F.J.T. en portage"

"Pres. C.R. Van Hise's coffee"

*From Dorothy Turner Photo Album*
*Courtesy of the Huntington Library*

The University of Wisconsin in 1884
*(Turner's handwriten notations on the back of the photograph identify the buildings)*

MAIN BLDG" "LADIES HALL" "NORTH HALL" "LIBRARY HALL" "SCIENCE HALL *....burned & replaced by new and better*

Turner's Room at Johns Hopkins *c.* 1889
*Courtesy of the Huntington Library*

Two of Turner's Teachers

"... the gentlest, justest, most scholarly man I ever knew. . . ."
*(Turner to Herbert B. Adams, Dec. 10, 1889)*

William F. Allen

Ely's ". . . method is (1st) to understand Mill; then compare him with . . . others . . . ."
(*Turner to William F. Allen, Oct. 31, 1888*)
Richard T. Ely

*Courtesy of the Huntington Library*

Founding Fathers of the State Historical Society of Wisconsin

"... Draper spent a half a century in collecting . . . ."

*(Turner to J. Franklin Jameson, August 10, 1895)*

Lyman C. Draper, Secretary of the Society, 1854-86.
*Courtesy of the Harvard University Library.*

"Thwaites' instincts were toward the romantic side, and toward editorial publication."

*(Turner to Constance Lindsay Skinner, March 15, 1922)*

Reuben Gold Thwaites, Secretary of the Society and Superintendent, 1887-1912.
*Courtesy of the Huntington Library.*

Turner's friend, Henry Morse Stephens, professor of history at the University of California, invited Turner to teach summer sessions at Berkeley and made several unsuccessful attempts to persuade Turner to accept a permanent teaching post on the Berkeley campus.

*Courtesy of the University of California Library, Berkeley, California*

Turner's lifelong friend, Max Farrand, *c.* 1931

*Courtesy of the Huntington Library*

Turner and his wife, Caroline Mae Turner, *c.* 1893, when he read his famous essay at the Chicago World's Fair.

*Courtesy of the Huntington Library and Dr. and Mrs. James G. Edinger*

Turner as a graduate student at the University of Wisconsin in 1887

*Courtesy of Dr. and Mrs. James G. Edinger*

Frederick J. Turner

1

Chapter I. Introduction

The history of the United States is the history of the occupation of a vast wilderness in a brief period. Nearly one hundred centuries of recorded history passed by while America lay unknown to the Old World, concealed in the wastes of the Ocean. It is only four centuries since Columbus planted the standard of Spain in the New World, and but three since England laid the foundations of the present United States by the settlement at Jamestown, Virginia.

But, though the time is brief, the nation which has evolved is as remarkable in its power and in its contributions to civilization, as it is in its youth. The area which it has occupied is vast. If Europe were placed upon the United States, the western coast of Spain would coincide with the coast of southern California; Constantinople would lie near Charleston, South Carolina; the southern extreme of the Italian peninsula would touch New Orleans; and the Baltic Coast would be in the latitude of the southern shore of Lake Superior. In other words, the United

"The history of the United States is the history of the occupation of a vast wilderness in a brief period."

The first page of Turner's unfinished "College History of the United States"

*Courtesy of the Huntington Library*

Herbert Eugene Bolton, one of Turner's former students, travelled over Southwestern trails as part of his research on the history of the Spanish borderlands. "Sometime you are going to complete your Parkman-like work," Turner wrote Bolton, January 20, 1916, ". . . . but you must water your rum, and offer it in a small glass to the man who is brought up on Parkman light wines —"

*Courtesy of the University of California Library, Berkeley, California*

Turner at home, 1923

"...I shall miss the opportunity to be your colleague, as I retire next September."
*(Turner to Arthur M. Schlesinger, December 18, 1923)*

Turner's home at 7 Phillips Place, Cambridge, Mass.
*Courtesy of the Huntington Library*

"That I have been associated with you, is one of the real pleasures of my life."
(Turner to Carl Becker, January 14, 1932).

Carl Becker *c.* 1930

*Courtesy Massachusetts Institute of Technology*

class. There is a thriving La Follette Club in Harvard, and I have agreed to talk to it sometime later. I think I shall speak of the session of Wis. legislature in 1911, which was a wonder, and which is a concrete example of tendency—also not a partisan subject!

If you want my own guess, Roosevelt will come in at the 'steenth hour and *fair-deal* the convention into another nomination to save the party. Possibly, if this doesn't occur, there will be a party split. In any case the danger is a conservative adoption of the democratic party —If the Republican party gets together on a tariff proposition that means supporting an American industry whether it deserves to live in the 20th century conditions or not, I shall probably vote the dem. ticket again, in spite of a deep distrust of its later actions; but there are some democrats I'll not vote for.

## *Historical Misconceptions*

Turner, writing to William E. Dodd of the University of Chicago, praised Dodd's *Statesmen of the Old South* of 1911. But Dodd's "bold forceful statements" sometimes, it would seem, resulted in oversimplification; and Turner was not altogether happy about the sources of some of Dodd's evidence: the testimony of Roger A. Pryor, Confederate politician and general, who had portrayed Davis as a man of moderation and peaceful intent, was perhaps somewhat suspect.

### TO WILLIAM E. DODD

153 Brattle St.
Cambridge, Mass.
Oct. 13, 1911

Dear Professor Dodd:

Did I write you how much pleasure I had in reading your *Statesmen of the Old South?* Its suggestiveness and its readability as well as its scholarship impressed me. I naturally like your interpretation of Jefferson particularly. On the Calhoun I should dissent at points, while thankful for new light; I have long been interested in Calhoun the politician, and in your general interpretation of him as shaping sectional alliances for the advancement of himself as the national leader I agree. Von Holst did not understand Calhoun, because he understood neither the South or the West. I hardly think you state Polk's attitude on unrestricted advance in Mexico with the limitations which you would attach to the statement in a fuller treatment. Nor does it seem to me that if Calhoun had come out for all of Mexico his presidential chances (nomination) would have been improved.

Your economic and sectional interpretation of Davis is very interesting, and the words regarding Davis' reluctance to start secession and war are more emphatic than in your life of Davis, where I read them with profit first. But the Pryor matter is new to me. I suppose you feel you can rely on his testimony.

In general, while I disagree with your judgments occasionally, and sometimes feel that the bold forceful statements go too far, yet in general with the underlying mode of interpretation I am so much in sympathy, and for your political grasp I have so much appreciation that these are minor points.

Broadly I think you present the case somewhat as the South itself saw it, without complete recognition of the difficulties arising in the Northwest to the program of statesmen like Calhoun and Davis. But you bring out more adequately than is generally done the existence of a Southern following in the Northwest. Perhaps on a more careful reading I should revise my feeling that you speak too appreciatively of the possibility of the Calhoun and Davis line of policy. You do not develop some phases which I should emphasize, but you present very much which I should have seen at too long a range to really comprehend.

Of course, I don't agree that the nation was a "league of states," by Davis' time at any rate. But the whole book is a bully corrective to the traditional treatment.

With good wishes and thanks,

I am

Yours truly,

Frederick J. Turner

When the superintendent of schools of Stambaugh, Michigan, H. M. Armstrong, wrote to Turner several years later concerning statements attributed to Abraham Lincoln on "liquor traffic," Turner answered on April 30, 1915, as follows. "Utterances attributed to President Lincoln usually require critical investigation, for he is credited with many sayings which belong to others."

Turner's 1915 letter to Richard Henry Dana, New England lawyer and amateur historian, raises the whole question of whether ancient history can shed light on modern problems. Turner argues that the further back we go, the more unsatisfactory is our knowledge of the past. Ancient history, based upon fragments of evidence, probably represents an approximate reconstruction of what happened. Modern and contemporary history provide the best guidelines for coping with the future.

TO RICHARD HENRY DANA

The Harvard Commission on Western History
Harvard University Library,
Cambridge, Massachusetts
May 3, 1915

Mr. Richard H. Dana,
113 Brattle Street,
Cambridge, Mass.

Dear Mr. Dana:

I have read your article with interest and profit. On specific questions of European history I am not qualified to point out any "misstatement." In general my suggestion would be that conditions in ancient history and, indeed, in much of the history of the past are so different from those in the present that lessons derived from anything but recent history are apt to be misleading. I have often thought, in observing the use made by the fathers of the republic of the experience of Greece, and Rome, the Helvetic republics, etc., that it was both deceptive and, on the whole, ineffective in really shaping the result. At any rate, I am sure that the present question of an adjustment at the end of the European war is not likely to be solved or put in the way of solution by remote historical examples. This may seem to you rather strange, coming from a student of history, but my own opinion is clear that the differences are so great as to invalidate any scheme based primarily upon remoter historical experience; and, even if that were not so, that the temper of the people who will have to be won is such that the plan will have to stand on its present merits rather than be based upon history.

In place, therefore, of one of the historians, it seems to me that a trained economist or a business man familiar with the larger aspects of world commerce, banking, etc., should be substituted.

I also venture to suggest that the committee would assist in the solution of the problem if they were to undertake a careful analysis of the elements of collision between nations such as have been influential in bringing about the present war. Such an analysis would undoubtedly reveal economic ambitions, as, for example, the Bagdad Railroad and its sphere of influence, as well as racial and general national ambitions. A workable scheme must be based upon a clear appreciation of the difficulties in the way of the scheme.

Our own history does seem to afford a basis for judgment in this matter in view of the fact that we have occupied a region as large as Europe and have kept the peace rather better than Europe has in the course of this development,—unless one regards our Indian policy as an exception. Our sections have taken the place of European nations. If it had not been for the Constitution, which operated upon individuals rather than only upon sections or states as such, and particularly if it had not been that our party organizations ran *across* sectional lines, I do not see how we could have kept the peace. Whenever party and sectional lines became practically identical, as in the case of New England Federalism and pro-slavery Democracy toward the end of the struggle, we have faced conditions very similar to those of Europe. Because Europe has not found any central organization capable of penetrating beyond the boundary of the *nation* itself, and because there have not been parties international in their scope, we have the bare impact of nations or allied groups of nations upon other nations or groups of nations. This means wars instead of peaceful adjustments by laws. Just what could take the place of American political parties in any conceivable readjustment of European organization is not easy to see. It is conceivable, however, that to some central organization might be assigned not merely judgments in respect to a restricted field of activity, at first, to be enforced upon separate states by other groups of states, but to be enforced also by direct contact between such a central power and the individual. It is also conceivable that to such a body might be assigned jurisdiction with respect to problems of international transportation, and business intercourse, such as tariffs, an international currency, banking systems, etc. It is, perhaps, not *in*conceivable that such a body might be given the power to regulate international trade and corporate development, and questions of labor and capital; but if it is not entirely inconceivable, it is, at least, very remote.

Assuming the possibility of such an organization, however, then *parties* would naturally form, in which the common interests of groups of men in England and Germany together, for example, might be greater than their distinctive interests as Englishmen or Germans. This would substitute a *federal state* for *Europe*.

I am not making this last suggestion with the idea that you should accept it or incorporate it in your paper. Possibly I shall include it merely as illustrative of the significance of our own development in a paper which I am preparing for the American Historical Review on "Sectionalism in American History." I mention it rather because it indicates the kind of analysis of the problem and the lines of solution which it seems to me such a committee might take up more profitably than to examine the remoter historical experiences of nations before the age of commercial intercourse under the new conditions of world trade, large scale production, colonial rivalry under the new conditions, etc.

Summing up my comments, the only criticism that I am inclined to make is that you over-emphasize the possibility of remoter historical examples and do not sufficiently urge the necessity of examination of present conditions.

With thanks, I am,

Sincerely yours,
Frederick J. Turner

In the period following his retirement from Harvard, Turner frequently referred in his letters to fallacies that had grown up around particular sections of America. The "golden age" of New England, for example, was the invention of historians: "James Truslow Adams' 3 volumes of New England history, put the history of that section in a new (and outsider's) light. They are worthwhile as an antidote to the golden age conception of our forefathers, but aren't muckraking." (Turner to Edward T. Hartman, Jan. 5, 1926).

In a letter to Andrew C. McLaughlin of the University of Chicago (Feb. 26, 1926) Turner criticized his former colleague, Edward Channing, for talking about the "solid south" before the South as a section even existed:

Writers like Channing in his discussion of the election of 1828, e.g.—speak of a "solid south" which did not yet exist. The trans-

Alleghany area, for example, was still the "Southwest" if not the "West," and had not conformed; the Up-country had not been assimilated to tidewater. The slavery and representation and taxation questions agitated in the North Carolina and Virginia conventions, the politics of Georgia . . . all mark divisional lines. Kentucky and, to a large extent Tennessee, still thought of themselves as "Western" in state classification.

In 1927, in a second letter to McLaughlin, Turner discussed the relationship of "the shrinking space element" to national unity on the one hand, and to sectional self-consciousness on the other.

### EXTRACT FROM TURNER'S LETTER TO ANDREW C. MC LAUGHLIN, JUNE 8, 1927

Hancock Point, Maine
June 8, 1927

Dear McLaughlin:

I always like to have a letter from you, and hear you "think out loud"; but as I left just as your letter came, I brought it on here with me.

I don't for a moment doubt that the shrinking up of the space element by transportation, communication and trade makes for nationalism and that economic processes are foundational (but not "determinative") beneath the influence of men like Henry Clay. Both the man and the conditions are included, I think, "the sport," in biological phrase, and the persistent tendencies—the leader and the voice and the movement which represents and stands for, as well as guides,—all this sounds durned serious, don't it! I once timidly enquired of Woodrow Wilson in our Baltimore boarding house: "Is society an organism?" and he took me one side, holding my coat lapel, and whispered: "Yes, but keep it in the dark!"

But while communication, in the broad scope of the word, tends as a whole toward unity, there are times and conditions when it accentuates sectional rivalries and I do not think it ever will obliterate regional or sectional consciousness. Witness the Bagdad railroad issue; the Great Lakes–St. Lawrence deep water way now; the Long & Short haul question; the reaction of the changes made by the Panama canal; the Baltimore, N.Y., Boston, & Philadelphia contests in the Interstate Commerce Commission hearings—and such!

"*Adjustment*" of sectional disagreements is the task of the real statesman who visions the thing nationally as Clay did. But Webster, Clay, Jackson, and all the rest of them have taken their nationalism with a sectional flavor, as I think you will agree. Their sectional background & interests and personal advantage happened to coincide with a national course. Not so with Calhoun in his later years, but he tried hard.

Some time our concealed sectional realities will achieve formal recognition in an intermediate organization of governmental regional federative units intermediate between state and nation.

## *Turner and World War I*

After 1914 Turner's letters show an increasing concern with the war that was being waged in Europe. Here, in an extract of a letter to Carl Becker, written March 10, 1916, Turner comments on American Midwestern reaction to Germany's aggressive policies.

I love my Middle West, though just now I am rather pained at the explanations I am forced to make for her failure to back up the President when Germany cracked the whip. The issue is an undesirable one on which to go to war; but the attitude of the Mid West will persuade Germany that she governs it—and that's neither good for the self respect of the M. W.—nor for the peace of the world. Since the Germans have "assumed the task of Fate," perhaps you will tell us in your next, what they are spinning for the "heart of the Republic" between the Rockies and the Alleghanies—Will they placate you while they blow us up?

By 1917 Turner was wholly absorbed in the work of the National Board for Historical Service, an organization headed by historians James T. Shotwell of Columbia University and Waldo G. Leland of the Carnegie Institution, Washington, D.C. It is strange to think of Turner as a dedicated member of a group which used history to win support for England; yet at the same time Turner stressed the need for objectivity in treating contemporary history and did not seem to feel that objectivity was incompatible with his work on the Board. In the following letter to Max Farrand in 1917 Turner argues that professional historians can perform a useful national service by counteracting anti-British propaganda with historical facts and arguments.

TO MAX FARRAND

National Board for Historical Service
1133 Woodward Building
Washington, D.C.
May 5, 1917

Dear Farrand:

Leland tells me of your letters to him. I entirely understand your doubts. The underlying idea is that both in the matter of public opinion and national policy in respect to the war, and in regard to the American interests and principles respecting conditions on which peace may be made, American historians ought to have useful contributions to make. Like enough the events will move so rapidly that public opinion will rather follow than create them. But, nonetheless, there is in American habitual ideas much that needs enlightenment from men with the historical temper and historical point of view. When times of real suffering and sacrifice come, it will be possible for shallow historical argumentation and for sinister manipulators of public opinion to cloud the essential historical facts and conditions. We need to bring into relief particular conditions that underlay the disputed aspects of American history that will be discussed. England's attitude, for example, in the period of the Revolution and of the Civil War can be made to serve as irritating and poisonous material by evilly disposed minds, to a degree unwarranted by all the facts, considered in the modern historical temper. The actions of the government of England were offensive enough. There was then and there will be now, special English interests and programmes inconsistent with our own. The *degree* of the offense, however, and the *extent* of the difference in interests and aims should be examined, if it becomes necessary to refute misrepresentation. The distinction between *the England of those days* and the England of today needs historical statement, with due attention to facts of governmental organization, and economic and social conditions. The attitude of the *people* in contrast to the *government* should be considered; and the recent changes in the place of democracy in England set forth.

There will be falsification of the facts of history by some, and misapprehension by others, e.g. Champ Clark on conscription in the confederacy. If the historians, including *local* teachers, brought into relation with scholars on the disputed points, cannot be helpful in the formation of correct thinking on such topics, who can?

We believe that the Board should not become anything like a professed repository of historical orthodoxy; that there should be no warping of history to serve a special end; that there should be no historical machine with its governing levers here. Rather this Board should be a center of information of the areas and the subjects wherein there is obvious misrepresentation of history; that it should, with its correspondents, try to *foresee* points of misrepresentation and find men who could help to examine the *facts* and the conditions that underlay the facts. That it should not only help to put the problem and the scholar into touch; but that it should be useful in informing journalists, lecture bureaus, perhaps congressmen, regarding men qualified to give historical testimony, sources of evidence, etc.

Beyond this primarily historical service of the profession, there is work to be done in the field of discussion of large policies to which the historians should be called. Conferences and correspondence on problems of the *terms of connection* with England, France, & other nations at war with Germany; and interchange of ideas regarding the merits of the terms which England, or France, or Russia think fit and necessary before peace should be declared. The argument will in part proceed on historical ground. If primarily by Europeans it will lack objectivity to say the least. How far do *American* interests, considered largely, not narrowly, require us to support the particular aims of these countries as conditions of peace.

These are statesmen's topics. But the historical training ought to be of use to Americans who write of them. Of course the *Board* shouldn't do these things. But may it not be a means of interchange of ideas among many men?

I could give you a long list of specific topics which ought to be discussed by the historian as a means of helping public opinion; but you can as readily state them. We shall have to make sacrifices. What sacrifices, concretely and in enough detail to be visualized did our forefathers make for American ideals?

We are setting up ideals of democracy, rights of small nations, visions of a world more nearly peaceful, leagues of honor. These are not new ideals. They might profitably be historically traced. So might our own federal and sectional evolution in an area equal to all Europe be examined with reference to its bearings upon Europe's problems.

Why did European immigrants look upon the United States as a house of refuge from Europe? What were the historic ideals that are worth dying for? These are in part at least historical questions; not to be answered alone by flag raisings and cheers, but by examination and illustration; by quotations from the men honored in our history; by interpretation of these quotations in the light of the times of their utterance.

I am myself likely to have to go to Cambridge later in May. I have only the desire to help to suggest activities, not to administer or to direct them. I do not expect to continue on the Board after it is *started*. But I do hope to help throughout.

If there is no need of any such organization; if the replies indicate that it would better be abandoned, I know the men here will feel that having freed their own conscience, they can turn to such individual avenues of service as they may open for themselves, and be glad to do the better thing. But unless such an enquiry is first made, many men will not feel that they are free from a duty as men who have made a study of history—European as well as American. They will feel a sense of treason to their cause if they are silent while pacifists set forth the meaning of American history, its lessons, and its finger points to committees of congress, in the public press, in lectures, etc.

*Some* people will use American and European history to affect opinion and action. Such history as is used by whomsoever, should be real history, the search for the truth, the truth in its full significance and in relation to its times. No Board can administer or possess this truth. But it can be an intelligence office to find the best seekers after it, and it need be but one such office among many others.

This is indeed a Polonius-like sermon. I am ashamed of it already; but it indicates my feeling. We none of us have a perfectly clear-cut picture of the job. We are seeking to enlist counsel and suggestion rather than handing down solutions, as yet. I myself think this search is the best thing we can do. Possibly *all* we can do is involved in it.

Yours truly
Frederick J Turner

In a letter to his former student, Herbert Eugene Bolton of the University of California, Turner tells something of the work of the Board, and urges that students be given assignments with a contemporary slant; essays emerging from such assignments might be used by the Board in its educational program.

TO HERBERT EUGENE BOLTON

NATIONAL BOARD FOR HISTORICAL SERVICE

James T. Shotwell, *Chairman*
Victor S. Clark
Robert D. W. Connor
Charles H. Hull, *Vice-Chairman*
Carl Russell Fish
Waldo G. Leland, *Secretary-Treasurer.*
Gaillard Hunt
Frederick J. Turner
Charles D. Hazen

1133 Woodward Building
Washington, D.C.
May 11, 1917

My dear Professor Bolton:

European historians have long had the quickening, though at times dangerous, consciousness that their modern historical problems were instinct with life; that their topics for research involved sensitive international relations, were live wires connecting with stores of dynamite, were liable at any moment to pass from history into present action.

Are not American historians learning that some of the important facts in our democratic development are more intimately connected with present urgent choices of domestic policy and foreign relations than had been commonly appreciated?

Is it not possible that in research work during the present summer and winter, at least, we ought to make fuller use of our realization that out of history there are issues of life to-day?

Can we not give greater zest to our research work, both in seminary and as individuals, by dealing with phases which are directly or indirectly connected with present problems? Shall we not feel better justified in following the scholars' calling if by our investigations we furnish material useful to Americans in determining their decisions in the great issues which now confront them and which will, in changing forms, confront them for a considerable future?

These are matters, not only of presenting the results of previous study and writing; they are matters for new and unforeseen adjustments of old to new; for research, and for research under the pressure of instant demand for information.

In the first place it is important to be able to furnish a background for news items. Our Board is already in a position where we shall often have advance information as to what will be news in certain lines some time before the event. This advance information would give a student familiar with the field and bibliography of the suggested subject time to produce an article which, though not final, will yet possess an intimacy of touch and an orientation impossible to a reporter.

If, for instance, we know that a seminary is being conducted in the general field of the administrative history of the Civil War, and we find that a committee of either house will in three weeks time report in favor of forming a committee on the conduct of the war, we may reasonably ask such a seminary to give us an article on the subject at ten days' notice, and we can notify the press that we will be in a position to give it to them, when the subject becomes news.

In the second place there are certain aspects of history with which the public should be familiar, but the significance of which is apparent only to one with a long perspective. In such cases the historians of the country should take the initiative, not waiting for the press.

In his speech at the Gridiron Club dinner, in Washington, February 26, 1916, President Wilson showed how deeply he was influenced by the historical mode of approach to his problem. He said:

"You can never tell your direction except by long measurements. You cannot establish a line by two posts; you have got to have three at least to know whether they are straight with anything, and the longer your line the more certain your measurement. There is only one way in which to determine how the future of the United States is going to be projected, and that is by looking backward and seeing which way the lines ran which led up to the present moment of power and of opportunity. There is no doubt about that."

The historical research and thought of the country should surely be concerned with this work of surveying American tendencies and ideals. It is important for us to know what, in the opinion of the profession, such subjects are, and to know whether they are being studied and if so, where. If they are being neglected we may be able to promote their study, and if they are being studied, we are in a position to bring the concentrated results before the public widely over the country.

The third function of research is one in connection with which the Board can do little, but the leaders of research in the country by correspondence and intercourse may do much. It is obvious that the problem of world reconstruction will not cease to be vital to the next generation. Not in detail but in general, it is possible to foresee the kind of questions which it will ask of its historians. Ought not a good proportion of the young scholars in our seminaries be directed to interest themselves, whatever their fields, along lines which may contribute to the wise solution of these problems which will be the pivot of politics and legislation during their lives? An illustration may be made in the fact that the devotion and skill which have been given to a study of the Napoleonic Wars, and even of our Civil War, have yet left almost untouched many subjects which throw most direct light upon the difficulties of to-day. Will it not be possible for us to do something—we all realize how little prophetic we are—to make this loss of experience as slight as it may be for the future?

As a first step will you not write the Board any ideas you may have on the general subject and any contribution you may be prepared to make?

After we receive information, we shall be glad to communicate with you, noting whether certain topics seem to be in need of attention by historians. In case of subjects actually under study we shall be glad to be of use in giving a national currency to the concentrated historical results. Will you not convey the ideas of this letter to such of your colleagues as you think willing and able to assist in the work?

Very truly yours,
F J Turner
For the Board.

## *The Complexity of History*

Turner wrote the following letter to Professor Dixon Ryan Fox at Columbia University in 1919. In it we find an excellent discussion of the various kinds of factors that may cause voters to vote as they do.

### TO DIXON RYAN FOX

7 Phillips Place
Cambridge
March 27 1919

Dear Mr. Fox:

I am always glad and fortunate to get your papers, for they are directly useful in my own studies.

I have just been doing a series of maps, as vacation amusement, on the distribution of political majorities in the period 1844–1856 incl. with some attention to the persistence of these groups, especially of course the *northern,* in 1884 and 1916. My maps so far are limited for the purpose of this study [to] the Miss. Valley states, tho in other form I have them for the whole country. These maps by *counties,* are correlated with others, on the same scale showing geological factors, soils, illiteracy, wealth, areas of interstate and foreign migration, roads, railroads, etc., as well as density of population. They are extremely informing, for they show the same relationship which you stress in N.Y., the class aspect of Whig and Dem. contests, and later Rep. and Dem. But they also show the regional distribution of the preponderances. The two things are related—even within the cities.

For an economist's estimate of the significance of the period about 1840 in relation to a leisure class and a labor class, foreign immigration, decline of birth rate etc., I found F. A. Walker's Phi Beta Kappa address at Brown useful. I think it was republished in a vol. of essays by him.

My reading of the newspapers of the 40's, and the debates in state constitutional conventions of the period 1840–50 etc., shows that the main proposition of importance of class control is correct *and* that it was contemporaneously recognized at least in the Miss. Valley.

See the whole history of the infiltration of Locofoco ideas into the Democratic party after the crisis of 1837. Harrison recognized his own position as in fact the candidate of Jacksonian pioneers as well as of Whigs. The Whigs undoubtedly camouflaged that election (1840) with log cabins, as Benton's "log cabin bill" forced the leaders to disclose.

Jackson explained the result of the election of 1840 in Tenn. as due to the Census takers, enumerating ducks etc. etc. to the disgust of the honest farmer.

Clay laid his defeat in 1844 to foreign voters.

There is danger in any simple formula for expressing party affiliation or success as you point out in your comments. . . . [A writer may give]* his readers the impression that men rather consciously cast up the advantages and disadvantages of their party attitude toward their own particular pocket book and acted in accord with the conclusion. This impression, for I don't suppose he would frame his own views

* Brackets and ellipses are in the manuscript, which is a typescript copy of the original.

of party action thus, lays too little stress on the unconscious predilections of the group, the intuitive sympathies and oppositions of classes, —not even class-conscious in much of that period. I suppose that the average voter saw rather the weak points of his opponents than his own special and selfish interest. The Whig or Republican—speaking roughly—saw the Democrats as unwashed, or illiterate, or unsuccessful men, not to be trusted with the conduct of the affairs of county, state, or nation; the Democrat saw in the Whig or the Republican of later days, a man who was of a privileged class with special interests, a belated Federalist or an incipient aristocrat, who was violating the principle of popular rule, rotation in office, etc. In both parties were men of the opposite classes, and sometimes, as perhaps in the up country of North Carolina, or the southern Alleghanies more generally, there seems to be a large influence of mere antagonism to the low country. Whigs are Whigs there partly because they may be on lines of intercourse and trade, partly because they need internal improvements to bring them a market, partly because they are non-slaveholders, but also I believe partly because they were "down" on the low country region on general principles and found that region tending to Democracy in their neighboring counties. The factors are sufficiently various to make plausible any one of several explanations, as in a refined analysis of a geological region the investigator must apply the "multiple hypothesis" and note the coexistence of more than one influence. When they combine they produce their strongest effects. When they are in antagonism there may be unstable results. And the party leaders always try to make a platform of more than one issue in order to hold their varied following, varied in regions and in classes. Roosevelt's "square deal" nearly swept the whole country in 1904,—but the application of the square deal was as difficult as the *details* of a League of Nations! And when all was said and done the Republicans split into Progressives and the rest, and Wilson came into power.

Your statistics of newspaper circulation are useful tools, if you don't trust them too far—for newspapers misrepresented their circulation, and there were appreciable numbers who didn't vote as they read (For instance I take the Boston Transcript!). But your general use of this data is, I think, sound. I have a student at work on the Boston press, 1830–50, and her study of the editorials, type of news, etc., tend, I think, to confirm your own view of the relations of the penny press to democracy and the reverse.

Regarding city statistics, there is a useful paper by Horace Secrist on the distribution in N.Y. City about 1828 which confirms your views. I think it was published in the Wis. Acad. of Arts and Sciences, under the title The Auction System.*

Recent history and every politician's knowledge of ward preferences tell the same story. I think your figures convincing.

Whig slogans of opposition to executive interference etc. etc. were like the debates in the ratifying conventions of the 1787–9 era, better ammunition than frank statements of class interest, and they believed their slogans too—at least in part!

And after all there is also room for the idealistic issues especially under *strain*. Men will vote at times from patriotic, or religious, or moral motives against their personal interests. But it is so easy to construe one's patriotism and his ethics consistently and unconsciously with one's other interests, that such occasions are high water marks.

When I started I meant to write but a page or two!

Yours truly

Frederick J. Turner

The copy of an important letter Turner wrote to Charles A. Beard about this time is not among Turner's papers, but we know that it contained a restrained and perhaps even a cordial comment on Beard's scathing review of *The Frontier in American History* which appeared in the *New Republic* (25 [1920–21], 349–50). Beard's main criticism was that Turner had failed to deal with conflicts between labor and capital, but his reply to Turner's letter indicates that there were other areas of disagreement between the two men.

FROM CHARLES A. BEARD TO TURNER

New Milford, Conn.,
May 14, 1921.

My dear Mr. Turner,

I was in Europe when my review of your book was published and your letter passed through many vicissitudes before it reached me a short time before I sailed for America. This explains the long delay

* *The Anti-auction Movement and the New York Workingmen's Party of 1829* (Madison, 1914).

in acknowledging your kind note, for which I am very grateful. On reading again my review and examining carefully your letter, I am impressed with the elusive character of words. In what a sad state our historical terminology is and must be!

I fear we must agree to differ about the influence of the West. Undoubtedly slavery, capitalism, and free land were woven in one national mesh and free land contributed a unique factor. Still, as I see things, slavery would have been slavery and capitalism capitalism in essence even had there been no free land with its accompaniments.

On Americanization, I surrender, for frankly I do not know what the term means or ever has meant. About the only test I can apply is that of plain loyalty in a crisis, and certainly Germans of long standing in the West fell down rather badly. I would put it this way: free land makes free farmers; America has had more of them than any other country; hence a free farmer is more characteristically American than an industrial worker.

On the "conditioned" clause, I am inclined to stand pat, especially as you have inserted "practically." Still I am inclined to say that Eastern capitalism "conditioned" land legislation, the slavocracy helping. Neither of them relished the growth of a free landed class. Capitalism feared the effect on wages and slavocracy on the balance of power.

As to "loose construction" we seem to be agreed. As I read American history both individuals and classes are for or against loose construction according to their view of their interests. The West was no exception. You say that Calhoun did not represent his section in 1816. Well, if you will read his tariff speech again you will note that the main thing he wanted was a market for Southern products that could not be interrupted by European wars.

I hope that I may sometime have the pleasure of going over some of these matters personally.

Yours sincerely,
Charles A. Beard

In 1922 Arthur M. Schlesinger sent Turner a copy of his *New Viewpoints in American History,* and Turner responded with an autobiographical account of his own intellectual development. Turner seems rather flattered that Schlesinger regards Reuben Gold Thwaites and Milo M. Quaife (both of whom had served as directors of the State Historical Society of Wisconsin) as his disciples. But he points out that both scholars, as well as Clarence W. Alvord, who had completed a valuable study on *The Mississippi Valley in British Politics* (published in two volumes in 1917), had worked "on their own."

TO ARTHUR M. SCHLESINGER

7 Phillips Place
Cambridge, Mass.
April 18, 1922

My dear Professor Schlesinger:

I have received from Macmillan, by your courtesy as I suppose, a copy of your *New Viewpoints in American History*. Let me thank you both for the interesting book, and for your very generous references to my work.

You have undertaken an attractive, and by no means easy task, and from such reading as I have been able to give the book, it seems to me that you have done a useful work well. I am always impressed with the slowness with which "new viewpoints" really get into the educational system and the public mind. Just now I am working on one of my own, a somewhat different conception of the word *sectionalism* in our history than is usually presented. I have unfolded it at various meetings of historical and geographical societies and hope I am now ready to make a more formal presentation.

What you say of my frontier studies being fundamentally an economic interpretation interests me. Personally I don't know. There is in this country such an interrelation of ideals, economic interests, frontier advance (or recession, if you prefer), and regional geography, that it isn't easy to separate them. One whose activity has been more continuously in an urban environment would no doubt lay more stress than I have in my published essays on the importance of the economic revolution substantively, but I am aware of its importance and although my essays have been more related to the influence of the free lands and the frontier in a large sense, they show my appreciation of the economic changes. I was especially impressed by them in writing my survey of the United States, 1865–1910, for the Encyclopedia Britannica, and in my lectures I have emphasized them more than in my addresses. The truth is that I found it necessary to hammer pretty hard and pretty steadily on the frontier idea to "get it in," as a corrective to the kind of thinking I found some thirty years ago and less. But I now hope to add a companion piece (the *Section*) to the *Frontier,* and if I live, to attempt a coordination of these old and new viewpoints in a general sketch of our history, emphasizing the dynamics rather than the statics: the genetic element, and the *flow* of it all.

Apropos of your list of what you call my "school," I should be delighted to be able to enroll such men as Thwaites and Alvord and Quaife; but aren't they rather Western scholars, working "on their own"? I should be glad to know that I influenced any of them; but I imagine they may not be ready to say *ad sum* when called.

You may be interested to know that my work really grew out of a preliminary training in Mediaeval history, where I learned to recognize the reactions between a people in the gristle, and their environment, and saw the interplay of economic, social and geographic factors in the politics, institutions, ideals and life of a nation and its relations with its neighbors. My first advanced courses were on successive periods in the "Social and Economic History of the United States," out of which grew the course on the history of the West.

But, too much of myself! I am not sure but more, and perhaps independent attention should be given to the history of agriculture, including migration of crop areas, sheep, cattle, etc.; and to their influence on Europe and its policies by their export of surplus; to the history of public lands and land tenure; to the phenomena of great city development and the results and problems in many fields incident thereto, as well as to the topics which you reserve because of their not being matured.

But being just now engaged in the boiling down process and finding it absurdly hard to select and compress, I can easily know your answer. Besides you do mention these matters. It's only a question of emphasis or of elaboration, and here the matter of space is compelling.

I hope your book will stir up discussion of Viewpoints, perspective, etc., and that you will have solid enjoyment as well as appreciation for your work. With thanks and

With regards I am
Sincerely yours
Frederick J. Turner

### *America and Europe*

Following his retirement from Harvard in 1924, Turner moved to Madison, Wisconsin; here he gave a series of lectures at the University and at other places in the Midwest. In the summers of 1924 and 1925 he lectured at the State Agricultural College at Logan, Utah, a beautiful part of the Far West that Turner and his wife particularly enjoyed visiting. During the spring of 1925 Turner corresponded with Edgar Eugene Robinson about the possibility of giving additional lectures on the Pacific Coast. In writing to Robinson on March 31, 1925, Turner discussed topics that might be included in lectures at Stanford: "In Illinois and here," he wrote:

> I have given an address on the Significance of Sections in the United States. . . . I could modify this, and if I had an extra half an hour, add some lantern slide illustration, chiefly maps of sectional voting and culture. Perhaps I could give a lecture on Recent Sectionalism. But this would be coals to New Castle! and not high grade ore at that! I might be able to write a new lecture on Lessons from the Puritan and the Pioneer, emphasizing the need of individualism and the call to duty as against the present tendencies toward uniformity and the danger of community conformity. But this is nebulous in my mind and I shrink from preaching as well as taking the time and mental wear and tear to write it.

Turner's Wisconsin lectures of 1924 met with rather a cold reception. He complained to Robinson that his audience was "rapidly diminishing" in size. In the following extract of one of his letters to Robinson, Turner expands a point he had made in an article, "The Significance of the Section in American History," published in the March 1925 issue of the *Wisconsin Magazine of History*.

#### EXTRACT FROM TURNER'S LETTER TO EDGAR EUGENE ROBINSON, APRIL 22, 1925

My reference to the League of Nations had a two-fold object. In the first place, to point out the differences which exist between the League as constituted and our own sectional conditions, and, second, as a suggestion of what might be possible (but improbable, I admit) in the way of modifications of the League along the lines of American practice. Since this would require the development of international political parties it may well be impracticable though not impossible. As for the powerful executive, our own history shows that that is not essential and that it is likely to come under the stress of necessity. The tradition of central power could only grow up with time. I feel confident that the present arrangement will meet with the same difficulties with which we should have met in the United States had not we developed parties and our type of government. But, after all, "sham battles" with all their futility, are better than real battles between nations.

However, my purpose was to produce a way of looking at our own problems and our own solution of them rather than to rearrange Europe. The suggestion that we must develop a council of advisors for the President made up of sectional representatives is an interesting one and one which you will recall was in substance advocated in the Constitutional Convention.

In a rambling 1925 letter to his old friend Charles Homer Haskins, (a letter which Turner revised, then marked "not sent"), Turner discussed his theory of sections and how it might throw light on the European situation.

EXTRACT FROM TURNER'S DRAFT OF A LETTER TO CHARLES HOMER HASKINS, MAY 19, 1925

Part of my job has been in trying to explain that aspect of American history and it can be applied also to European history. But I will not try to write out an analysis of the importance of *space* in history, nor [try to explain]* why, even, even aside from the matter of the political system, I think that the matters of extent of surface, distances involved, remoteness from contacts, freedom from intimate economic and social entanglement, and a lot of such other things as the vital importance (at times) of great regions sectionally disposed, even though sparsely held, due to their treasures of raw material, food, mines, forests etc., widely extended into space. Relation of population to the square mile, even total population are not the only—at times, not the important—consideration in such cases, when particularly the vast area has developed a sectional thought of itself and of its place in the

* Turner's brackets.

nation, or of the continent (in the case of Europe). Germany presents a beautiful case of sections *within* a nation. I think it is somewhat different than the sectionalism revealed in the United States, where distance (e.g. transportation) and space itself are factors, on a continental scale. However I close with a C major of agreement on the importance of the application of the sectional hypothesis generally, and that one must not assume that a grouping at a particular election is more than temporary. I have tried to grapple with this question pretty carefully in the United States, so far as means and time permitted.

Marcus Lee Hansen was one of Turner's gifted students who, after completing a doctorate in 1924, embarked upon a comprehensive study of the European origins of American immigration. Hansen, who seemed to recognize instinctively those areas in which research could be expected to bear fruit, died in 1938, but some of his most significant writings were published posthumously, including *The Atlantic Migration, 1607–1860,* which appeared in 1940 with a foreword by Arthur M. Schlesinger.

In the following letter to Hansen Turner comments on the extent to which historical investigations must go into detail, the extent to which a subject should be treated exhaustively.

TO MARCUS LEE HANSEN

2214 Van Hise Avenue
Madison, Wisconsin
Jan. 7, 1926

Dear Hansen

It was very pleasant to receive your Christmas letter,—much more acceptable than what our over-worked postman called "them cards!"

So far as I can see, your project of exclusion is your only road to safety, but incidentally, when you see and turn down material useful for *American* history in general, why not jot down a note of it, for other studies.

For a definitive monograph, of course, concentration by period or place is necessary, but for a setting forth of the larger aspects in a way to preempt the field and to make its larger lines clear, it isn't necessary to do the German type of thesis. Bryce's Holy Roman Empire —*in its day*—was worth a whole lot of minute studies of mediaeval institutions—particularly since most of them have gone the way of much historical writing, by the discovery of new material and by the changing Zeitgeist in historical conceptions of what is worth while and what are the real meanings of the thing in relation to the larger movements. So I have felt it necessary in my own work, to dig deeply in spots, to know how to dig, and to test others diggings, and then with the reserves that digging compels and with the knowledge of tested spots through the whole field, try to envisage the historical landscape, without feeling compelled to plough up and sink wells every few inches in the territory. Of course there is a chance of going wrong if one doesn't uncover every inch; but there is more chance of hopeless confusion—mere spade work for someone else to use.

I should be glad to have you receive a second year's try at the subject. Let me know, of course, if I can help.

Germany is immensely interesting just now. When you can do so without cutting in to your job, I'd like to hear your reactions.

Cordially
Frederick J Turner

In his reply Hansen comments on the admiration for American democracy that he detected in Europe.

FROM MARCUS LEE HANSEN

7 Gordon St., London W.C.I.
May 24, 1926

Dear Prof. Turner:

Your letter of Jan. 7 reached me in due time and the delay in acknowledging it is no indication of the way in which it was appreciated. But I took literally your suggestion that I should not let letter writing interfere with professional duties. However today presented an unknown holiday in the form of Whitsun Monday, and with the Public Record Office closed correspondence comes as the next on the program.

First of all let me inform you that the Social Science Research Council has renewed my fellowship for another year and has approved my plans for continuing the study of my problem down to 1890. This will make it possible for me to transform my investigation into a history of the origins of the "old immigration" which will coincide with the colonization of the Middle West. In fact the more I study the question as it evolves on both sides of the Atlantic the more unity I see in the whole process and that I hope to make the theme of the completed study. Before autumn I plan to take a whole month off to do nothing but mull over my notes and arrange a semi-permanent outline, hoping thereby to be able to arrange the last few months of research more intelligently. When that outline is completed I would like to send you a copy of it for your comments if it would not be imposing too much upon your time. The PhD thesis will hardly be recognizable as most of that scaffolding has been torn down.

The four months that I spent in Germany were very pleasant and profitable. Though the political cauldron did not boil over it was continually seething, and the daily rumors of contemplated Monarchist and Bolshevist coups added a little spice to the routine of research. With our late enemies my relations were most pleasant. Towards Americans as such there was absolutely no hostility manifested. In fact the Germans seemed to blame all their troubles upon two men —the Kaiser for getting them into the war, and President Wilson for not getting them out. Getting most of their information from German-American sources probably accounts for the general impression that the Americans have repudiated Mr. Wilson and all his works. It makes the position of visiting Americans distinctly friendly, unless they try to enlighten their chance acquaintances too fully.

American prestige is remarkably high, especially in business matters. The impression is general that there is only one thing that can save the nation industrially and that is the adoption of the latest methods especially in production. And for them they look to America. Several students told me their ambition was to be able to spend some months in commercial houses in New York or in factories. A film dealing with Henry Ford and his establishment was shown several times a week in one of the downtown movie houses all winter and always seemed to be well patronized. The windows of the bookstores were always displaying the lives of American capitalists or more scientific treatises on American organizations; and I never rode on the subway during the rush hours without seeing some young man with his head buried in one of these books.

To me this fact suggested a very interesting parallel. The more I study the origins of the emigration movement in the middle of the last century, the more I realize what a tremendous reputation American democracy had in Europe at that time and the interest with which all its developments were followed by the common man. I am almost beginning to think that Nineteenth Century European Democracy owes less to the "leaven" of the French Revolution than it does to the practical experience of the United States during the first half of the century—an example that came before them every day in the newspapers. I have a suspicion that you suggested this idea on one occasion in seminar. I am finding many evidences of its truth. So once having been a model to save Europe politically we must now be an example to save them industrially. You see I haven't lost any of my hundred percentism by living abroad.

I expect to return to Germany and Scandinavia next fall but in order to keep a proper balance to all sides of my rather varied fields I have thought it best to bring the study of the British emigration down to 1860 before going more deeply into the continental. The Public Record Office with its papers of the Emigration Commissioners and the reports of the consuls in the American ports provides what I some times fear is an inexhaustible mine. But I will probably not stay here later than Sept. first. On this next trip to the continent I hope to spread my labors considerably in order to get as much experience as possible. Before returning home I hope to have worked in all the leading libraries of Europe with the exception of those in Spain. Even Rome has its sources.

England presented to me unexpectedly another phase of my education by allowing me to be an innocent bystander during the General Strike. I must revise much of my Economics as a result of those observations. For the General Strike which I always was taught was a weapon which would from its very nature lead to such public despair that they could do nothing but submit turned out an entirely different atmosphere; and the English whom I always thought took even their pleasures sadly took their General Strike as a picnic. Had it lasted for weeks the volunteers would have lost a little of their good humour, but, as it was, their pleasure in working was so contagious that at the end of ten days the strikers already bored with their leisure wanted to share in the fun. So to prevent a general stampede back to work the T.U.C. capitulated. This may not be a scientific analysis of the fiasco, but it is what an observer could see.

Wishing you a pleasant summer season, I am

Yours Sincerely,
Marcus L. Hansen.
7 Gordon St. London W.C.I.

Prof. F.J. Turner
Madison, Wis.

Turner was enthusiastic about Hansen's progress in pioneering a challenging new field in American social history.

TO MARCUS LEE HANSEN

Hancock Point, Maine
June 20, 1926

Dear Hansen,

I am glad to hear that your fellowship was extended and am expecting valuable results. You have a fine field and you are a good historical farmer! There is opportunity to make a national, indeed international, reputation in the history of immigration to the United States, and I am particularly pleased that you are examining the matter of American influence on European ideals, expecially in reference to the spread of democracy. This was one of the things that seemed clear to me from the study of the testimony of those who came to this country and I remember presenting it, hypothetically, to the seminary; but it could not be tested properly without doing what you are doing—namely studying the reaction in Europe itself. This one point, if fully established, would make the reputation of your book and give you a "place in the sun."

Your report of German and English conditions is exceedingly interesting, and in some respects quite different from what we think of them in this country. When Haskins gets here in a few days, I shall share your letter with him.

I am slowly recuperating from an attack of the middle ear control of equilibrium while on my way here from Wisconsin which landed me in the Stillman Infirmary at Cambridge for a while.

With warm regards and good wishes,

Yours sincerely
Frederick J Turner

Why not publish—say in Am. Hist. Review,—some of your preliminary results soon? I want to see them before it is too late, and I think the campaign of the Am Hist Asso for funds for endowment of research would be facilitated thereby. Immigration was among the things which the Committee stressed, as needing such research. The interest aroused by this campaign will lead others into the field. You have a good lead, and should, I think publish preliminary reports—as the geologist does of his reconnaisance.

T

### *The Frontier Theory: Favorable and Adverse Criticism*

On May 2, 1925, Schlesinger wrote to Turner about an article criticizing Turner's ideas on the frontier, "The Shibboleth of the Frontier," by John C. Almack, which appeared in the May 1925 issue of *Historical Outlook*. "Such an article will deceive no one," Schlesinger wrote, "and I hope you will not allow it to disturb your mental serenity in any way."

In his reply to Schlesinger, Turner shows that his confidence in his work is not to be shaken by adverse criticism. He complains that his theory has sometimes been misinterpreted, but he is confident that his work on the frontier and the section will survive the test of time.

TO ARTHUR M. SCHLESINGER

2214 Van Hise Avenue
Madison Wisconsin
May 5, 1925

Dear Professor Schlesinger:

I haven't yet seen the article in the *Historical Outlook;* but I am indebted to the critic for calling out so pleasing an expression of your friendship! My use of the frontier conception has not always been understood by readers who are careless, so I am not surprised at the news that such an attack has been made. Beard (taking the edge of settlement as it is to-day, or at least as it was *after* the publication of my paper on the frontier up to 1890, and apparently not having read my essays in which I noted the changes in the Western attitude in the years that followed) attacked the essay as though it had been written to describe the frontier after the railroad, the later immigrant, the shift from individualism that came toward the close of the era of free lands and after the changes that came about the close of the nineteenth century.

Of course Frontier and West are not identical but I used Frontier as (so to speak) the barometric line that recorded the advance of settlement, the creation of new Wests, not merely as the area of Indian fighting, vigilantes, annexations, etc. It would help to an understanding of what I tried to do, if one were to note the prior different conception of Western history, as a record of territorial annexations (without, by the way, any considerable attempt to sound the economic aspects of the diplomatic contests), or as a field for marking trails, Indian sites, etc. (see the resolutions proposed by Clarence Bowen and passed by the A.H.A., as quoted in my address called "A Plea for the Study of the West," or some such title, in the Am. Hist. Asso. Report about 1896). For a good many years the Frontier paper did not have much general acceptance, then it rather suddenly became so generally accepted that I seemed to be plagiarizing myself when I developed a phase of the theme—or, as sometimes happened in Harvard, I was criticised for seeming to follow too closely the work of some of my students! Or as "old stuff."

What was really surprising to me was the slight amount of criticism that I got when historians began to take note of the interpretation, so that a reaction was to be expected. But I am sorry if, as you report, a teachers' magazine has allowed a man of straw to be pummeled; what is writ is writ, but I should like readers really to know what I said; when I said it; and what had been the status of the subject when I began my own attempt to change the perspective, and to stress the interior as a necessary element in an understanding of the America of the time, and also to urge the vital connection of economic and social history with political history. We shall also have to pay a lot more attention to historical geography, psychology, etc.

I imagine that some of the attempts to minimize the frontier theme, in the broad sense in which I used it, are part of the pessimistic reaction against the old America that have followed the World War—the reaction against pioneer ideals, against distinctively American things historically in favor of the Old World solutions of "the promise of American life"—to write in terms of European experience, and of the class struggle incident to industrialism. There seems likely to be an urban reinterpretation of our history. But we cannot altogether get away from the facts of American history, however far we go in the way of adopting the Old World! I do not wish to crystallize my contributions, to oppose other innovators, for I was an innovator myself to some degree, nor do I wish to avoid criticism. But I am happy that you understand my attitude and that you write with sympathy and encouragement.

Maybe I am wrong, but just now I am possessed with the idea that twenty years or so from now my Sections paper will travel along with my Frontier as interpretations, even if in the future the importance of regional geography in American *History* should be less than in the past, which I am far from expecting will be the case. But I am not a prophet!

My warm regards and good wishes.

Sincerely yours,
Frederick J. Turner

Turner's interpretations had also influenced the writings of Norman Foerster, professor of English at the University of North Carolina, who made use of the frontier theory in a provocative piece, "American Literature," published as the lead article in the *Saturday Review of Literature* of April 3, 1926. Foerster argued that the mainsprings of American culture could be traced to "two heads: European culture and American environment. American history, including literary history, is to be viewed as the interplay of these two tremendous factors." Foerster argued further that the pioneer spirit of a "frontier nation" could be discerned in the writings of Emerson, Whitman, and Mark Twain. In a letter to Foerster, Turner expressed his approval of the way in which his theory had been applied.

EXTRACT FROM TURNER'S LETTER TO NORMAN FOERSTER, JULY 27, 1926

If one takes the frontier in the large sense that I have thought it should be taken, as not merely "the edge of cultivation," but at the same time the barometer of a society expanding into the wilderness, into the field of unexploited resources, unsettled lands, etc., with its reactions on the settled societies behind this moving edge, and its influence through inherited ideas upon regions once frontier, but no longer,—I think that your thesis is unassailable. Indeed, I am not sure that much of our "realism" and some of our "romanticism," go back to the same national experience, in the special forms they have taken in our literature. But some people have supposed that the "frontier" was to be taken in the narrower sense of the word, and have quite misunderstood its significance as the *marker* of our mobile and expanding nation, and of our pioneer experience.

Turner was delighted to hear that his frontier essay had been republished in a periodical edited by the Harvard economist Charles Jesse Bullock, in a socialist magazine and in a pedagogical review, and that the new governor of Wisconsin, Philip Fox La Follette (son of the famous senator) had quoted Turner in his inaugural address. Joseph Schafer, to whom the following letter was addressed, had studied under Turner. He was the director of the State Historical Society of Wisconsin.

TO JOSEPH SCHAFER

Henry E. Huntington Library and Art Gallery, San Marino, California
January 19, 1931

Confidential

Dr. Joseph Schafer
State Historical Society
Madison, Wisconsin

Dear Schafer:

Thank you for sending me Governor LaFollette's Inaugural. My "Frontier" has been republished in a socialist magazine, in a pedagogical review, and in Bullock's *Writings in Economics* [and Bullock is of the anti-socialist group],* so that I am not unwilling to see myself mentioned in so handsome a way also by the Progressive governor! In point of fact, while LaFollette, Sr., was governor I found myself in agreement with his general policies, and I think that he was an important influence in shaping American tendencies in his time—although he shaped a course that I could not altogether agree with in his later years. Nor do I agree with the attitude of Senator Robert LaFollette, 2d, in his attacks upon Hoover. However, to be mentioned and quoted in the opening sentence of an Inaugural is an honor that was quite unexpected.

The acceptance of the frontier idea, by these clashing groups, of course, leaves them open to their own respective substitutes for it now that it has gone—as a determining influence in American life. Into that problem I do not venture just now! I don't want to be anybody's patron saint! Can't fill the bill!

I am always very glad to hear from you and of the progress of things at Wisconsin. I am now working at the Huntington two hours daily, but am yet far from being in fighting trim.

* Turner's brackets.

I was happy to hear of the good record that your sons are making, and my wife and I both send our greetings to you and Mrs. Schafer.

Cordially yours,
Frederick J. Turner

In a friendly letter to another former student, Guy Stanton Ford, Dean of the University of Minnesota Graduate School, Turner comments on American society since the passing of the frontier.

TO GUY STANTON FORD

Henry E. Huntington Library and Art Gallery
San Marino, California
March 25, 1931

Dean Guy Stanton Ford
Graduate School
University of Minnesota
Minneapolis, Minnesota

Dear Ford:

Thank you for sending me your paper on "The Mental, Social and Historical Sciences." So far am I from thinking that I could have done the subject justice, that I feel, after reading your paper, that you have done a much better job. The changing conditions since the closing of the era characterized by a moving frontier have, of course, presented themselves to me, and I also have seen that the work of the social scientist is highly important in the process of readjustment; and I agree, too, that the problems are "too large for solution by any single individual." In fact, I somewhat suspect that they will be met by a process of *drift,* under the earth movements of social and economic, as well as political, tendencies; but that is not to say that leadership is not highly important and needed.

Again thanking you, I am

Cordially yours,
Frederick J. Turner

Turner's frontier theory was attacked at this time in an article appearing in the Winter 1931 issue of the *Yale Review* (pp. 349–65); it was written by a young Harvard instructor in government, Benjamin F. Wright, who believed that Turner's theory distorted

American history: backwoods democracy had played only a minor role in the development of America, and in any case the influence of the frontier had been unfortunate, for it had tended to isolate American democracy "from the general course of western civilization."

That this attack should appear in the *Yale Review,* which had published Turner's own "Sections and the Nation," was particularly unpleasant. In the next decade Turner's work was to be frequently attacked by historians who, like Wright, aimed their critical shafts at the visible chinks in Turner's theories. Turner, who died in 1932, had to leave the defense of his works to other scholars.

In the following extract from his letter to Frederick Merk, a former student then in charge of American Western history instruction at Harvard, Turner questions the validity of Wright's attack. He also comments on critical remarks made in an article by the geographer Isaiah Bowman, who questioned what he assumed to be Turner's assumption—that the frontier had ended in 1890. Although Turner was not mentioned by name, the implication was that he was in "error." The article by Bowman appeared in the January 1931 issue of the *American Geographical Review* (pp. 25–55), a periodical which Turner, as a subscriber, received regularly.

### EXTRACT FROM TURNER'S LETTER TO FREDERICK MERK, JANUARY 9, 1931

I had not seen Benjamin F. Wright's "assault" until your letter, but have since run over it in the *Yale Review* here. I suppose that it is not unlikely that in my desire to modify current historical conceptions of American history I may have seemed to overemphasize the purely American aspects of our democracy; but I think Mr. Wright fails to realize that what I was dealing with was, in the first place, the *American* character of democracy as compared with that of Europe or of European philosophers; and that, secondly, whatever may be said regarding the writings and activity of coastal men in promoting it, they had as a background the American Western experience and were influenced thereby. At any rate, it was not my idea that the Revolution was fundamentally a work of the West. So far as the colonial phase goes, I think it would be possible to show that in New England, for example, the interior towns and their problems had a very important influence in modifying the form of government that the original Puritan leaders imposed; and that in Virginia the development of the representative assembly, for instance, was deeply shaped by the opportunity, and indeed the need, of giving concrete form to such speculations as those of Sandys and of adjusting government to the idea of an assembly from particular plantations. These are phases of the subject which I have briefly touched upon in my class lectures and into which I have gone farther in my investigations and notes, but which I have not dealt with adequately in print. However, the data is existent, and I think if Mr. Wright had considered it fully he would have been less confident of the primary influence of European democracy and philosophy in shaping the actual form of the American type, in the seventeenth century and later. Now, however, I must not turn aside from my present work (which will be hard enough to bring to an outcome at best, in view of my health) to deal with the views of Mr. Wright. If he is correct in his strictures on the conception of the frontier as a fundamental factor in American history, a whole lot of rather able men have been misled by it; and if the frontier conception has real value such men should be able to make any defense that may be called for. How important Mr. Wright is, I do not know.

I notice that I. Bowman, in the last *American Geographical Review,* in an article entitled "The Jordan Country [Montana],"* dwells upon the "error" of thinking that the frontier ended with 1890. Of course the frontier did not end in 1890, but, as he takes pains to point out, it was rather the census-map *line* of the frontier. Occasionally, I think, I have been careless in using the phrase "frontier *ending*" for "*line* of frontier ending"; but I have always realized that there was that difference and that the frontier did not come to an end "with a bang" in 1890. However, the importance of the frontier movement as a large factor in American history did reach its close about that time, and an examination of legislation, economic development, social traits, etc., would make this clear.—So much for frontier!

Later in 1931 Turner received a copy of Isaiah Bowman's new book, *The Pioneer Fringe* (New York, 1931). Turner, somewhat piqued by the implied criticisms of the frontier theory in Bowman's *American Geographical Review* article, decided to argue the

* Turner's brackets.

case for the defense to Bowman himself. It was not in fact Bowman's book but his article that annoyed Turner. The book, composed of a series of essays on rural life on the American great plains and other such areas in western Canada and South America where similar frontiers were to be found, pleased Turner because it suggested that his theory could be applied on a worldwide scale.

TO ISAIAH BOWMAN

December 24, 1931

Dr. Isaiah Bowman
American Geographical Society
Broadway at 156th Street
New York, New York

My dear Dr. Bowman:

I have received a copy of your very stimulating and informing *Pioneer Fringe,* and have been much interested in examining it. The scope of your inquiry greatly impresses me, as well as the acute observations in which the book abounds.

I have no desire to prove my consistency in the matter of a pamphlet written some forty years ago, but I notice that, on page 111 (and, if I remember rightly, in an article of yours in the *American Geographical Review*), you emphasized the fact that the frontier is far from having vanished; and it might be inferred that that early paper of mine had had some influence in spreading an error. Not, therefore, in the way of criticism, but simply from a desire to be understood, I should like to say that, in that paper, I quoted the remarks of the Census Bureau regarding the frontier *line* and dealt with that phase of American history that resulted from the continuous westward extension of a line having marked continuity. I tried to suggest that this continuous progress of the nation into vast areas of unoccupied land had been more fundamental in the shaping of our history than historians had as a rule perceived. The idea, of course, was not so much a new one as a neglected one; and I tried to show that this general advance through so many decades had had profound influences both in the shaping of the society of the new geographical provinces that were thus entered and in the reactive effects upon the more eastern regions, upon Congressional legislation, and upon the American way of looking at the world. Doubtless it was an inadvertence on my part to have used the sentence at the end of the article: "And now the frontier has gone." As the paper itself shows, I was aware that considerable areas of the country had not yet lost their frontier characteristics. My point was that, as an effective factor in shaping American history, the end of the frontier line, as described by the Census, marked the end of a real chapter in our history. In the use of the word "frontier" at the end, therefore, I still had in mind the frontier as described in the previous Census maps and in the Report of the Census for 1890. You are quite right, of course, in drawing a distinction between the frontier line and the frontier; and, in my class lectures (see, for example, Turner and Merk, *List of References on the History of the West;* Cambridge, 1922 and earlier), I made this clear. But, as a fundamental factor (although not the fundamental factor) in American history, the period around 1890, marked by the end of the frontier line, was a real turning point. Although this has sometimes been doubted, I think that the fact could be clearly demonstrated; and I notice that, in his recent *Epic of American History,* J. T. Adams also takes this view, although he incorrectly thinks that I had made the frontier phenomenon the one key to American history. It *was* a key, and a neglected one. With regard to such regions as some of those dealt with by you in your book and in your article, where frontier conditions still show themselves, it seems to me, from my point of view, that they are local indications of survival rather than factors in the fundamental course of American development.

With all this you may not agree, but I would wish a scholar like yourself to understand that we are in agreement as to the distinction between frontier line and frontier, but that my emphasis upon the phenomenon was with regard to its shaping of the general course of our history and, consequently, that a region like the Jordan country, dealt with by you, does not seem to me to have been sufficiently important in its effects, or in its area, to overturn the conceptions of that earlier paper of mine, considered in the way that I have explained above.

However all this may seem to you, you will let me say that the interest which your book shows in the pioneer fringe in so many countries has given me pleasure as well as profit. Sometime I hope to see the subject developed more fully in regard to the effect of the advance of these pioneer fringes upon economics, politics, and society. How far did these different "fringes" resemble each other in these respects? how far did they differ? and, particularly, how far did the racial factor affect the manner in which these pioneer fringes formed and spread? Some studies in this direction have been brought to my attention—for example, that by Professor James Westfall Thompson, of the University of Chicago, who has dealt with the expansion of medieval Germany; and various others, dealing with Canada, South America, South Africa, etc. Probably there may be adequate studies for these aspects of the Russian advance toward the east, but I cannot recall that they have come to my notice.

With personal regards, I am

Very sincerely yours,

Turner's generous remarks on the *Pioneer Fringe* brought a somewhat unexpected response from Bowman on January 5, 1932: an expression of thanks and an invitation to review the book. Here are two extracts from Bowman's letter, and Turner's reply declining the invitation.

Dear Professor Turner:

It is a great pleasure to have your letter of December 24 with its comments upon the *Pioneer Fringe.* I had forgotten that you closed your article with the statement that the frontier had gone. My spear was leveled not at you but at those who use the phrase in an uncritical sense. Your own use of it was amply safeguarded.

. . . .

Would you not like to review my book for the *American Historical Review* or the *New York Times,* if they have made no other arrangements? In making these requests I am not looking for praise, which I deplore, but for critical comments of the sort that your letter contains and that you can supply in fuller measure, no doubt, after you have read the whole book.

San Marino, Calif.
Jan. 12, 1932

Dr. Isaiah Bowman
American Geographical Society
Broadway at 156th Street
New York, New York

Dear Doctor Bowman:

Your letter of January fifth has given me real pleasure.

As I have been for some months confined to my bed during most of the day, and am dictating therefrom, I am not in condition to undertake a review, which, otherwise, I should be inclined to do, although, for some years, I have declined to review and might, therefore, get into trouble with others if I were to attempt to deal with your interesting work. I am greatly obliged to you for having sent the volume to me.

Very sincerely yours,

# 5

# Problems in Writing History

## *Introduction*

Turner was no Francis Parkman, no poet-scholar whose stylistic verve sweeps the reader through a multicolored past. "So far as my style goes," wrote Turner, who was nothing if not realistic, "I apprehend that a good deal of it will seem in the future to be rather out of the mode of the twentieth century; but whatever may be the thought about that, it was really an outcome of my own earnest interest in the subject rather than an attempt to emphasize literary form" (to Frederick Merk, Jan. 9, 1931).

That Turner concerned himself so little with literary style is hardly surprising, for he found the job of getting his ideas down on paper extraordinarily difficult. One of the problems he encountered as a writer was, he said, lack of time. He complained repeatedly that the American university system failed to provide sufficient time for research and that it stifled the creative energies of younger teachers with too heavy a teaching load. Yet year after year Turner took long summer vacations during which he indulged his passion for fishing. His complaint seems, therefore, at least in part an attempt to rationalize his own lack of productivity.

A far more convincing reason for Turner's failure to write is to be found in the unmanageability of the material with which he worked. To describe the numerous factors leading up to any historical event, to unravel in words the tangled strands of the American past so as to create a reasonably accurate model of bygone events—this was a job to daunt any scholar.

But the main problem, as Turner knew, was not simply lack of time or refractory and many-sided material requiring an almost unheard-of combination of talents in the man who would treat it satisfactorily; rather it was Turner's cast of mind. He enjoyed gathering data, building up a vast store of raw material which, in its untreated state, resembled an amorphous mass. The accumulating of data was a much more congenial task than ordering and presenting such material in a form suitable for publication. Ulrich B. Phillips, a close friend and colleague, described Turner's dislike of writing in a letter of October 13, 1925, to Carl Becker (Becker was preparing an essay on Turner* at this time): "He has never been able to 'compose' except when under the lash. Writing his own stuff is agony to him. . . . He has not so much written books as made a school and created a tradition."

Writing was an agonizing process for Turner partly because he was convinced that the very acts of classifying, ordering, and manipulating masses of material into communicable forms involved a distortion of the stuff to be communicated. Consider the following comments, which Turner wrote to Carl Becker on November 7, 1898, justifying the rather informal instructional methods that he used at Wisconsin:

> our method is to take the student into the workshop where the chips are flying and where he can see the workman cut his finger and jam his thumb, as often as occasion arises. It is a little damaging to the dignity and poise, but it has two decided advantages for advanced work. In the first place, you don't have to write your lectures, which takes time from more engaging occupations, and which is apt to commit you to a settled body of doctrine—which is chafing; and in the second place,—as you I think see,—it gives an impetus to the student's own construction, and develops his critical faculty!

These words express more than Turner's views on teaching methods; they reveal a rooted antagonism towards the codifying and organizing activities of scholarship. For writing books, quite as much as preparing lectures, he saw, would "take time from more engaging occupations" and "commit[s] you to a settled body of doctrine." Yet while Turner was willing to defend his use of the workshop method in the classroom, he did not, as he might

* First published in *American Masters of Social Science,* ed. Howard W. Odum (New York, 1927), pp. 273–318. The copy that Becker inscribed for Turner is in the Huntington Library, Rare Book No. 139511.

have done, use a similar defense to justify his relative failure to transform his own research into book form. He did not defend himself in this way because on a more rational level he fully accepted his obligation to put his studies in more permanent form—indeed, he regarded the publishing of the results of original research as one of the first duties of a scholar and one that ought not to be pushed aside by classroom or personal pressures.

The letter describing Turner's workshop method was written in 1898. The year before, Turner had written to his publisher about his plans for a college textbook: "Next year, I propose to concentrate my teaching almost entirely upon the colonial and revolutionary period, and I shall organize my material in text-book form" (June 11, 1897). Clearly Turner recognized that a careful organization of his teaching material would be a great step toward publication; and just as clearly, the best intentions provided insufficient impetus. The college textbook, along with other works that would most certainly have strengthened his reputation as a historian, were never to appear.

This lack of productivity was a matter for regret on the part of Turner's friends and professional associates; Turner himself must have suffered considerably from his own professional shortcoming, for he was a man who valued fame more highly than might at first be apparent to the reader of his letters. In spite of his modest references to his own contributions to historical scholarship, he cared a great deal about getting credit for his work. When Harry Elmer Barnes' book, *The New History and the Social Studies* appeared in 1925, Turner eagerly searched through it for mention of his own name, and in his personal copy corrected the index in cases where references appearing in the text had been ignored in the index. He took pains to make sure that future biographers should be properly informed about his affairs, and often scribbled explanatory notes on letters and manuscripts. Frequently he wrote his name over and over again on folders or on the boxes housing his collection of notes and file cards.

Turner's desire for recognition did not prevent him from lavishing on his students the fruits of his remarkable mind. One of his students, Avery Craven, wrote of Turner's willingness "to share his great learning." He always gave more than he received, Craven wrote, "sometimes even to the detriment of his own work. No man of our day had been more 'borrowed from' and more 'imposed on' by those who could 'get' but give little" (Craven, Draft for Turner Memorial Service, Mar. 19, 1932). Yet very little of Turner's own work was in published, permanent form, and perhaps this explains why it mattered so much to him that he be recognized as a pathbreaker, an original thinker; he was offended when he felt that colleagues had feasted too richly on his preserves.

Turner regarded his writings almost as a monument to himself —as a reflection of his thought at a given period; he did not, therefore, care to revise his essays when they were about to be republished, for each one had its place in time and in his own intellectual development. Moreover he displayed no false modesty when it came to commenting on his own writings: in several letters to former students he spoke about his essays as marking a turning point in American historiography. He maintained, for example, that the only earlier historian who had successfully woven economic and social data into American history was Henry Adams, in the first volume of his history. But it was not done, Turner said, "in my way." Economic and social questions were kept separate from political and diplomatic history. Turner attributed his own "unwritten books" to the difficulties of recording complicated relationships—this kind of writing was not "easy" (to Merle Curti, Aug. 15, 1928).

In a letter to Constance Lindsay Skinner (Mar. 15, 1922) (see above, pp. 55–62 for full text of letter), Turner made yet another attempt to define his contribution to American historical scholarship: he had, he wrote, attempted something previously unattempted—an analysis of the westward movement and of frontier expansion in terms of the larger framework of institutional history. No earlier American historian, he observed, had made a serious effort to delve into geography, geology, and related disciplines.

Fulmer Mood, in his introduction to *The Early Writings of Frederick Jackson Turner* (Madison, 1938) stresses the special importance of the 1892 article, "Problems in American History"; it marked, in his opinion, "a revolution . . . in American historiography." Turner shows in this article how economic and social history must be considered in relation to sectional and frontier development, and urges historians to free themselves from the limitations of a traditional approach to history.

Turner's theorizing about the complexity of history was to some extent the result of his attempts to find a path through the jungle of data that surrounded him. Housed at the Huntington Library are Turner's research materials; huge rolls of paper on which election figures were recorded, dozens of maps with detailed markings and shadings, boxes of glass slides, thousands of 3" x 5" reference cards, and several dozen large file drawers of notes. After wrestling in the late 1920s with a mass of statistical data on sectionalism, Turner reached the conclusion that the work could best be handled by a team of historians. The task of writing a book on the political bases of sectionalism, county by county, was, Turner wrote, "too big a job for one man" (to Charles O. Paullin, Nov. 20, 1928). It is in the light of this constant struggle with unyielding material that we should view Turner's attitude towards his own work; in this context his pride in his own accomplishment is both understandable and excusable.

Turner's sensitivity on the question of ownership of ideas was responsible for a certain tension between himself and Max Farrand which continued over many years. On various occasions Farrand wrote Turner to make sure that this or that piece of writing did not trespass unacceptably on Turner's historical domain. On October 16, 1907, for instance, Farrand wrote: "The first thing I want you to tell me, and I want you to tell me frankly, is whether this is not encroaching too much on your ground. You know I have refrained from doing any extensive work in that field until after you have published, but now that my Constitutional work is approaching completion I find it hard to keep my hands off much longer." Turner's answer was reassuring, if not enthusiastic: "Of course I have touched upon this incidentally in one or two places—(especially in State Making in West in Rev. Period) . . . but I think the field is open for bringing this matter of unjust apportionment and franchise out more clearly as a means of testing the sincerity—and earnestness of the revolutionists in using the revolutionary doctrines. This would give a certain unity and definiteness of purpose to your paper, which possibly one finds defective at present" (Nov. 24, 1907). On other occasions Turner made more explicitly clear his opinion that Farrand is free to pursue his historical bent:

With regard to the admission of new states, I hope that you will not in the least hesitate to make as much use of my suggestion as you care to. I have no immediate intention of doing an article on The West in the Federal Convention, although I shall give *incidental* treatment of this subject in a book which I hope to have ready this year. This should not in the least, however, interfere with your using the material for purposes of bringing out the "compromise idea"; and, even if I had the ambition to monopolize the subject, it would be absurd to try to keep any scholar from the sources found in Madison's reports! [October 17, 1903]

On October 19, 1909, Turner touched on the same subject in a letter to Farrand:

Second, regarding the delimitation of spheres—I shall shout *bon voyage* to whatever trip you make in the historical ocean, and I know your ship will bring a rich freightage back—you should not hesitate a moment to go into any field—But I am not sure enough of my own future plans to mark out my course yet. My craft goes tramping about so many ports that I feel unable to chart out a sailing route, as a well ordered ocean liner ought. I hope to cover (some time) the period from Adams to Rhodes. My little book gave me a desire to rework that field as a preparation for the study of the period that follows and my seminaries have been running in recent years from Monroe down through Tyler. I don't think at present that I shall try to do the Mexican war, but there is much development of American society between 1840 and 1850 which I do hanker after as a field of work, and which I must do to supplement my studies of the western movement.

In short, you ought not to hesitate at all to follow your own bent, and the world will be the better for it. The whole period needs many workers and can't be handled by any one man.

I hope you see clearly that I don't dream of being a trust magnate, in the historical domain—I wouldn't hog anything if I could. I am simply too uncertain of my own wishes or future interests to decide on any definite limitation now. You may—(and doubtless very properly)—think it high time that I should do this. But until my studies go farther I can't be sure that it would be wise for me to eliminate any period into which I may need to go in the development of my bent. This is doubtless the vagrant disposition of the "pioneer"!

Notwithstanding statements such as these, Turner did care intensely about personal recognition. He preferred that his distinct contribution to historical scholarship reach posterity unmarred by the overlapping work of other scholars. The tension between the two men persisted until 1915 when the question was finally talked over at a friendly conference. A letter from Farrand on December 23 of that year begins: "You don't know how thankful I am for the talk we had last Thursday. It will, I hope, keep me from doing anything more which might be regarded as trespassing on your preserves."

When in 1917 Farrand was asked (at the suggestion of Turner) to prepare a textbook in American history, so aware was he of his old friend's sensitivity on this subject that he felt unable to go ahead until Turner had specifically given his approval. Turner's approval, when it came in a letter of May 8, 1917, was cautious; Farrand could proceed with the book, but it must be his own book, containing his own, and not Turner's, views:

This in order to explain that the case seems to me to stand where it did at the time of our conversation. You do not ask or want me to *give* you any thing in the way of an interpretation of American history that is legitimately my own. If I did so I should be debarred from its use in my own productions; and I have so published and lectured that I couldn't deliver the goods even if you wanted them. On the other hand there is every reason why I should not stand in the way of your doing *your own* piece of work and it would be a wrong to historical scholarship if I should be in this position.

Turner's sensitivity to questions involving the ownership of ideas sometimes caused him to take rather extreme positions. In the following extract from a letter to Woodrow Wilson, for instance, written December 24, 1894, Turner decides not to read a manuscript that Wilson has asked him to examine:

I would gladly know what you think of many problems that I have been working on in that same period—Indeed this makes the difficulty in the way of my reading your work. I am likely to publish at least monographs in the same field myself before your book is in print, and I know that our point of view has so much in common that I could not help absorbing into my own work many of your ideas—It is with real regret that I come to this conclusion,—but it seems to be a choice between enjoying your book before others, and abandoning my own publication—I suppose I ought to begin to write—

Turner's concern for his scholarly reputation and future fame should be judged charitably in the light of two ameliorating circumstances. First, the difficulties that he experienced in bringing a portion of his researches to their final stages made him more attached to what he had written and fiercer in his desire to protect it than might have been the case in a man more prolific. And second, Turner's skill as a teacher, his generosity with ideas for investigation (documented in the last part of this book) meant that Turnerean concepts and Turnerean interpretations were repeatedly confronting him in the writings of other historians. Yet Turner was glad that his methods and approaches were being widely used. He did not regret this state of affairs, for in spite of his desire for a modicum of fame, he was not petty in his relations with others. Turner is in any case not the first scholar to long for fame, and he has the very great virtue of deserving it.

## *Turner's Publications*

The following letters and extracts of letters cover the years 1883 to 1928 and help us to trace Turner's development as a writer of history. As early as April 16, 1883, on the advice of Lyman C. Draper, a founder of the State Historical Society of Wisconsin, he wrote Louis B. Porlier, descendant of an old fur-trading family, for information that was to provide the basis for his first published article: "History of the 'Grignon Tract' on the Portage of the Fox and Wisconsin Rivers" (*Portage State Register,* June 23, 1883). In the following letter the twenty-one year old Turner attempts to obtain "the inside history" on these complex land transactions.

TO LOUIS B. PORLIER

Madison, Wisconsin
April 16, 1883

Dear Sir:—

Mr. L.C. Draper informs me that you being the son-in-law of Mr. Augustin Grignon, may have some knowledge of a subject in which I am at present interested.

In 1823 Mr. Grignon presented a claim before the Land Commissioners of Detroit (signed by J. G. Porlier, Justice of the Peace), for the tract of land at the portage of the Fox & Wisconsin Rivers—where the City of Portage now stands. His claim stated that in 1821, the heirs of Ecuyer (or Lecuyer) had sold the property to him. But these heirs also made a claim to the same land evidently denying the above named sale. The U.S. patented the claim to Mr. Grignon reserving the rights of the heirs of Lecuyer, and both parties finally disposed of their titles to Whitney.

Can you tell me any of the inside history of this matter, such as why Lecuyer's heirs denied the sale to Mr. Grignon; whether the mere transportation of goods across the portage, as a business, formed any basis for these claims, or whether both Lecuyer's heirs and Mr. Grignon occupied this land. Do you know whether both the titles finally passed to Whitney, or were there some claims still on the land after his purchase.

It is possible that you may be able to give me some of these points, or others in this connection; if so you would confer a great favor by a reply as soon as convenient.

Very truly yours
Fred J. Turner

Address—
Fred J. Turner
Davidson House Madison, Wis—

In 1895 Turner wrote J. Franklin Jameson, editor of the *American Historical Review,* about his forthcoming article in the *Review* and the problems he had in evaluating the masses of documents in Lyman C. Draper's collection of Scotch-Irish manuscripts.

EXTRACT FROM TURNER'S LETTER TO
J. FRANKLIN JAMESON, AUGUST 19, 1895

With this I am mailing about one-half of my paper on "Western State-Making in the Revolutionary Era,"—or, if you think the title more appropriate, "Western Attempts at State-Making in the Revolutionary Era."—I have put it as nearly into the desired limits, as at present I can manage, and I am afraid I have squeezed all the juice out of it in trying to do so. The fact is that I undertook a bigger task than I anticipated when I began; and there is some uncanny spell about these Scotch-Irish manuscripts in the Draper Collection—Draper spent half a century in collecting them, and expected to write a book every year in that period! The threads that run in and out of them are interminable, and you may be able at your distance from their influence to cut the meshes with your blue pencil. If you find it unadvisable to print the article in full, let me know and I will give you my ideas on amputation.

Two years later, in 1897, he informed Henry Holt and Company that he was not able to name a definite date for the completion of his history textbook.

EXTRACT FROM TURNER'S LETTER TO
HENRY HOLT AND COMPANY, OCTOBER 2, 1897

In reply to your letter enquiring about the college history of the United States, I will say that the only fair thing to you is to advise you that I find it impossible to bring my reconstruction of the subject into such shape that I am ready to fix it in a book within such a definite period that I can expect you to wait for it. As I wrote you in my last letter, I want to push my western studies somewhat first, and I find that these studies force me frequently to reconsider my general view of American history. The subject is growing *as a whole,* and is just now in so formative a condition in my mind that I find it impossible to crystallize any particular portion. My methods of work require me to see how I wish to organize the field as an entirety before working out the details.

Turner complained that lack of money as well as lack of time kept him from completing his various scholarly projects.

EXTRACT FROM TURNER'S LETTER TO MAX FARRAND, JANUARY 3, 1905

As my uncompleted books—*unwritten* would be more to the point! —loom up before my imaginative vision, I grow more & more covetous of the freedom from University work needed to bring them about, and I am impressed by the idea that a man ought to have either the wealth of Rhodes or Henry Adams (with their pluck in sticking to their job) or University connection for only a part of the year, to enable visits to the various libraries and for writing. This breaks up the home life badly, however, and I "guess" the best thing a man can do is to quit pipe dreams and go to work on that salvation of all needy professors, a kindergarten history in words of one syllable, phonetically spelled! I am certain that this is the only way whereby the profession can be saved financially.

In another letter to Max Farrand in 1905 Turner extolled the virtues of his editor, Albert Bushnell Hart, to whose persistent prodding the completion of *The Rise of the New West* was probably due.

TO MAX FARRAND

629 Frances Street
Madison Wis
Dec 29 '05

Dear Farrand

Thanks but I am not really so mad as you are! The fact is that I realize the hard problem that an editor has, and while of course I kicked on some of his decisions, I realize that I was so belated with my *MS* that the fellows who got their kick in first had the advantage. It's heaps of comfort to know some one cares enough to get *mad* for you!

One thing I do owe to Hart, and that is the steadfast way in which he has worked the reel and finally landed the *MS*. It's a poor sucker instead of a trout, but it fought like the devil against coming to the landing net—it looked so much more like a trout in the water that it was really a pity to bring it to the surface—but he did it nobly. And he has painted some red spots and stylistic rainbows on it, cut its mouth and trimmed its tail until some people may really take it for a trout—but you will probably recognize it for a fish—Still I really think Hart has helped me to make the book better, everything considered, and I think it only just to say this, in spite of my kicks,—and I rather like the little fish after all.

I am now working two stenographers on my final revise. The thing goes to Hart for publication January 1. You will be interested in my maps. The maps of votes are too reduced in size to be most effective, however.

I don't doubt that you and the other critics will poke holes in them and the book too—but I hope I have given in some respects a logical and occasionally a new interpretation to my decade

Cordially & wishing you a happy New Year

Yrs

Turner

Turner's correspondence with Albert Bushnell Hart in 1905–06, however, reveals that their work did not proceed without a certain amount of friction.

EXTRACT FROM ALBERT BUSHNELL HART'S LETTER TO TURNER, MARCH 14, 1906

My dear Turner:

Your criticism on my introduction came in this morning. Of course the author knows better than anybody else what he wants to say, but I thought the book had as I hoped it would a distinct Western slant. I think it would have been simpler if I had written the book, and you had written the introduction, but I have telegraphed to hold up the introduction till I can straighten it out.

Two years later, faced with the prospect of a summer of writing, Turner's thoughts turn with longing to the wilderness:

EXTRACT FROM TURNER'S LETTER TO CARL BECKER, JUNE 26, 190[8]

My plans for the future are limited at present to cleaning up some of the obligations I have undertaken for a text book; but I am interested very much in the period 1820–1850—It is the best opportunity for a new work in a period, and it happens to fall in a period when the West needs especial study,—which as yet it hasn't received—But I find it very hard to write, and suspect that I need to break for the wilderness and freshen up—rather than tie myself to the chair—

Writing on October 19, 1910, to his former student Homer C. Hockett, who was beginning his career at Ohio State University, Turner explains why the university teacher has an obligation to publish: "I know how hard it is for a busy man to produce. But don't yield to the temptation of doing your duty as a teacher *solely*. Your growth and the *stimulation* of your teaching depends in part on your continuing to investigate and publish." Though Turner practiced what he preached, he was not altogether satisfied with the results, as the following rather wistful lines to the colonial historian Charles M. Andrews, a college friend from Johns Hopkins days, illustrate: "Thank you for the copy of your paper on the *Boston Merchants and the Non-importation Movement.* Like all of your studies it shows the practised hand and insight that we have come to expect from you. I am always glad to receive your papers and only regret that I have not the means of making adequate return in like currency" (Feb. 10, 1918).

In 1919 Turner made plans for the republication of a number of his essays in book form. Quite remarkable are the grounds on which he decided against revising the essays, which appeared under the title of *The Frontier in American History* (New York, 1920). On April 24, 1919, he wrote to Edward N. Bristol of Henry Holt and Company.

I have intended when the time was ripe to bring them together into a revised and fused form; but until now there hardly seemed a sufficient demand; and *to use them as materials for a new structure* now would somewhat confuse matters: first, because the essays have a certain value in the history of self-consciousness of Americans at successive years, in our reactions between changing conditions and older ideals and conceptions. I have in some sense been an indicator of these things, and to that degree there are historical reasons for presenting the essays as they came. Second, these essays have a bearing upon the kind of influence which I have had, outside of my class room, upon the formation of a conception of American history. If I revise them, even to accord with the investigations and lectures which I have been giving students, (many of them now writers) in the two or three decades since the first appeared, I shall lose the right to my evidence of pioneering, and be open to the intimation of moulding them to others' work—

Despite the persuasiveness of Turner's argument, one suspects that another factor was involved: reluctance to devote time that might be spent fishing or working on another project to something as unpleasant as the work of revising his own essays.

In the following letter to Guy Stanton Ford, Turner once more justifies his decision not to revise the essays republished in *The Frontier in American History*.

### EXTRACT FROM TURNER'S LETTER TO GUY STANTON FORD, NOVEMBER, 27, 1920

There was so much (as it seemed to me, at least) duplication of general ideas in my various essays that I hesitated for some time whether to try to re-write them into a consistent whole, absorb them into a more general history, or let them stand as they were in their original places of publication. But the general history plan seemed slow in maturing and would have required so much omission of material that I decided not to let it interfere. To re-write would expose me to the thought that I had taken over the work of some of my later disciples and would seem old stuff. So I decided to let them stand much as originally printed with some omissions of duplicate passages, and with such indication of time of original publication as would clear up questions of priority, if any one were interested, and at the same time indicate the conditions of the time which affected the interpretations of the various papers. On the whole I was rather pleased and surprised at the degree of continuity that appeared in the scattered essays brought into a single book, for which they were not originally intended.

The general reader had to be considered, from the publisher's stand point as well as the student, and I feared the article on *Problems,* which you mention, might seem not only repetitious, but also that it would seem to be taking my work pretty seriously to trace its childhood.

Writing to one of his advanced students, an instructor at Williams College, Turner touches on an occupational problem which not infrequently plagues scholars—whether to publish studies that are doomed to become obsolete, or whether to publish only that which one believes to be definitive: "Some of my own difficulty in publishing arises from my realization of the many factors essential to a fundamental treatment, and a dislike to issue a partial survey. But we must build foundations, and furnish *real* bricks for those who come after us, and profit by our mistakes and half-sight. And there is a real danger of merely thinking 'by-and-large'" (to Arthur H. Buffinton, Feb. 26, 1921).

The following letter was written in the spring of 1921 to Lincoln MacVeagh, an officer of Henry Holt and Company who was attempting to extract from Turner the manuscript of a college history textbook. Turner analyzes his strengths and weaknesses as a writer of history:

### EXTRACT FROM TURNER'S LETTER TO LINCOLN MAC VEAGH OF HENRY HOLT AND COMPANY, APRIL 5, 1921

It is in narrative history that I am least experienced or (I fear) competent. And in *condensed* narrative especially—My strength, or weakness, lies in interpretation, correlation, elucidation of large tendencies to bring out new points of view and in giving a new setting. This appeals to the student who already knows the conventional narrative; but less to the general reader. I get on better (to put it specifically and with reference to my *trade* as a University instructor) in presenting my data to graduates already equipped with a course in American history, than to beginning undergraduates. I'm not a good saga-man. But when I get the thing moving I may find power coming to me in these respects. Only, you and my friends must not expect too much.

And finally, as I once wrote Mr. Bristol, I have, whenever I tried to go ahead under full steam,—and this is the way I write most effectively—for I must write passionately if I do it well and originally—(I am not able to sit down to so many hundred words a day as a regular accomplishment)—Whenever, I say, I have tried to really *push* ahead I have landed in the hospital; and now my physical condition, though better, demands great moderation if there isn't to be a blow up of the type of Mr Wilson's—to put a tragic event along side of—my little personal drama.

This, not by way of apology or justification, but simply that you may have the situation in mind.

If I get free from teaching, if only for a hf. year each year for the next two or three years, and can find means for adequate stenographic assistance, I have some confidence. If I could relinquish lecturing to classes entirely I should have more. I can't teach and write at the same time. In this respect I have a "temperament," as well as physical limitations. *If* the Carnegie plan of relief from teaching at the end of 25 years service had not been reversed, and *if* the value of money hadn't been cut in two, making such income inadequate, and *if* various possibilities of retirement on a living income had materialized some years ago, I should have been in better repute with Henry Holt & Co. as a Keeper of Promises. But these are the ifs, which are useless to recount, and there is no "angel" in the offing!

Miss Anna M. Clark, to whom the following letter was addressed, was National Secretary of the Young Women's Christian Association. She was in 1921 compiling a booklet on American rural social life.

### EXTRACT FROM TURNER'S DRAFT OF A LETTER TO ANNA M. CLARK, NOVEMBER 4, 1921

In my *Frontier,* I was primarily concerned with a process in American life which starts in the seventeenth century and extends from Atlantic to Pacific, and then back to the Rocky Mt and Great Plain States. I have freely generalized on this Western movement and its effects on the nation drawing broadly and emphasizing main tendencies, rather than dealing in detail . . . My essays tend to select what was most significant and useful for later American democracy and ideals, rather than to paint in detail either what was common to rural life in all parts of the country or the special variations.

On November 15, 1922 Turner wrote William E. Dodd indicating that he might seek early retirement in order to complete his writing projects: "Whenever conditions in my own income shall permit it, I hope to retire, in order to clean up a lot of stuff that ought to be written before I am much older and more worn out in the harness. At present this is only a wish rather than anything that I can count on, in view of the cost of living and my neglect of the text book route to independence. I am writing this frankly and confidentially . . . ."

By 1923 Turner had set aside his textbook and was attempting to complete his history of the United States, 1830–50, which was finally published posthumously in 1935.

EXTRACT FROM TURNER'S LETTER TO LINCOLN MAC VEAGH OF HENRY HOLT AND COMPANY, MAY 1, 1923

So nearly as I can now see, the book will run to 120,000 words, of about 12 chapters. Is a greater length permissible if I find when I come to complete the last two or three chapters that I need to divide them and also increase the number of words? Are the chapters too long if they run to 9000 or 10,000 words?

I will send the title page and table of contents with the first two chapters. Both are tentative, and, naturally, subject to modification at the suggestion of the publishers.

I have lived with this thing so long, that now that I try to boil the details down I find that the process is painful—The stuff "doesn't jell," as the housewife says, and I question, sometimes, whether when the details are squeezed out, the book will not seem to follow the routes traversed by others; and whether it has the quality I should like to put into it. This may be reaction; or it may be insight!

The following letter to historian-cartographer Charles O. Paullin, who wished to use the sectional approach in his research, deals with the difficulties that Turner was meeting with in his work on the period 1830 to 1850.

EXTRACT FROM TURNER'S LETTER TO CHARLES O. PAULLIN, NOVEMBER 20, 1928

Here I am completing a book on the period 1830 to 1850, attempting to exhibit the sectional and regional (in distinction from sectional) aspects of our history in those years, first outlining each section's geography and development, economically, socially, and politically in the period, and then showing the interplay in Congressional debates and votes and in the attitude of the leaders of the various sections. I am more and more aware of the difficulty of the task and am getting very humble.

I mention these personal matters in order to say that my own work has convinced me of several things. One of them is that when one tries to deal with the sections statistically he is practically forced by the groupings in the Census either to use its Divisions (New England, Middle Atlantic, South Atlantic, etc.) or to attempt a rearrangement by *counties* or *precincts,* which involves work that some future group of investigators may undertake for the whole of our history, but which is too big a job for one man. On the whole, I think the Census Divisions are wisely made and not misleading. The naming of sections as "Southeast," "Southwest," "Middle West," etc., has the difficulty that the meanings of these terms change with the periods of our development and that, even in the same period, they connote different state groups in the writings of different authors, and to the reader. At least a very definite statement of states included in whatever term is used is important, as I am sure you realize.

I am finding that I have to distinguish *regions,* within a section or across several sections, from *sections* as groups of states. Both have important influences. Second, I am finding also that the period of twenty years on which I am working at present involves much more knowledge and research into the economic, political, social, and cultural aspects and their mutual relations than I had thought when I began the study.

I am more impressed than you seem to be with the number of studies of particular states, or topics, that have already been produced concerning regionalism in the separate states. There is quite a long list of them, including the work of geographers. Sectionalism in the larger sense has not been adequately treated. Formerly it was conceived of as North against South, or less often East against West, but these big sections mislead the reader. Their complexity, as you know, is even more important in shaping the historical outcome.

Therefore, it seems to me that you are setting forth on a long journey, if as a piece of scientific research into all the sectional phases of American life (including such important aspects as the literature and church organizations, for example), you take the whole of United States history on the lines of your plan. A reconnaissance or suggestive sketch of the field is not impossible, and if my working days permit I may myself also try some such thing, on the basis of my previous studies.

Your fine work on the Atlas is an important preparation. But if I may suggest, I should (for correlation and interpretation of the forces behind maps) take a special period, rather than essay the whole course of our history. But you are younger than I am, and the courage of youth is a big factor in success. Apart from the considerations above outlined the scheme is sound, I think, and important. God speed you, whatever choice you make!

# 6

# The Generous Critic

## *Introduction*

It is not simply a pleasant coincidence that this final part of the book is longer than the earlier sections; the letters containing praise, criticism, encouragement, and counsel do in fact form a substantial portion of Turner's total correspondence.

Turner's reputation reached its height during the years following his 1910 election to the presidency of the American Historical Association. During these years Turner—now a professor at Harvard and a leading figure in his profession—was bombarded with requests for his opinion on a wide variety of subjects, and capable students flocked to his seminars. Yet in spite of the many demands made upon his time, Turner acknowledged books and articles sent to him with letters that were frequently long and detailed and nearly always generous in tone. The detailed suggestions for reading and investigation that he sent to students must astonish less dedicated teachers. Even a casual inquiry about the qualifications of a young historian might elicit from Turner a lengthy reply.

How is it that a man with Turner's professional obligations could find time for such letters? The answer lies in Turner's broad definition of the historian's role: the historian, as he saw it, is obligated to carry on studies in his subject and make his findings available in published form; second, the historian must concern himself with the state of historical learning in his society and, more particularly, he must take an active role in training young historians qualified to continue the search for historical truth; third, the historian must contribute to the health of his profession by encouraging contacts and exchanges between scattered scholars; and finally, he should foster historical study along scientific lines, keeping in mind the spirit and problems of the age in which he lives.

In this listing of Turner's views on the duties of the historian, social obligation plays a big part. The historian has a duty to society in general, to his students, to his fellow historians. He must be in touch with the problems of the day and in times of crisis must put his special knowledge at the disposal of his country. Even Turner's view of scholarship partakes of this societal bias. Just as many of the most necessary historical investigations could best be carried out on a group basis—each scholar contributing his special talents to the group effort—so historical scholarship itself was, in essence, a group undertaking: Turner's own studies would, he realized, be superseded by later studies built on the foundations that he had provided. History was, he felt, so complex and challenging that no one individual could accomplish much without the help of others. It was therefore important to encourage young historians to undertake studies likely to enrich the main channels of historical knowledge, and to guide careers of gifted students so that their talents not be wasted. Furthermore, it was necessary that mature historians maintain close professional contacts with one another, for without cooperation historical research would lack coherence and purpose.

Obviously a man with views such as these must lay great stress on constant contact between teacher and student, historian and fellow historian. Turner took upon himself the responsibility of producing a new kind of historian and of encouraging among his colleagues a new kind of history. A natural tool for these purposes was the letter.

Many of the following letters were written to graduate students on the threshold of a career. By the late 1920s a number of Turner's former students had achieved a degree of eminence; indeed a copy of the program of the 1928 meeting of the Mississippi Valley Historical Association (preserved in Turner's papers with annotations in his handwriting) at Des Moines, Iowa, shows how Turner's students and Turner's ideas almost completely dominated the scene. In that year Joseph Schafer, one of his most dedicated students, was president of the Association, while another former student, Louise P. Kellogg, took an active part in the program, and later became president of the Association. Turner was proud of the record of his students, and carefully put a check beside each of their names in the printed program.

Of course some of his students never succeeded in making a name for themselves as scholars, and some even had difficulty in completing the requirements for the doctorate. For students of the latter kind in whose ability he nevertheless had confidence, Turner was prepared to go to enormous trouble. Arthur H. Buffinton was a case in point. Turner did all that he could to get Buffinton to finish his dissertation as quickly and painlessly as possible, and he helped him in various other ways as well. He assisted Buffinton in obtaining a library stack card, he put his name forward for membership in an historical society, and he cheered him up when the trials of a young teacher at Williams College seemed almost overwhelming. Equally important, Turner did what he could to improve Buffinton's lot as a college teacher, recommending that he be given an improved teaching assignment.

Turner's broad concept of his professional obligations was backed up by a naturally friendly and kindly disposition. We know from his letters that his contacts with students were a source of human as well as professional satisfaction. Max Farrand said of him: "His attitude was not that of an instructor—he was himself a student among his fellows."

Mature scholars as well as students repeatedly wrote to Turner for advice, perhaps because he had the knack of being truthful without giving offense. His comments could be critical and unflattering, yet they rarely offended, for his complete lack of vindictiveness and obvious desire to help seemed to take away the sting.

Yet Turner's criticism had not always been well received. In the early years of his career Turner had written a number of book reviews, including a review of Woodrow Wilson's *History of the American People* (published in the July 1903 issue of the *American Historical Review*). The break in his friendship with Wilson brought about by the review caused Turner to give up this activity. In future his criticism was to be confined to letters, where an author might benefit in private from constructive suggestions. According to Turner's secretary, Merrill H. Crissey, Turner wanted no more friendships severed as a result of "adverse comments" in book reviews (see the Crissey memorandums, preserved among the Turner papers at the Huntington Library). Thus critical comments in Turner's letters are especially interesting, for they provide us with a substitute for the book reviews which he no longer cared to write.

Turner was adept at putting his criticism in a context which ensured its acceptability. On July 16, 1893, for instance, he wrote Woodrow Wilson (in a letter printed in this section): "Some of the chapters [in Wilson's *Division and Reunion*] are destined to live with the classics of our literature and history." Praise such as this more than makes amends for the specific reservations that follow. This mixing of praise and criticism was designed to spur the recipient on to further efforts—hence the preponderance of praise. Turner's letters of recommendation were discreet and tactful; they reflect, as much as anything, his own good nature. Carl Becker's letters of May 16, 1910, and October 24, 1920 (printed in full in this group), show that Turner's devotion to his students was matched by the affection and loyalty of the students for their teacher.

Becker was only one of the many students who felt a keen sense of obligation to Turner for the excellent training he provided and for the selfless way in which he furthered his students' careers—with encouragement, with advice, and with letters of recommendation. Homer C. Hockett in his last years liked to describe how Turner's shadowy figure would slowly rise behind the opaque glass of his office door when student visitors interrupted his work. Turner's informality and accessibility made a deep impression on his students. In a letter written to Mrs. Turner on April 3, 1932, shortly after Turner's death, George Clark Sellery, Wisconsin dean and history professor, told of hearing Turner as a lecturer at Chicago: "I knew him in his late thirties, when he gave us his weekends at the University of Chicago, and I have never met so charming, companionable and inspiring a teacher . . . I shall always keep the letters he wrote me in the spring of 1901."

The letters Turner wrote Sellery in 1901 are friendly notes regarding Sellery's appointment to the Wisconsin faculty and are not included here. That Sellery preserved these letters with such care, eventually depositing them in the Huntington Library, is some measure of the devotion which Turner was capable of inspiring, even in students who had done no more than attend an occasional lecture.

## *Letters to Woodrow Wilson*

One of Turner's earliest letters to Woodrow Wilson was written in 1889; in it he agrees to provide what help he can in identifying important sources on Western history.

### EXTRACT FROM TURNER'S LETTER TO WOODROW WILSON, AUGUST 31, 1889

On my return from a brief absence from the city I am very much pleased to find your kind letter of the 23[d]. Replying in the order of your queries, I will first say that I shall be glad to help you to the material you mention as far as is in my power. Mr. Thwaites had already told me of your connection with Longmans, Green and Co's new work, and I am especially glad to know that you are to do the important *third period.* So few writers have grasped the historical importance of the West in this period that it is gratifying to know that in the present undertaking it will fall to one who appreciates the matter. There is no lack of *self-consciousness* on the part of the West. The trouble will be rather in *selection* than in the finding of material for the history of its "self-expression." But I fear that I shall not be able to help in the important work you are about to do, as much as I could wish to. You know I have fifteen hours a week here to say nothing of my studies for a degree at JHU, the examination for which occurs in May next. Moreover, just before leaving Balto. I promised Dr. Adams to take the Northwest in the proposed text book in American history on the co-operative plan, which he is to edit. You are probably familiar with its scope and purpose. (It is not yet to be made public). With a view to working up this field I shall offer a Seminary in Northwest history this fall—to continue through the year. If I can find a few good students to work under my direction I can accomplish more than I could with only myself to work at the unorganized material. If you are content with the arrangement I will put one of my students at work on the collection of the material you wish, and give what attention I am able to spare additionally to the matter. I need not assure you that this will be as large a measure as I can make it. It would be still larger were I not under this prior pledge to Dr Adams, to whose scheme, of course, I owe first allegiance—Of course if I make the arrangement with a student he will first agree that he is merely collecting material as a discipline under my direction, not for purposes of original work.

The following letter to Wilson was written shortly after Turner had completed writing his famous essay of 1893. Turner hopes that Wilson's projected history of the American people will favorably compare with John Richard Green's excellent *Short History of the English People* (1874).

TO WOODROW WILSON

Chicago University
July 16, 1893.

My dear Wilson:

I received your letter while in the final agonies of getting out a belated paper for the Am. Hist. Association and since I have been here I have not found opportunity to write you as I wish to. I go home in a day or so and will write you fully then. Let me say now simply that I am delighted to learn that you contemplate a history of the United States. I believe no one is so well qualified to do for us what Green did for England, and I shall be glad to be of any service. I am one of the enthusiasts over your *Division and Reunion*. In style it is your most attractive work, and in treatment judicial—Some of the chapters are destined to live with the classics of our literature and history —I will write you in detail later, but will only say just now in criticism of your book that I think you hold the doctrine of survival of state sovereignty in too absolute a form. Admitting the dominant particularism in 1790, it is yet true that the South (and the South is *complex* in respect to the doctrine) intensified, systematized, and modified the doctrine to suit her changing economic conditions—The South did remain behind the procession of American advance, but she did not remain *preserved* by the ice of slavery like a Siberian mammoth. She changed greatly. I will write you what I mean soon, and will send you a copy of my syllabus on Colonization, and my paper before the Am. Hist. Assoc.—

With warm regards, yours
Frederick J. Turner

Wilson's *Division and Reunion* appeared in 1893, and met with Turner's approval.

EXTRACT FROM TURNER'S LETTER TO WOODROW WILSON, DECEMBER, 24, 1894

I have been rereading your Division and Reunion—It is a wonderful little work—at once a contribution to knowledge and an example of the wedding of a good literary form to historical writing—There is a vitality,—a flesh and blood form—to the book that I like very much—Your full history will be *the* American history of our time, I believe—Did I ever tell you how much I enjoyed your calendar of Great Americans? I tried the same kind of a test on Franklin once, in a review of Hale's Franklin in France, I, in the *Dial,* coming to the conclusion that he was the first typical great American.—great as America was great.

With this I send you an old photograph of my map. I hope you can use it. The exaggeration of the vertical scale conveys false impressions, especially for the Cordilleran region, but on the whole the map is the most suggestive for historical use of any relief map I have used —except that great one, built on the curve of the sphere by Howells, I think, of Washington—and for photographic use, mine is quite as serviceable perhaps. The most history I ever found in any map, however, I found in the contour maps of the U.S. Geolog. Survey—nine sheets, without any names, or political boundaries on the map—giving lakes, rivers, and contour lines only. It is a revelation. The same thing is published with county and state boundaries, names of towns, rivers etc—But this destroys its value as showing the part played by physiographic conditions—Address Mr. Gannett, U.S. Topographer, U.S. Geological Survey, Washington, D.C. It is not for sale.—

Turner responded to a letter from Woodrow Wilson raising the possibility that Charles Homer Haskins might be induced to leave Wisconsin for Princeton with the following comments.

EXTRACT FROM TURNER'S LETTER TO WOODROW WILSON, DECEMBER 3, 1896

I do know Haskins thoroughly. I wouldn't trade him for any other Professor of European history in the country. You remember him when he was hardly more than a boy at Johns Hopkins. He has outgrown his nervousness and while he is not a "facile talker," he speaks freely, forcibly and lucidly, and holds the closest attention and respect of his classes. I regard him as an exceptionally good class lecturer. He has one elective class of 80 or 90 in Mediaeval History, to which he lectures three times a week with entire success. He has exceptional solidity of judgement and clearness of historical insight. In his seminary work he is all that you could ask for, and his year, spent chiefly in Paris, has given him a great incentive in his work. It may help you to an understanding of him to know that he is as enthusiastic over the *lecturing* of such great teachers as Lavisse, in the Ecole Normal, as he is over the criticism of men like Langlois. He is one of the strongest reasoners and effective debaters in our faculty meetings.

## *Letters of Advice*

In 1896 Turner took the trouble to advise young Carl Becker about preparing for advanced study at the University of Wisconsin.

TO CARL BECKER

*Bulletin of the University of Wisconsin*
Madison, Wisconsin
July 3, 1896

Dear Mr. Becker:

If you can do so, it is wiser I think to go right on with your graduate study, as you intend. The fellowships are awarded, other things being equal, chiefly upon thesis work; the instructional work is regarded by the faculty as of secondary importance to the investigation —But of course we remember that part of the fellow's work is in the class room, and that he is in training for the instructor's chair—In your case I would not advise you to prepare definitely on a given study for the *instructional* purpose. If you have time for some reading, take a historical classic like Mommsen, or Gibbon and read it through— The fellow's work is usually in English history or Ancient history—

To get up Green, with excursions into Stubbs, would be excellent work on England. The idea is, you see, to read a considerable block of history by a great master—the exact period is not so important—

Regarding your minors: the old union between history and literature is now broken in all the growing colleges. So, if you consider the probable demand for instructors, I should not advise you to make a *first* minor of literature. I am not sure that there will not be a reaction and a return to the combination sometime. You might very well make a *second* minor in literature. For a first minor I would take either Economics, or Political Science. You will find a good general knowledge of both essential to historical study, if your work is not to become dilettante, and this could be gotten in the course of your work, even if you take your second minor in literature—

It would give me pleasure to see you win a fellowship. We have to settle them purely on the basis of competition, but I should be glad, other things being equal, to see one of the men trained entirely by us win the honor. Of course I cannot make any promises, and you, I understand, are not asking any.

I think that a number of our graduates are to be with us in historical study next year and I am looking forward to a year of most pleasant associations—

Yours cordially
Frederick J. Turner

In 1901 Turner suggested that Carl Becker investigate the possibility of a position at Washington University in St. Louis.

TO CARL BECKER

School of History
University of Wisconsin
Madison
Nov. 1, 1901

My dear Becker:

When I was in St. Louis the other day, Professor Snow, of the history department of Washington University there, told me that they contemplated adding to their force an instructor who should be in line for the chair of American history. Professor Snow expects to have the work divided, and their recent gift of a valuable *terminal railroad line,* has enabled them to erect a lot of new buildings and they expect a rapid expansion under the new regime. I think it is a good center to go to. When he said that their department would require next year an instructor in American history and political science, I naturally thought of you, and recommended you to Professor Snow.—He has just written for further particulars.

I doubt whether the amount now at their disposal will enable them to make you any tempting offer, if they decide to write you. But I think the place has possibilities and it may be well to make some sacrifices to be in line for the future development of the institution. Professor Snow is a charming gentleman, of the set of John Fiske, Mr. Hosmer, Justin Winsor, etc.

I have no idea just how much they can pay; but at least it can do no harm to put you in touch with the opportunity, in case anything comes of the letter of further enquiry which Professor Snow has just written to me.

Yours cordially
Frederick J. Turner

In the following letter to Max Farrand, Turner gives a concise summary of those aspects of New England history that, in his opinion, called for further investigation. He also suggested that Farrand examine Joseph Schafer's M.A. thesis, published in 1902, which developed the idea of the continuing "colonization" process in recent American history.

### EXTRACT FROM TURNER'S LETTER TO MAX FARRAND MAY 14, 1903

I am decidedly of your opinion that there is an excellent field for study in the expansion of New England into the West, and I should be sorry to have you think that I underestimated the importance of New England influence. Being of Connecticut origin, *remotely,* myself, it is a matter of patriotic pride to point out the importance of that section, and I am a little grieved that I failed to impress you with my enthusiasm in the matter. I am especially convinced of the importance of the New Englander *after* he has left his native heath!

What is particularly needed, (in my judgment), is a study of the local conditions in New England, economic, political, and religious and social, that led to the larger movements away from home, and in the second place, the methods of circulation of information respecting the West and the organization of colonization societies. I believe that an interesting study in the survival of colonial methods could be worked out by noting the points of resemblance and difference between the earliest New England colonization, the colonization of interior New England, and the colonization of the Middle West and the Pacific coast from New England. In illustration of this idea I suggest that you look over Schafer's thesis, published in the Bulletin of the University of Wisconsin, on the "Origin of Land Grants to Education."

In the following note Turner acknowledges two monographs sent him by the young Frederic L. Paxson of the University of Colorado (winner of a Pulitzer Prize in 1924 for *The History of the American Frontier*).

TO FREDERIC LOGAN PAXSON

University of Wisconsin
Madison
Department of History
Jan 12, 1906

Dear Professor Paxson:

I wish to thank you for the two valuable monographs which you send me, showing both your grasp of the significance of western history, and your ability to handle a problem.

I am particularly pleased with your presentation of the opportunities for work in the field of Colorado history. The opportunities are indeed great, and the rest of us, (anxious to see the evolution of the United States in relation to its various physiographic provinces, worked out), will all rejoice when the good work which you sketch shall be fully entered upon by those who take up your program.

Not until all the varying kingdoms of our American empire are studied shall we be able to know the historical meaning of the United States, or even comprehend it today.

Good luck to you and to your fellow workers in the realm of the Rockies!

Thank you for the personal compliment suggested, also; but the main thing is to see this vast field really attacked by trained scholars. If I can figure in any rôle as a minor prophet, or any out of a Pisgah, I shall be content.

Cordially yours
Frederick J. Turner

In January 1908 Turner received an unexpected letter from Max Farrand, who had decided to leave Stanford for Yale.

EXTRACT OF A LETTER FROM MAX FARRAND TO TURNER

Leland Stanford Junior University
Department of History
January 24, 1908.

Professor Frederick J. Turner,
Madison, Wisconsin.

Dear Turner:—

Are you, or are you not, surprised that I have decided to accept an offer from Yale? If you are not surprised, I am. I did not suppose that I would go east, nor did I think that Yale could make an offer to attract me; but when George Adams came out here the first of this week and laid the proposition before me I found how mistaken I had been, and within forty-eight hours I told him I was ready to accept an offer made to me on the lines he indicated. This must be regarded as strictly confidential, for negotiations are only through the first stage, but I wanted you to know of it from me, and at once. . . .

I wish awfully that I could have had a talk with you over the whole matter, but I had to make my decision all by myself, and I pretty quickly concluded that I ought to accept.

You know something of what it means to me to give up life out here, and some of the plans I had in mind; but there comes an equally great relief from certain conditions. With my usual optimistic point of view I have thus far taken only the cheerful side of the case and have left the difficulties and troubles to be met as they arise.

Trusting you will approve of this move, for if it does nothing else it will bring us a little closer together, I am,

Sincerely yours,
Max Farrand

If Farrand had certain reservations about moving to Yale, Turner's reply to his letter was calculated to dispel doubts. Farrand would make new friends at Yale and perhaps become acquainted with the classicist George Hendrickson, whom Turner had known at Wisconsin.

TO MAX FARRAND

629 Frances St
Madison Wisconsin
January 28, 1908

Dear Farrand—

It *is* sudden and rather takes the breath away; but it is very natural for Yale to desire you and to put the matter up to you in good Yale fashion. I am not at all surprised at their decision. Nor, am I entirely at your own, for ever since your talk at the Town and Gown on *isolation,* I have known that there was an undercurrent that set eastward in your bosom—

Sometime you will tell me the other things.

I am writing now, simply to tell you that I am very glad, if you are glad. But it will be a loss to western history on the ground; and this I don't like. Besides I'm sorry for Stanford. But Yale is a great University—and you will have a wide influence there.

I hope it will really mean that we shall see more of you—though I doubt this, for California is about as near to Wisconsin as is Yale, for all purposes of running in to chat.

You will find at Yale one of my warm friends, George Hendrickson, formerly of Wisconsin, who has this year left Chicago for Yale. I hope you will get acquainted.

Will you take to fishing for tom cod and rock fish? Or will you come with me some time to the Nipigon?

I told Mrs Turner and Dorothy under the pledge—(they are safe) —Mrs Turner's pleasure was tempered by her admiration and sympathy for Stanford. Dorothy whose interest in California is concentrated in Glen Alpine, was filled with great joy tempered only by the superior admiration which she has for Harvard as compared with Yale—the *why* of which she hasn't explained

Well, here's *to* you and your new voyage. Like Benton's statue, you point to the west, and say "in that way lies the east."

I have labored to get into touch on the wit of the book you kindly sent me. But my laughs run off into a sort of lumbago-like twinge. I can count the spots of too many blisters and I know where too many pills went to really enjoy it. As the dying man said to the friend who sent him brandy peaches, "I thank you; I can't eat the peaches, but I appreciate the spirit in which they are sent." When I reach the degree of mental depression that will make a tooth ache a blessed relief I'll try the book again. Dorothy however wants me to tell you that I know nothing about fun, and that the book is a joy.

Best regards and congratulations from us all

Yours

Frederick J. Turner

## *Tokens of Esteem*

One of the most remarkable letters received by Turner was written by Carl Becker in 1910, at the time of Turner's move from Wisconsin to Harvard. Becker expresses his gratitude to his former teacher for arousing in him a sense of the significance of the past. What impressed Becker most about Turner's teaching was the way in which he managed to impress upon his students the value of interpretations underlying historical facts.

### CARL BECKER TO TURNER

Lawrence, Kansas,
May 16, 1910.

My dear Professor Turner,

It was in 1894 that I took my first course with you—that general course based upon the Epoch Series. Until then, I had never been interested in history; since then, I have never ceased to be so. For this effect, I hold you entirely responsible;—the things that impressed me, that remained with me permanently, were incidental to the course, but inseparable from the teacher. I learned but few facts. So far as I recall, I answered correctly only one question during the year. The answer was 1811; the question I have forgotten. I think you gave us to understand that no one, not even Mr. Thwaites, knew "exactly what happened," that you did not yourself know; but to me at least you seemed mightily interested in selecting, from the infinite number of things that were said to have happened, things that had meaning and significance. Some of the things you said, often enough but casual remarks, my mind has held fast, and they have since become keys to open many locked doors. I do not remember whether South Carolina nullified the laws of the United States; but I learned that minorities are everywhere likely to be nullifiers; and the latter point opened up so much the larger field of speculation than the former, that I have never ceased considering it. It seems that minorities can at best have only right on their side, whereas majorities have generally fact on theirs, and in the end therefore invariably prevail; which has puzzled me much, so that I have sometimes asked whether there is any difference between fact and right. I do not remember whether sovereignty resided with the States or with the Nation in 1789; but I remember you drew a diagram on the board to illustrate the problem, (which I had never seen anyone do except for geometry) and that you said you hadn't a logical mind, which one ought to have if one wanted to be positive about such a question. That remark I have often recalled, and have pondered, in a desultory way, the difference between the logical and the historical mind; and have come to the conclusion that logic and history are two distinct ways (and perhaps the only ways) of apprehending "reality," history being, however, the more comprehensive, since there is no logic of history but [there] is a very interesting history of logic. Then I remember you said once that it was all very well to poke fun at the Philosophy of history, but that after all it was impossible not to have some kind of a Philosophy of history, the vital point being only whether one's Philosophy amounted to anything. And more than once I have heard you say: "History is the self-consciousness of humanity." That, at the time, meant absolutely nothing to me, but the phrase must have been working in the "fringe" of *my* consciousness all these years, for I have recently hazarded in print the thesis that "we must have a past that is the product of all the present." That, I take it, is the same as saying that history is the self consciousness of humanity. Thus you see you are responsible even for what I publish, although, as they say in the prefaces, while quite agreeing to give you the credit for the little good there may be in it, I hold you in no way liable for the much that is bad. I remember that you tried to interest us in the Blue Ridge, and the Cumberland Gap, and the Old Cumberland Road, (or some such road.) What it was you said, I have forgotten; but I remember precisely the manner in which you said it: it was a manner that carried conviction—the manner of one who utters moral truths; and somehow it has ever since stuck in my mind that the Blue Ridge, and the Cumberland Gap, and the Old Cumberland Road, (or whatever road it was) are threads that will unravel the whole tangled skein of American history.

To me, nothing can be duller than historical facts; nothing more interesting than the service they can be made to render in the effort to solve the everlasting riddle of human existence. It is from you, my dear Professor Turner, more than from any one else, that I have learned to distinguish historical facts from their uses.

With best wishes, and most cordially,
Carl Becker

In the following letter Turner thanks Homer C. Hockett for his essay "Federalism and the West," which was printed in *Essays in American History Dedicated to Frederick Jackson Turner* (New York, 1910).

TO HOMER C. HOCKETT

175 Brattle St.
Cambridge, Mass$^{tts}$
January 3, 1911

My dear Hockett,

I was sorry not to be able to thank you in person for the essay which you did me the honor to include in the volume issued on the occasion of my presidency. I like it very much and have learned much from it. It is no repetition of things which I told you—you are telling me things, and that's the pupil to be proud of—indeed that is the kind of thing I find and like in the volume as a whole. I shall lecture out of your essay in a day or so!

I wish you could see the beautiful form in which it is printed and bound; and I am as pleased as a grandfather with a new grand baby! My students will now relieve me of the odium of not writing more and I am inclined to take to the chimney corner and watch them grow; but not just yet!

We all send our warm regards to you and your family

Cordially yours
Frederick J. Turner

Becker's thought-provoking essay, "Kansas," which also appeared in the volume dedicated to Turner, aroused the interest of the University of Michigan historian Claude H. Van Tyne, who wrote to Turner on February 16, 1911, about the possibility of bringing Becker (then at the University of Kansas) to Michigan.

One of the men we are considering for the position in Modern European history, which Hudson's retirement will leave open, is Carl

Becker. I have met him several times and have not found him prepossessing. He struck me as curt, indifferent, and wanting in the social amenities. His work on the Pol. Parties in N.Y. before the Revolution seemed to me a thorough, scholarly, patiently but heavily executed work. Now, however, appears his essay, in your memorial volume, which is a brilliant, interpretative bit of work, written with real literary charm, and withal sound and convincing. It has revolutionized my opinion of his intellectual possibilities. Will you let me bother you to the extent of telling me your impression of his personality. You have known him longer, and have a better foundation for judgment.

Turner's report on Becker was distinctly favorable but he suggested that Van Tyne also obtain appraisals from Professors Frank H. Hodder of the University of Kansas and Wilbur C. Abbott of Yale.

EXTRACT FROM TURNER'S LETTER TO CLAUDE H. VAN TYNE, FEBRUARY 24, 1911

Becker doesn't show for his real worth on first acquaintance, and he never will by his exterior manner really present *himself*. But he is not really curt or indifferent—rather, he is *lacking* in indifference and hides some sensitiveness under a crust. He was one of the most scholarly, if not *the* most scholarly undergraduate student I ever had, and he took a year of graduate work with me. He has a rich vein of sly humor, a critical power that is very exceptional, and as his "Kansas" shows, a sympathetic appreciation that is of a high rank of usefulness when combined with the critical ability. If you read his Walpole paper in the *Review* you saw how he can handle a seminary problem, and his Atlantic article on History shows unusual literary gifts. Jameson is quite moved by his ability.

I don't know personally how well Becker *teaches* or *lectures;* but I have heard that his electives are large, that he gets hold of his men etc. Hodder and Abbott (Yale) can tell you about that. Hodder is always conservative in his judgments of men, and Abbott is no enthusiast. Let me add that they report at Kansas that Becker is a strong man in administrative work on committees—that is, a helpful faculty man.

I had already mentioned Becker to Haskins here as a man well worth considering for a vacancy at Harvard. The *personality* side is not one that would make him an *offensive* colleague I am certain. Rather he would win your affection I think. At least that is the way I feel about him. How quickly he would reveal his real worth to a class is a matter dependent upon the kind of students; and the record which he has made in Kansas. I am certain he will go far in his reputation as a historical scholar and writer. His doctor's dissertation is an illustration of a delicate conscience and a training under Osgood, fighting successfully against a literary instinct. His "Kansas" shows how he can win out! I think you would not regret taking him. If you needed to combine colonial and modern history you would find him well fitted.

Despite Turner's generous recommendation, Becker did not receive an offer from Michigan. On March 10, 1911, Van Tyne wrote Turner about the unfavorable reports President Harry Burns Hutchins had received on Becker.

I am greatly obliged for your letter about Becker. President Hutchins at once wrote to both Abbott and Hodder, but the replies of both men were so unfavorable on the personal and teaching side (I am telling you this in strictest confidence) that he refused to consider Becker further. I told Mr. Hutchins that, if I were an absolute despot here, I should call Becker notwithstanding. Abbott's letter was the most crushing, and I thought I detected a personal animus. Hodder merely said that Becker was a recluse, and that students did not warm up to him, but it was plain that Hodder did not wish to lose him. I believe that your estimate was nearer the truth.

Time would bear out the accuracy of Turner's assessment of Becker's potentialities. In 1917 Becker moved to Cornell, where he was at last recognized as one of the most accomplished historians of our time.

### *Praise and Criticism*

Turner's letter of thanks to Max Farrand for a three-volume edition of his *Records of the Federal Convention of 1787*, published by Yale University Press in 1911, contains much praise and a little gentle criticism.

TO MAX FARRAND

Harvard University
Department of History
Cambridge, Massachusetts
March 23, 1911

Dear Farrand

Your three stately and beautiful volumes are more welcome than I can express without unbecoming extravagance. I thank you heartily for your gift and for the gracious words which you wrote on the fly leaf. No one knows better than I do that such work as yours will permanently associate your name with the records of one of the enduring documents in the world's political history, and that my interpretations will become airy nothings as time goes on, and what I have seen discerningly becomes a commonplace, and what I thought I saw and didn't really see, becomes happily lost in the ruck. I haven't had time to do more than delight my eyes with the general appearance of the books and approve the plan of arrangement, and to discover by the indexes that you have opened new materials on various topics in which I am especially interested. Your succinct presentation of the status of the Pinckney plan, e.g. is a model of statement. Your criticism of the text, especially your discussion of votes, seems to me a permanent contribution to the literature of the convention, and I am sure in advance that your care has given us the best textual rendering of Madison—though I wish you had explicitly *said* you had collated it with the manuscript.

A long line of scholars will be your debtors for this collection of the sources and I'd envy you your monument if I didn't feel a sort of partnership in it by reason of our friendship. It was a happy and appropriate thing for you to dedicate it to Jameson, to whose scholarship we are all so much indebted both by the things he has done and by his attitude toward historical scholarship and his intellectual acumen and integrity.

We are sorry not to see you sooner, but understand your desire to be with your mother when you can; and you will be welcome whenever you can come—Mrs Turner wants to have you and Haskins and Andrew McF Davis with a few others in to a white tie dinner sometime while you are with us, but our main desire is to sit about the camp fire and tell fish stories and visit.

Cordially yours
Frederick J Turner

Max Farrand was one of the first to perceive a serious shortcoming in Turner's published work—his tendency to repeat himself in essay after essay. In the following excerpt from a letter to Turner of May 30, 1911, Farrand casually draws his friend's attention to this weakness.

In reading over your paper in the *Proceedings* of the Mississippi Valley Historical Association [1910–11], on the "Significance of the Mississippi Valley in American History," I found a few items that were new, although most of the points you bring out I had already gotten from you before. Do not imagine from that that I do not think the paper is worth while, for it seems to me to be distinctly so. Only I am so familiar with your work and ideas that there was not as much new material in this for me as I generally find in your papers.

One of Turner's most candid letters was written to Merl Longfellow Gochenour, a former Harvard student who in 1912 was teaching at Oklahoma State Normal School. Despite Gochenour's plea that Turner "confer a big favor upon one of your old students" (Gochenour to Turner, June 4, 1912), Turner decided not to recommend the young man for a position at the University of Pittsburgh.

TO MERL LONGFELLOW GOCHENOUR

153 Brattle St
Cambridge, Mass
June 7, 1912

My dear Professor Gochenour:

I really can't testify to your "ability in going to the bottom of a piece of research, however big." There are few men for whom that can be said!

Your study of "Indiana and the Tarrif" (which is usually spelled "tariff" in these parts) showed interest and application and had promise in it. I am willing to say that. But it was not brought into such literary form that I can honestly say it showed more than what you call "meagre talent as a writer," and that wouldn't help you!

I should prefer to be more responsive, but frankly it seems to me that you are making a mistake in seeking the Pittsburg place at this stage of your progress, and that you are asking somewhat more than your work justified in the way of endorsement. I say this in the kindliest spirit, and hope you will credit me with this, whatever you think of my judgement.

Sincerely yours
Frederick J. Turner

Gochenour, recognizing the friendly tone of Turner's "very kind and candid letter," was not offended by Turner's less than flattering judgment of his capabilities. The former student wrote that he remembered "with gratitude the painstaking examination you made of my piece-meal manuscript . . . I shall see that 'tarrif' is spelled tariff . . . I hope you and Mrs. Turner have grown to love Cambridge." Gochenour appears never to have completed the work for his doctorate.

In 1912 Turner wrote a detailed letter of advice to one of his most talented students, Edgar Eugene Robinson, who was just beginning his long teaching career at Stanford.

TO EDGAR EUGENE ROBINSON

Frederick J. Turner,
153 Brattle St.,
Cambridge, Mass.
October 29, 1912

Dear Professor Robinson:

No, your paper didn't go astray. I did. I wandered off into lobster harbors, and stray islands, and thrush-haunted woods, and rose lined lanes, and lost myself in the ice water of the Maine coast, and strayed into the back yard and chopped wood. In between times I did some hack work, and refreshed myself by reading your paper. And unless my memory has gone astray, I wrote you a letter about it and told you I liked it. Then I came home here and went astray among the confused days of opening, and your paper still lies on my table. But it goes to you today by registered post.

I think the Columbia man and you are not at real odds. The western sectionalism of Andrew Jackson's democracy had an eastern alliance in the labor class and as it grew it permeated eastern politics and became a national phenomenon to some considerable extent. So with the Progressive movement.

My advice is to carry it down to the present campaign; making, if need be, two papers, and presenting the grouping of votes on all the leading measures in which the Progressive movement expressed itself. I should also analyze somewhat more in detail the various elements of Progressivism, noting the leaders of each subgroup, the economic & social & political environment of the leader, and how that helps explain the reactions (chemical figure!) of the politics involved.

I should re-draw the chart, so as to present the votes by sectional (census) grouping of states; and I should use black and white symbols entirely—get engineering or architectural assistance if necessary. I should select a few maps. Probably several could be put on one page —reducing the size.

Then I should submit it to the Am. Hist. Review. I will back it up. But it may be refused; probably will be, on the ground that it is too recent, and that the cost of reproducing maps & chart, and the size of the chart, renders it unsuitable. There remains, (if this occurs, in spite of my advice), the Political Science Review; or the Stanford publications; or printing privately as a little book.

I think the chart, as an illustration of method of historical and political exposition, the most original and in some respects, the most important feature. Don't expose yourself to the criticism of selecting with any bias. (I don't say you have. But give it careful consideration.) Give due mention in the text at least, of the amount of regular *party* voting of the Progressive Reps. & Dems.

The paper is too good to lie fallow *long*. But I think it will be possible for you to strengthen it along the above lines, and I shouldn't be in a rush.

You will probably do too much if you push this along with your shepherding of such a western flock. The Californian knows better than the tenderfoot how to take the stimulus of his climate. The man who drinks champagne pretty regularly and who takes care of himself gets along surprisingly well compared with the man who doesn't "purge and live cleanly" at intervals between his occasional excesses. Behold a parable. The moral is adjust. Take *restful* exercise, moderate in amount, and enough outdoors to counteract the nervous stimulation. Think in terms of years rather than in terms of days— If you don't, you will prevent yourself from reaching your goal by your very eagerness to get there. Accumulate sufficient reserved steam power between lectures to put your best into the class room, yourself with physical vigor behind yourself. And if pushing this revision interferes don't push it!

Cordially yours
Frederick J Turner
*Preacher*

Turner in 1913 found much to praise in Max Farrand's new book, *The Framing of the Constitution*.

TO MAX FARRAND

153 Brattle St
Cambridge Mass
April 10, 1913

My dear Farrand:

Many thanks for the volume on the framing of the Constitution. I have read it over rapidly already and my thanks are not solely for the book itself, though it is a beautifully made book, nor for your presentation words, but quite as much for the admirable presentation you have made of a complex subject. I thank you as a student as well as a friend.

It seems to me that your clear cut statement of the results of your long continued studies makes a real model, and that you have set forth many points with greater clarity than previous writers. Where you change the emphasis, I am confident that your work will withstand criticism—You have wisely avoided the metaphysics of the sovereignty question——just as the framers did!

Cordially yours
Frederick J Turner

Three years later Turner sent the following blunt yet encouraging letter to his former student, Herbert Eugene Bolton.

EXTRACT FROM TURNER'S LETTER TO
HERBERT EUGENE BOLTON, JANUARY 20, 1916

I am glad to be remembered with so substantial a contribution to my Western books, as is your *Texas in the Middle of the Eighteenth Century*. It is unmistakeably a product of the most original kind of research, including collecting, organization, criticism, interpretation and all that is involved in construction.

Sometime you are going to complete your Parkmanlike work by putting your material in a form of interpretation and generalization suited to the general reader, not primarily for the *sake* of the general reader only, but because by doing this you will make clear to eastern and northern scholars also what a rich field you are working and what its bearings are on general American history, in the large sense.

Some of us are converted already, even if we are not adepts, but you must water your rum, and offer it in a small glass to the man who is brought up on the Parkman light wines—Or words to that effect! —You get the idea.

Thomas P. Martin, one of Turner's advanced students, was in 1917 employed as an archivist for Turner's Harvard Commission on Western History. Without consulting Turner (at the time on academic leave as a research associate at the Carnegie Institution in Washington), Martin wrote to Edgar H. Wells, secretary of the Commission, demanding secretarial help: "If you commissioners wish to get the maximum mental service out of me, you must provide me with some clerical assistance . . ." (March 7, 1917). A mild scolding from Turner caused Martin to acknowledge the brashness of his behavior, and to apologize.

### EXTRACTS FROM DRAFT OF TURNER'S LETTER TO THOMAS P. MARTIN, MARCH 12, 1917

613 The Brighton
2123 California St.

Dear Martin:

This letter is personal not official, the letter of a friend who wants to help you. I shall not try to tell you how astonished and sorry I was that you wrote the first letter to Mr. Wells.

Do you not now see that it was a letter to your superior officer, written in a brusque and lecturing fashion entirely unsuited to the relationship between you and lacking in courtesy? I can say this to you as an older man and as your friend.

Mr. Wells had been at the foundation of the Commission. His unpaid unselfish interest, wide acquaintance, and large influence among the Harvard alumni whose aid we need have been important factors throughout.

I do not think you realized what you wrote. You assumed to put him in his proper place in dealing with you, but in doing this you failed to comprehend the relations between you as archivist and Mr. Wells as Commissioner.

. . . .

It is the irony of the affair that you wrote this letter to Mr. Wells at the moment when he of his own suggestion, after full consideration of your good work, and after a consultation with me was starting a campaign to collect funds to supply you with a stenographer, assistance, reasonable travelling expenses and so on. He was engaged in this in the midst of the pressure of Red Cross duties which have piled up because of the approaching war.

I did not tell you of these plans because they had just been arranged and as your own position and salary were involved it was improper to awaken expectations that we might not be able to fulfill. Your letter hit the man who was doing his best to serve your own interests, and whose questions to you were due to his desire to have an intelligent grasp on the whole condition. I am sure that you must now see that if you suspected Mr. Wells of an intention to *drive* you, or if you thought there were too many executives, you should first have talked the matter over with Mr. Coolidge, or Roger Pierce, or (in view of our own intimate relations) to me by letter before you wrote to Mr. Wells in that vein. A dozen words would have sufficed to clear it up.

Writing to Frederic L. Paxson afterward, Turner explains Martin's impetuousness as arising from overwork and immaturity. Martin's positive qualities are such that Turner recommends him for a post at the State Historical Society of Wisconsin.

EXTRACT FROM TURNER'S LETTER TO FREDERIC L. PAXSON, DECEMBER 13, 1919

He M. hasn't yet matured, and *once or twice* he has shown a little capacity to put his foot in it, by writing impulsively and without full consideration of the amenities of the situation—with a bit of *gaucherie*. But these are exceptions, based on his misunderstanding of the situation, and I think that they arose from an excessive load without corresponding care in giving him his head and an assured and effective position. However, they showed inexperience in the *mode* of expostulation in "good form," rather than any deep seated inability to work with men. He is sensitive, high spirited and ambitious, under an appearance of shyness and some deference. He has powers not fully developed, and when conditions haven't been what they ought to have been for such freedom of development he hasn't always known exactly how to suggest modifications with easy grace. One had to know his essential good will to understand that his mode of stating his views was simply less adroit than it might have been. In every case, however, he had been loaded with too heavy work considering his duties as student, archivist, or assistant, and he retained the confidence and friendliness of all of us. I think he learned by the experience—.

In 1917 Turner was able to help his student George M. Stephenson obtain a teaching post at the University of Minnesota. In the same year Stephenson revised his thesis for publication as a book (*The Political History of Public Lands from 1840 to 1862* [Boston, 1917]). Turner helped him along with the following advice.

EXTRACT FROM TURNER'S LETTER TO
GEORGE M. STEPHENSON, FEBRUARY 11, 1917

My impression is that the book should be published; but I believe it will be much improved if you can find time to go over it again, with the needs of the reader in mind more,—condensing in general and eliminating also some considerable part of the detailed citation of footnotes, especially where the citation doesn't *require* a mass of references, most of which physically could not be tested by the reader, even though a scholar. In the last resort their value depends on your accuracy and intelligence. Therefore,—except where the exact words of a given newspaper are important evidence; or where some new and radically different point of view or judgement on your part seems to demand ample evidence of the thoroughness of your search, —you could make a reference to "Bibliography section G" (by way of imaginative illustration of my idea)—wherein should be listed the Southern or Western &c &c newspapers used. Your original MS thesis should be preserved—one copy ought to be deposited in Harvard, if not now there, as evidence of the care and detail of your investigation, to be referred to in case of dispute. You did much condensation of citation on my suggestion during the progress of the thesis, but you can do still more without real loss,—if your *MS* is preserved.

You should not try to write a popular book for a large general public. But after the interval between its composition and now, you can now see it in a better perspective. In re-reading you will be able to raise into the high lights the things that seem important, the new points of view, new evidence etc, as well as give more mature vision of the general proportions of the subject.

In other words it has gotten cold, and you are in a position to see it from a more detached position.

The book was published later in the year. Turner's copy was covered with red and black annotations—he used it as a reference work for his history of *The United States, 1830–1850*. In a letter accompanying Turner's copy, Stephenson apologized for not revising the book more thoroughly along the lines Turner had suggested: "I can't say that I am so well pleased with it—some of the disappointments are the fault of the publisher and some must be laid at my door. But I suppose we all learn by experience." In the preface Stephenson expressed his appreciation for Turner's "illuminating criticism" and "never-failing encouragement."

Carl Becker, a talented writer, was, of all Turner's students, best able to express his gratitude for the help and encouragement he had received. In 1920 he wrote his former teacher to thank him for the copy of *The Frontier in American History* that Turner had sent him. In the following letter from Becker, Turner marked with a red pencil the sentence containing this comment: ". . . I have appropriated your interpretations."

FROM CARL BECKER TO TURNER

Modern European History
Cornell University
Ithaca, New York
October 24, 1920

Dear Professor Turner,

Your book came yesterday, and although the Nation had already sent me a copy, I was glad indeed to have your autographed copy, with its generous expressions of regard. Your 'share' in my stock, whatever the stock may be worth, is no small one, as I have often assured you. Whatever I have written in American history shows the influence of ideas which are expressed in these essays and addresses; and in my last book, as you will see if you look at it, I have appropriated your interpretations without scruple, without fear, also, without reproach I hope, and certainly without research. This share in my stock is I fear not very profitable to you, since I have thus embezzled it. But you have other shares less palpably docketed, but not I hope less worth while. It was you more than anyone, you and Haskins, who shunted me into the scholar's life. I always wanted to write. From the age of twelve I had the writer's itch, the models which then fascinated me being the wonderful fictive adventures appearing in the Saturday Night and the New York Family Story Paper, and such journals of established reputation; admirable stories no doubt in their kind, but perhaps not after all representing the 'best that had been thought and said in the world.' Later I became interested in the realistic novel, the sort that, without chapter headings, were intended to illustrate the 'art for art's sake' theory of life and letters. In fact I had in me the making of a scrubby journalist and a third rate literary fellow. The literary fellow I still have with me; but I try to keep him in his place, and I hope I succeed passably. If I do not it is because I got at an early age a kind of grip on the idea of scholarship. The holy fear of the dishonest and the second best, of words without sense, of easy generalizations unballasted with knowledge—this is what I desperately needed, and this was what I got from you and Haskins, and from the study of history as you taught me to study it. You may be surprised to learn that to this day, whenever I write anything, sooner or later, before I let it go, I read it over, with you and Haskins and certain others at my elbow listening; and it often happens that one or other of you, or all of you together, send me to the library for further researches, or wisely suggest that this sentence be cut out, or that paragraph be recast, in order that the thing may not be too brash or superficial or otherwise unworthy of my good masters. You may say you would never have suspected it. Fact nevertheless; and if I have not profited more by the procedure, the fault is wholly mine. Thus your share in my stock is large and steadily increasing; and I live in hope that the stock may some day go to par, or perhaps above. All things are possible, and this may come to pass when we eventuate from our present involvements and retropedate back to normalcy.

I hope you may find it convenient to come on to Washington in December.

With best wishes,

Carl Becker

## *The Case of Arthur H. Buffinton*

During the early 1920s Turner wrote a series of letters to Arthur H. Buffinton, an instructor at Williams College who had completed his M.A. degree at Harvard in 1909 and had begun work on his doctoral dissertation shortly thereafter. The following extract from a letter to Turner of 1912 indicates that Buffinton was at that time already far along with his dissertation; all the more must we admire Turner's sustained efforts to get Buffinton to complete the requirements for a doctorate.

### EXTRACT FROM ARTHUR H. BUFFINTON'S LETTER TO TURNER, MARCH 14, 1912

Williams College
Williamstown, Mass.
March 14, 1912

Dear Professor Turner,

I am mailing to you separately the outline of that part of my thesis which I have completed. It is very detailed, as you will see, but I thought it better to make it so that Professor Channing might be able to get a good idea of what I have done. My manuscript at present comprises 265 pages and closes abruptly just before the end of Queen Anne's War. I intend also to take up the early feeling of the colonists with regard to the danger of the control of Louisiana by the French. I have some early expressions of opinion on the subject which are interesting.

I am enclosing with the outline a few pages of manuscript which I have written out as a tentative preface. They are of course only for your perusal unless you choose to show them to Professor Channing. From time to time various things have occurred to me that I desired to say in the preface, and I seized the opportunity afforded by Washington's Birthday to write them down before they escaped me. I have there attempted to define the purpose and scope of the thesis and wish to submit these few pages to you for revision.

My work this half year is much the same as that of last half, save that I am more familiar with the period we are covering. I have twenty fewer men to handle and so save about two hours a week correcting papers. Normally I should have three or four hours a week free to devote to my thesis. It isn't much, I know, but in the aggregate will amount to considerable by the end of the half year. There is plenty of material here for me to work on during the limited time I have.

And again in the same year.

FROM ARTHUR H. BUFFINTON TO TURNER

10 Sacramento Street,
Cambridge, Mass.,
Aug. 13, 1912

Dear Professor Turner,

I want to thank you for sending the recommendation for a stack permit. As you supposed, however, I found that it was unnecessary, instructors in other universities and colleges being granted permission to use the library freely.

This is my second week of work here, and I think I shall be able to stay the month out of it does not get too warm. The work I am doing now is more or less drudgery, but I am getting through a lot of material that must be gone through, and getting some hints as to developments from it. I think I shall be able to clear up all the printed material upon the period 1713–1763, and possibly most of that sort of material down to 1775. That would leave me only some work on newspapers and such work upon manuscript material as it seems best to do.

I enclose one or two items which may interest you, although probably you know of them already. The bit of revolutionary and pioneer political theory from the pen of George Mason is worthy to be set beside some of Jefferson's utterances.

Wishing you a pleasant summer I am,

Truly yours,
A. H. Buffinton

Then from Turner in 1915.

TO ARTHUR H. BUFFINTON

June 21, 1915

Mr. Arthur H. Buffinton,
Somerset, Mass.

My dear Buffinton:

I have been confined to my bed for a fortnight with a severe attack of erysipelas, and am still in the hands of the nurse and doctor. It does not look as though I should be able to be of much assistance to you or anybody else during the few days that remain before I am to leave for the West. However, you know the general point of view which I have tried to develop in criticism of your work. The thoroughness of it is beyond question. It needs condensation; emphasis upon the essentials; comment and interpretation on the focal points; as much illustration as your space permits for such focal points. For the rest, the running narrative should be cut down to such brief statements as seem necessary to carry the thread of events while not obscuring the main theme which you have in hand. If there is anything that seems to you to require personal conversation, call me up or drop me a note and I will arrange an interview if I am strong enough. I believe I still have one or two of your chapters here which I was unable to take up. My present plans involve leaving on the 4th. With good wishes I am

Truly yours,

Six years later Turner was still corresponding with Buffinton about his doctoral dissertation. In a letter of 1921, he urges Buffinton to publish his work with the least possible delay, lest the field be appropriated by other scholars—by, for instance, Clarence W. Alvord.

EXTRACT FROM TURNER'S LETTER TO
ARTHUR H. BUFFINTON,
FEBRUARY 26, 1921

I had noticed the articles, and I hope the "Westward Push" one may induce you to bring your thesis to a focus! There seems no reason why you should not ask Professor Alvord (now at University of Minnesota) whether he has the plan of doing a book in the field, and to learn Miss Broshar's plans. I have no doubt that Alvord's interests will carry him back to the period, but I imagine that Miss B's work was done in the way of the usual doctoral research. You may rely upon it, however, that some one will occupy your claim, if you don't work it.

As to the article, I should first learn from Alvord whether he has a book on the stocks, and then act, with the knowledge that when one prints an article it necessarily puts the idea in the heads of others so that it is advantageous to follow it rather soon with your book, unless you wish to see others absorb the idea, and related ideas, from the article and so take the bloom off the thesis. I know of no one likely to profit by an article *soon* unless Alvord has already worked on the topic. But before long they will do so. Can't you get out an article, or two articles, this year, and follow it up at once by the thesis also, leaving elaboration for publication later?—but not much later. I think you could kill two birds with your stone. Incorporate the articles in the thesis in substance.

In the spring of 1922 Turner again urged Buffinton to publish as articles studies eventually designed to form part of the dissertation. This dissertation was, with Turner's help, to be eventually completed.

### EXTRACT FROM TURNER'S LETTER TO ARTHUR H. BUFFINTON, APRIL 22, 1922

I had already discovered to my delight that you are very much alive, and I read your Albany study with renewed conviction that you ought to put together your printed papers, tie them up, fill in the gaps and get your doctorate. It ought to result in your getting out of the "handy man" group, for one thing, and you ought to publish your "opening to new fields" before some of the other people who are reaching toward the same goal get there first. Especially since you have shown the way. Even if you publish in parts, you ought to get your results out; but the book would soon follow. What you need is the courage to get your existing material out. The manner isn't anything you need to worry over, and the flow and persuasive and interpretative form will come increasingly as you write. I appreciate gratefully what you say of my influence upon your researches and am willing to back you up in breaking into print. All I have done is to say "*Go to it*" and bring out the main aspects.

Just now few people are deeply interested in anything really scholarly; but that's not a good reason for holding our hand. And I really believe there can be found a publisher for your subject.

I have taught general history, and mediaeval history, and English history, and recent modern history, and elocution, and have run a correspondence course in Oriental history! So I know some of your trials. But such things do broaden the view if you live through them, and better men than either of us have been all the better for having occupied a settee instead of a chair. Cheer up, and take Dr. Walter Camp's "Daily Dozen" Exercises (price 10 cents).

In the following letter of 1922 (a postscript about the death of a friend has been omitted), Turner sent Buffinton detailed instructions for completing his thesis.

TO ARTHUR H. BUFFINTON

P.O. Box 15<br>
Hancock Point, Maine<br>
August 29, 1922

Dear Buffinton:

I am writing hastily and briefly to say that I see no reason why you should not weave together your published papers, and submit them as your thesis. Personally I should be ready to accept a collection of them as they stand, without further work on them, as I think they show the quality; but this is not usual, and the Dean and others should be consulted as to the possibility of such a solution. But since they all lie along a common theme, I think you could without much hard work, and with some adjustment of title, furnish an introduction and conclusion, with brief connections, leaving elaboration for a later volume. It would be better for your own progress, and for your reputation, to print such a volume soon. You are no longer so young that you can remain without a book to your credit without doing yourself injustice. If the project above will hasten it, by getting you out of the stage of doctoral candidacy into that of writer, I will do all I can to assist! "Come on in! The water's fine!"

Perhaps some such title as "Chapters in Colonial Expansion" (or

"Imperialism"—or "—in Northern Expansion and Imperialism" (?)) would serve as a thread on which you string your studies. You could, in an introductory chapter, set forth the general theme, and the bearings of the chapters on it; and you could, by paragraphs concluding the successive chapters, or introducing the chapters, indicate developments and salient changes in between your studies; and, in a conclusion, present your thoughts on the movement as a whole, briefly, and as a *caveat.* These reflections could be made *tentatively;* but I see no harm in refraining from over-caution in the *thesis,* since your work has been thorough and careful, and you still can modify before publication.

Would you care to become a member of the Colonial Society of Massachusetts, if I can get you nominated by the committee? It is, I think, a rather carefully limited group—the dues are something like ten a year, if I recall, and the members have to have Massachusetts colonial ancestry. The list may be filled up; but if not, and if there are no difficulties, I think you might find it worth while, in view of your special field, to avail yourself of their publications, and to get into touch with an interesting body of Massachusetts men. Let me know how you feel about it, and I will then sound out the committee. Who were your forebears? (!)

I remain here until Sept. 20, or 22 so I shall miss you—to my regret. From Sept. 1 to 10 or so I am going into the northern Maine woods somewhere on a fishing trip.

Yours cordially
Frederick J Turner

Several months later Turner once more prodded Buffinton about finishing his work. He promised to speak with Dean Charles Homer Haskins about the possibility of permitting Buffinton to submit his articles as a dissertation.

### EXTRACT FROM TURNER'S LETTER TO ARTHUR H. BUFFINTON, OCTOBER 27, 1922

I shall take an early opportunity to talk with Dean Haskins and others on the subject of my letter to you of Aug. 29. Meantime, as you do not propose to come up this year, I advise you to consider the project of "filling in the gaps" by way of generalized results and analysis of your studies of the intermediate material, making drafts for such a survey of the field in case some such plan as I suggested should be acceptable. *Publication* of fuller detailed presentation could come later than the submission of the thesis for the degree—if indeed you find such detailed statement essential. Such studies could come in a later series of papers, provided you feel assured of the general correctness of the survey to be presented in the thesis. I am prone to believe that you are still influenced by your early, student, ideal of setting forth *all* the detailed facts, with which I always quarreled with you. But it is your mutton, and I don't mean to interfere with its cooking! Only I should like to eat the dish before I quit eating!

Turner continued to push in the following months, for Buffinton was close to completing his dissertation, and with it, the work for his doctorate.

TO ARTHUR H. BUFFINTON

7 Phillips Place
Cambridge 38, Mass.
December 21, 1922

Dear Professor Buffinton,

Yes, I should be glad to see as much of your thesis, before the end of the first week of February, preferably, as you may have ready.

And I like your centralizing thought. It ought to clarify and facilitate. Besides it has the advantage of making it possible to utilize a good portion of the work already published by you. I should so construe it as to allow incorporation of your study of the New England fur trade, even if you have to strain a point.

Let your thoroughness of detailed investigation appear clearly enough, especially in footnote citations and illustrations, and bibliography, to make it clear that the "grind" has preceded the grist.

I spend my brief vacation chiefly in New Haven.

A few weeks ago I had a little visit with President Garfield,* and suggested that you should have a chance at advanced work in American history if Professor Smith should have a leave. I think I interested him.

Merry Christmas to you and your wife from us.

Yours cordially
Frederick J Turner

* Harry Augustus Garfield, President of Williams College.

P.S.

I once did a club paper on the "imperialism" exhibited in the New England Confederation—based in considerable measure on your Fur Trade study. It was of interest in connection with the League of Nations' problems. I went through the League Confid. records. I think you might well go into this in your thesis, though the Dutch as well as the French are involved. Why couldn't you include Dutch as well as French in your title?

T

Buffinton finally obtained his doctorate in 1924, the year in which Turner retired from Harvard.

### *Turner's Later Years*

During the next decade Turner continued to correspond with advanced students. The recipient of the following letter, Eugene H. Roseboom, was to teach for many years at Ohio State University. At this time he was considering writing a doctoral dissertation on Ohio politics. Turner suggested that Roseboom consult Roy F. Nichols' *The Democratic Machine 1850–1854* (1923) and Dixon Ryan Fox's *The Decline of Aristocracy in the Politics of New York* (1919), but he warned the young man against taking Charles A. Beard as his model.

#### TO EUGENE H. ROSEBOOM

November 22, 1923

Dear Roseboom:

I am sure that the politics of Ohio, 1850 to 1860, particularly if you illuminate the politics by their relation to economic and social changes, and the regional party geography of the State in its political evolution, is an excellent thesis subject. Too many such theses are rather arid and barren, because they are political annals, without the informing factors of the changes and interactions in the general life of the state. They oppress us with a multitude of names of little men, do not bring the leaders and their people into vital relations, and fail to deal with party machinery and methods—in short

November 22 1923
Dear Roseboom:
I am sure that
the politics of Ohio, 1850 & 1860,
particularly if you illuminate the
politics by their relation to economic and
social changes, and the
regional party geography of the State
in its political evolution, is an
excellent thesis subject.
Too many such theses are
rather arid and barren, because
they are political annals without
the informing factors of the

"... illuminate the politics by their relation to economic and social changes ...."

A Portion of Turner's Letter to Eugene H. Roseboom, November 22, 1923

Courtesy of the Huntington Library and Eugene H. Roseboom

pass over the surface merely. I should like to see you do a study on a new model.

There is some manuscript material, as you know, in the Library of Congress, letters of leaders, etc. which should be consulted, as well as the Ohio newspapers and manuscripts, and I don't doubt that you can find manuscripts of others still in private hands. Often the less celebrated figure is as influential in the politics of a state as the men who go to Washington. Is there a type of Ohio politician? Is he discernible in your period of study? A different Democratic type from that of the Republicans or Whigs? What lies behind the groups and their leaders? Are there durable regional groupings? Are there definite *periods* in the party history of Ohio in those years? Are these domestic or national periods? How far does Ohio affect national party organizations—as in national conventions, in Congress, in the cabinet &c?

You see the line of thought. Nichols, in the Columbia Studies, has a volume on the national politics of the Fifties. I have only glanced it over. It is not sufficiently correlated with the various factors suggested above to be a model for you, but you could profit by examining it, as well as Fox's Decline of Aristocracy in New York. But of course I do not mean to suggest that you carry on your work in the *determinative* manner of Beard. I haven't looked into the Jameson list to see if any similar study is cited there; but you'd better make sure.

I am trying, in between the dominant activities of University duties, to finish a book on the United States, 1830–1850, but it is "hard sledding." At the end of this academic year I retire, and shall probably go to Madison, Wisconsin, where our daughter lives, and where I can exist on my diminished income, as I could not here. I hope to get some writing done if possible then. But I am relying on you younger men to "carry on" and carry farther!

Cordially yours
Frederick J. Turner

Shortly before his retirement, Turner assisted in recruiting new faculty. Harvard historian William Scott Ferguson had already written to Arthur M. Schlesinger of the State University of Iowa concerning a one-year appointment; Turner's letter underlines the advantages which such a year would have for the scholar from Iowa.

TO ARTHUR M. SCHLESINGER

Harvard University
December 18, 1923

Dear Professor Schlesinger:

Professor Ferguson of the department tells me that he is writing you asking you to come to Harvard for a year next fall. I sincerely hope you will do so, although I shall miss the opportunity to be your colleague, as I retire next September. You will enjoy the companionship of the history men here, and the library is a first class place in which to work, as you already know. The students are an exceptional lot, and you will bring them inspiration. I hope you will not let anything interfere with acceptance. Wisconsin permitted me to make a similar program for 1903–04 during Channing's leave of absence that year, and I know the new contacts made me more valuable when I returned. Iowa needs you, I am aware, but she needs you badly enough to concede something to your wishes. And I hope your wishes will be to get acquainted with Harvard and let the Harvard students get acquainted with you.

With best good wishes, I am

Sincerely yours,
Frederick J. Turner

Turner reacted with enthusiasm to Harry Elmer Barnes' *The New History and the Social Studies* (1925). The marginalia in Turner's copy of the book (Turner Collection, Huntington Library) show that he was particularly pleased to see his own name included among the leaders of the "new" historians.

TO HARRY ELMER BARNES

Hancock Point, Maine
August 12, 1925

Prof. H. E. Barnes
186 Elm Street
Northampton, Mass.

Dear Professor Barnes:

The publishers sent me, very kindly, a copy of your "The New History and the Social Studies," which followed me into Utah where I have been spending the time since the first of June until just now. I did not write to you at once, though I acknowledged the receipt to your publishers, because I wanted to examine the book more thoroughly than I could at the moment.

Now I have had the pleasure of reading many of the chapters and I can only say that I am deeply impressed with the extent of your acquaintance with the allied sciences, as well as with history, and that the treatment which you have given to my own little share, aside from the too generous recognition of my work, represents very gratifyingly just the thing I have been trying to do. I should hardly be able, in so brief a compass, to state my point of view so well.

I also loaned the book to one of my visiting colleagues at the College of Agriculture in Logan, Utah, who assured me that your treatment of the individual psychologists was remarkably intelligent *for a historian!* so my own appreciation of the contribution you have made is supported by the specialists in other lines! Seriously, I am amazed at the load of books which you carry and carry without being overburdened. Such a study of the interaction of the social sciences has long been needed and mightily appeals to me, as you may perhaps have seen by the closing portion of my presidential address before the American Historical Association—but when I see all the possibilities of those complex relationships which your book reveals, I am very glad that it is a matter for the younger generation to grapple with.

Of course, you will be criticised for some of the points of view presented, and occasionally I find myself still somewhat of a mid-Victorian in the matter of accepting at once some of the conclusions, as, for example, in the chapter on ethics and history, but I suppose there is a real advantage in rocking the foundations just sufficiently to set the historical mind to working in a new direction.

With thanks for your kindness and with cordial regards, I am

Sincerely yours,

Frederick J Turner

Turner was prepared to go to endless trouble reading and rereading the manuscript of a doctoral dissertation, and he usually examined with some care published books and articles that had been sent to him; but he declined to criticize drafts of prospective books. In 1925 for example he politely refused to read the manuscript of Samuel Eliot Morison's *Oxford History of the United States, 1783–1917,* a two-volume work that was published in 1927.

TO SAMUEL ELIOT MORISON

August 12, 1925

Prof. S. E. Morison,
Harmsworth Professor of American History
Fyfield Lodge, Fyfield Road
Oxford, England

Dear Morison:

I have just returned from two months in Utah and am not certain whether your letter which followed me around has been answered, and I have now, in the course of my packing and travels, mislaid it.

I shall be very much interested in seeing your proposed history, but I am forced to tell you that I have felt unable to read the manuscripts of such volumes from quite a list of my friends and former students, including Woodrow Wilson and various others. There are several reasons for this and I must beg you to believe that it is with the utmost reluctance that I have established this rule. I am sure that your own book will be a piece of scholarship. That it will be interesting, of course, goes without saying. Again and again I refer with admiration to your maritime history of Massachusetts. The little clipping on Tennessee culture that you were kind enough to send me is a delightful thing and entirely well founded. I have no doubt it was needed.

We came directly through from Utah, therefore did not get out to Harvard. The weather was warm and my wife's hay fever made it desirable to reach the pine belt at once.

Cordially yours,

Arthur P. Whitaker, author of two valuable books (*The Spanish American Frontier, 1783–1795* [1927] and *The Mississippi Question, 1795–1803* [1934]) in which he traced the trade, politics, and diplomacy of America's borderlands, was for many years professor at the University of Pennsylvania. In 1926 Whitaker had tentatively accepted a position at the University of California at Los Angeles (although he later decided to go to Florida instead), and Turner took the opportunity to advise him on the areas of research and the type of outlook best suited to the California environment.

EXTRACTS FROM TURNER'S LETTER TO
ARTHUR P. WHITAKER

March 31, 1926

Dear Whitaker:

I think that you did right. If you will adjust to the Californians and to California, remembering that it is necessary to hold one's self in leash until one really knows the other fellow, and the other place, I think you have a future there. Don't get mixed up in faculty factions, or regional disputes. Saw your own wood and make the California girls and boys trust and like you and above all stir them up to an interest in history, assuming that interest and the ability they may not know they possess. Yours truly, Polonius!

Please let Merk and the appointment office at Harvard know the change in your plans.

Even if later you go elsewhere, (which you should *not* plan to do), California will be a rich experience to you, and there are endless opportunities for research in Pacific Coast and Mountain States history. Try to get a sympathetic understanding of the Mormons and later to do something on the economic and social aspects of their settlement of the Arid region and the evolution of their very interesting and in many ways enviable social types. Postpone the consideration of their religion and deal with their secular history and social fruits. Read Harris and Butt, The Fruits of Mormonism, Macmillan, (1925). Stop over, if you can and visit Logan, Utah. For two summers I lectured at the State Agricultural College there, and Professor Ricks, (a Mormon), of their history department, trained in Chicago, can put you in touch with important sources and people and scenery! He will, I think, like to be polite to you if he knows that you were once a student of mine.

One final word. You are high spirited. . . . Hold yourself in, in time of trouble and try to see the other fellow's point of view. I am not recommending undue humility but largeness and sympathetic understanding and tolerance. Don't take offence at the advice. It will be worth much to you sometime. To other men, I have recommended self-assertion and I am pretty near through recommending to any body! I think you have a future and I should like to see you achieve it at the least cost of soul. I have had my own trials and I speak out of my own experience and my own need for self-discipline.

Good luck to you and a happy career and successful usefulness!

Whitaker summarized Turner's virtues as a teacher in writing to Mrs. Turner (April 1, 1932):

I first met him when I went to Harvard as a graduate student in 1915; and when I returned there after the war, I was his assistant in the History of the West and wrote my thesis with him . . . He had a quality of sympathy or understanding which did not take the form of condoning faults, but of encouragement and incitement to better things. Above all, he gave one a sense that there is in our own day a movement of ideas comparable to the movement of population so graphically described in his writings on the History of the West.

Fulmer Mood, an advanced student, also worked under Turner at Harvard in the early 1920s. On April 29, 1926, he sent Turner a detailed proposal for a doctoral dissertation on the literature of frontier promotion, which would include narratives, guidebooks, and booster pamphlets. Arthur M. Schlesinger, whom Mood had previously consulted, had stressed the need to limit the scope of a subject that might well begin with the Elizabethan era and extend through modern times. Turner was of the same opinion.

TO FULMER MOOD

May 1, 1926

Dear Mood,

The subject you have in mind naturally interests me, but I think you should first be sure that your Harvard instructors, who have to pass on it, are satisfied that it would do, if properly developed. I must not encourage you into something that might not pass muster in the committee. With this warning, I may say that such a study might, I think, cast light both upon the way the frontier call was presented and upon European and American responses to the frontier call at different periods, from, as you say, colonial times. Perhaps a single phase would be more satisfactory as a doctoral thesis, as for example, the colonial period, or some later one; or a given region carried through a period, and including not only the literature of general propaganda and the criticism called out by it, but also practical operations, like emigrant agents of states (which Blegen, of Minn. has more or less annexed for himself) and Railroad colonization, by means of land seekers' excursions, sale and advertisement of railroad lands, etc., state activity in land marketing, etc.

In any case it would be a mistake, I think, to plan to give "years of study" to it. It could either be handled as a broad study in analysis and interpretation of methods and results, through the whole frontier period—including the colonial—or it could be developed in detail for some special region or era or process. If you are up to it, there is more credit to be gained by the general survey. Here insight into the significant and the ability to grasp rapidly the *essentials* in a mass of evidence would be the test of its worth and the method of investigation. Masses of evidence would appear, but need not be incorporated or exhausted—rather sampled and appraised and fitted in to the larger picture. The other method would show faithfulness in detailed study, with some opportunity also for the exercise of historical skill in organizing and interpreting.

But I doubt the wisdom, or perhaps the "worthwhile-ness," of a *magnum opus* of *detailed* presentation of the whole period and of all America. Such a topic as the Railroad as a Colonizer has definiteness and concreteness and is enough in itself for a detailed study of a limited field, if that alternative is chosen.

Remember also that the literary aspect of American history, though highly important, is not yet fully recognized as a field for new work. You take the risk of a conservative inertia to be overcome when you try a doctoral thesis on the history of ideas as expressed in literature.

In short I think there is an opportunity, but at the same time a risk in your proposed topic. Part of the risk is because you have, yourself, to prospect and to "*find* the color." Part of it is in the danger that confronts any pioneer. Prof. Schlesinger's query is to the point. Will you get lost, or arrive? If you conclude to explore, the risk will be yours! and the "pay dirt" if it turns up. The more limited field is the safer.

Cordially yours

PS—There is also a chance for *comparisons*—as the methods of the Virginia Company and its clerical "boomers," Penn's propaganda, the American land companies—like the old, and the later, Ohio Company; Loyal Land Co., Mississippi Co., etc., the Emigrant Aid Society; idealistic community promoters, the railroad literature, the modern state efforts to sell abandoned farms, & cut-over lands; the German, French and English companies for colonization and directed immigration; real estate operations in the Far West, etc. Obviously also there is enough difference to sharpen one's wits in differentiation by periods, by places, and by the agencies involved—and there is something common to all these. In a still larger view one could contrast the American aspect of the thing with, South American, Canadian, African, European frontier propaganda, touching only the high points.

Another student who completed his doctoral work at Harvard after Turner's retirement was Merle Curti, a brilliant young scholar interested in the history of ideas who had begun to publish articles in the field of American intellectual history. Curti had yet to complete a doctoral dissertation, and vacillated between expanding an earlier thesis on American-Austrian relations in connection with the "Kossuth excitement," or embarking on a new topic, the history of the American peace movement. "That," Curti wrote Turner on May 11, 1926, "was the chapter in the old thesis which Mr. Schlesinger did like and which he suggested using as the basis for a new one." Curti hoped that Turner would help to bring "some order out of my thesis problem."

TO MERLE CURTI

Hancock Point, Maine
June 11, 1926

Dear Curti

Your letter has reached me here in my summer home. I am glad that your work is to see the daylight of print. Of course you are the one to decide the question of a new thesis. But I am sure that what you need to do is rather to concentrate on a chapter or phase of your thesis than to undertake a new subject. If you do this, it should not be necessary to spend two years at it: one should do, if you make your subject sufficiently definite and if you make your points with clarity and insight. *But* if I were you, I'd submit an outline of such a limited subject to Professor Schlesinger, or whomever you write the thesis with, in advance, so that your minds will meet on the general plan. I am of the opinion that Schlesinger will appreciate *quality* more than *quantity* and I think it would be a mistake to take so general a topic that two years would be needed to finish it. Don't forget that there is a special examination as well as a general—Some candidates with the best of theses fall down because they have spent all their time on the thesis and little on the examination.

I haven't been in very good shape this winter and I had a nasty upset on the train coming to Boston and had to go to Stillman Infirmary. The trouble—as told to me—is inner ear. I had no control over equilibrium and I still "skid" when I walk and am in no very lively condition.

Mrs. T sent her regards and I do

Yours cordially

After giving further thought to the problem, Turner wrote again.

TO MERLE CURTI

Hancock Point, Maine
July 10, '26

Dear Curti:

Just a line to say that the "multiple hypothesis" probably holds in the matter of the Peace Movement. My angle of suggestion was purely hypothetical, tho' I probably put it dogmatically in my haste! No doubt the thing is a complex with several factors—each to be tested and included if sound. I like your program.

Yes, I have been paying bills, ever since my Boston escapade, to specialists!

But the real trouble, I keep mum about—my advancing years and the drain on my energy during my rather active period. But I'm getting better and hope to [resume] fishing and writing before long!

Yours sincerely
Frederick J. Turner

On May 8, 1927, Curti wrote to Turner to report that he had passed his "special," or final doctoral examination, the prospect of which had filled him with anxiety. "In reviewing for my special," he wrote, ". . . I went through my notes in your work, and I rediscovered how very much that is best in my equipment I owe to you. Re-discovered is scarcely the word, for I never really forgot it."

Turner, in his reply warmly congratulated Curti on his success, but with a touch of humor discounted his own influence: "I think all students confuse their interest in history, the books that stirred them, and all, with the person of the instructor who offered them the key to the city . . . If your notes on my courses helped out on the special, you may safely file them away in some remote corner." He then went on to define more exactly his influence on advanced students.

EXTRACT FROM TURNER'S LETTER TO MERLE CURTI, JUNE 11, 1927

But I am glad my work was not too narrowly "Western" to help out in a special, for I myself think of the work as general enough to start something in agricultural history, the historical aspects of

American literature, diplomacy, and even religion!—for the country as a whole, rather than "the frontier" alone! At any rate I think political, economic, and social history is all tied together and the interaction of these factors must be considered in any investigation into one of them. And if I had any influence upon students it was by pounding hard on this conception, and then keeping pretty much out of their way, while they blazed out their own trails. At any rate they are carrying on, in many fields, widely apart, and *keeping it up* on their "own hook," in the history of all sections and in many aspects.

If you keep on writing and publishing I believe the problem of working where you would like in American history alone will, no doubt, solve itself. Meantime the breadth of a *settee* instead of a *chair* in that particular subject has its advantages. I think, in my own case, that the fact almost all of my college and graduate work, and my first teaching were in that broader field of European history helped a lot. Its a good foundation for later specialization—provided you are digging at some special problems in American history all the time, and making known your results.

Turner, in a 1928 letter to Carl Becker, referred to the satisfaction he derived from working with graduate students.

EXTRACT FROM TURNER'S LETTER TO CARL BECKER, OCTOBER 25, 1928

You may be sure that I appreciate very deeply the kind things you have said of me and the approval of the men whose agreement you mention. If I ever gave you reason to think that I didn't, it was because I can't realize that I deserve such good treatment and such friends. If I calmly accepted the praise, I should feel a bit as though I took myself too seriously. But have no doubt about the warmth of my feeling and my thankfulness that such things can be said by such men.

As I grow older the more I realize how much the companionship of my research students has meant to me. Not the *educational* aspect, not the teaching, but the companionship of men out on the adventure after historical truth, and incidentally the desire to help them to outstrip their guide in finding the trail and the new horizons—

In 1929 Turner gave the Huntington Library a large part of the books, notes, and reference materials he had brought with him to California.

TO MAX FARRAND

December 20, 1929

Dr. Max Farrand
Henry E. Huntington Library
San Marino, California

Dear Max:

Verifying our conversation of yesterday, I wish to say that I desire to give to the Huntington Library, at present, that portion of my books which is stored in the basement of the Library. It may be found that there are some books which, being duplicates or inappropriate, the Library may wish to dispose of, by gift from me to the California Institute of Technology or otherwise. With regard to such series as the *American Historical Review, Mississippi Valley Historical Review,* and publications of the Colonial Society of Massachusetts, the Massachusetts Historical Society, etc., it may be a question of whether the Library would not like to have duplicates for consultation in the reference room or for storage with a view to use later; but that, of course, I leave to you. With regard to books on government and economics, most of them are so closely associated with my own library for use in American history that I think it might be well to retain them for the convenience of research men in American history. Upon this you will, of course, use your own judgment.

With regard to my notes in the basement, concerning which we conversed, you will find that they are not systematically organized nor fully representative of my own inquiries, because I relied upon the Wisconsin and Harvard libraries and the Library of Congress to supplement them. Intermixed with material that is obviously intended for class use, there will probably be found pamphlets and transcripts of sufficient importance to be placed in the Library itself. Whatever organization the material has was topical and chronological, and I doubt whether it would be practicable to apply to these notes the combination of alphabetical references that you suggested. That, however, is a matter for your own decision after looking at them.

With regard to the books and notes at present in the study that you have so kindly assigned me for the time being, I should like to reserve them until later, as I may want to make use of them outside of the Library, and if I gave them to the Library now, this would be impracticable under the rules. It is my intention, however, later on to turn them all over to the Library.

If on investigation you think that the notes in general are not suited to the purposes of the Library, please let me know before destroying them.

With cordial appreciation of your kindness in this matter and recognition of the courtesy of the Huntington Library to myself in the matter of opportunity for research, I am

Sincerely yours,
Frederick J Turner

The essay by Merle Curti referred to in the following letter is "The Section and the Frontier in American History: The Methodological Concepts of Frederick Jackson Turner" (in *Methods in Social Science, A Case Book,* ed. Stuart A. Rice). The book by Cecilia Beaux which Turner mentions is the *Autobiography;* Mrs. Alice Forbes Perkins Hooper was, of course, his friend who had helped to finance the Western history collection in the Harvard Library.

TO MAX FARRAND

26 Oak Knoll Gardens
Pasadena, California
January 5, 1931

Dear Max:

I am turning over to you a copy of Stuart Rice (editor), *Methods in Social Science*—a Report to the Social Science Research Council.

My former student, Curti, has attempted (pp. 353 ff.) an analysis of my methods in college and in publications, which is, of course, the work of a much-too-friendly hand to win any general acceptance, but which may help you to a reconciliation of the Library's assistance to me in the past few years. I cannot take myself so seriously as his chapter does. I am also tempted to quit work altogether after reading the observation of Doctor Edwards, in his "Bibliography of the History of Agriculture in the United States" (U.S. Department of Agriculture, Misc. Pub. no. 84; Washington, 1930), p. 5, where he is using language not unlike that of Curti as to the effect of my "Frontier." However, the whole thing may have some interest to you; and perhaps you will care to turn the Rice volume over to the Library after you have looked at it. Some of the other chapters may have a value there for shaping the Library's activities in the direction of your report on the possibility of using it for a survey of Anglo-American relations in cultural history.

I have also received (from Mrs. Hooper, at Christmas) a volume by Cecilia Beaux, on her European and American experiences, which might interest you or Mrs. Farrand, and if so I should be glad to lend it to you if you have not already seen it.

Sincerely yours,
FJT

During his last years Turner continued to follow with interest the careers of former students. No detail of their lives was too small to interest him; to Frederick Merk at Harvard, for instance, he wrote (Jan. 9, 1931): "I am very glad that your administrative and secretarial duties are being shifted and that the prospects are that you may be able to push your writings and investigations next semester."

In the same letter Turner discusses the price charged by Harvard University Press for a booklet prepared by Merk and Turner jointly and used by Merk's students. Merk with justification concluded that the price was exorbitant, and Turner was inclined to agree, but unlike Merk he felt that drastic measures (bringing the case before a court) were unlikely to help matters.

### EXTRACT FROM TURNER'S LETTER TO FREDERICK MERK, JANUARY 9, 1931

Of course $1.50 does seem an excessive price for the pamphlet, particularly since it is used by your Harvard classes. Probably, however, the price charged by the Press was based on the theory that the entire sale would be to Harvard students; and there may have been for it a certain demand of a more general nature—which, however, would be unlikely to continue forever. The figures that you quote regarding the profits of the Press do seem to show that it has been absorbing money which (if I had any idea on the subject) I had thought would go to the Department for use in cheapening the pamphlet to your students or in making possible a cheaper rate for such things as the maps, etc. In regard to the claim of the Press that it had regarded "the pamphlet as its own," I do not believe it would be wise for you to carry the issue to a serious point—as to the courts. I do not know in how far the Press is a separate thing from Harvard University, but I certainly never had, myself, any intention of giving any share that I had in the pamphlet to the Press; nor had I any idea of a royalty from it, but I thought that it might be an advantage, at some time, to the Department, and particularly to your courses. The sum of the matter is that I should try, if I were you, to reach an amicable compromise. So far as breaking with the Press is concerned, you might have more to lose than to gain, in your relations with Harvard, if you did so—particularly if, in other departments, pamphlets are issued for class use by the Press rather than by some other publisher. With these general considerations, I must leave the matter largely to your good judgment. Before you decide what you plan to do finally, however, I suggest that you talk with such a person as Professor Beale, on the ground that you are a friend and former student of mine, and with colleagues in the History Department who would be able to advise in the matter.

In the following spring, Turner received an unexpected telegram from another of his former students, Louise P. Kellogg, president-elect of the Mississippi Valley Historical Association.

WESTERN UNION

1931 MAY 2 AM 5 49

SA35 45 NL=LEXINGTON KY 1

PROF FREDERICK J TURNER=

CARE HUNTINGTON LIBRARY SANMARINO CALIF= THE MISSISSIPPI VALLEY HISTORICAL ASSOCIATION HERE ASSEMBLED OCCUPIED ONE SESSION WITH A DISCUSSION OF THE FRONTIER HYPOTHESIS THE MEMBERS OF THE ASSOCIATION MANY OF WHOM ARE YOUR STUDENTS ALL YOUR FRIENDS UNANIMOUSLY RESOLVED TO SEND SINCERE AND AFFECTIONATE GREETINGS TO THE AUTHOR OF THIS HYPOTHESIS=

LOUISE P KELLOGG PRESIDENT.

Here is Turner's reply.

TO LOUISE P. KELLOGG

May 4, 1931

Miss Louise Kellogg
State Historical Society
Madison, Wisconsin

Dear Miss Kellogg:

Thank you cordially for sending me the deeply appreciated message from the members of the Mississippi Valley Historical Association. The telegram reached me after the meeting had adjourned, so that I was not able to wire my warm regards to the members and my good wishes for the Association's future.

I shall look forward with interest to the discussion when it is reported, and am confidently expecting the Association to till the rich field of American expansion, of which the frontier line was the symbol.

With personal regards, I am

Very sincerely yours,

*P.S.* I am dictating this letter, since my handwriting is no longer very legible.

F.J.T.

If convenient, place this letter in the Association's records, or in the report of the meeting in the M.V.H. review.

On the copy of her presidential address (published in the June 1931 issue of the *Mississippi Valley Historical Review* [*18,* 3–22]) that she sent to Turner, Miss Kellogg wrote "With greetings to my instructor who first encouraged me to continue research." This compliment did not prevent Turner from making clear in his letter of June 22, 1931, that in this case Miss Kellogg had gone beyond her depth, had tried to cover too much. Miss Kellogg, however, showed no resentment: "Criticism from you," she wrote Turner (July 9, 1931), "and such kindly thoughtful criticism—is worth more, much more than commendation by others . . . you immediately pierced to the weakest point of my address, the one I felt the least certain about myself . . . but I did want to round out the subject . . . ." Here is the letter in which Turner sets forth his reservations about Miss Kellogg's paper.

TO LOUISE PHELPS KELLOGG

June 22, 1931

My dear Miss Kellogg:

I think the separate you kindly sent me, on "France and the Mississippi Valley," is a notable contribution to the perspective of the subject; and, as you know, I am much interested in perspectives. I value highly your words of greeting, also.

I have not, of course, had time to examine the paper with the attention it demands, but I have already noted the importance of what you say about the ineffectiveness of the French policy of Indian concentration, the relation of this to the Indian and intercolonial wars, etc. Of course, the fundamental thing is that the French tried to make use of the Indians as a part of their colonization policy, while, on the whole, the English policy was that of pushing them out.

What you say regarding the attitude of France in the period of the American Revolution and just after, raises a question or two in my mind.

I see that you cite [Paul C.] Phillips and [Edward S.] Corwin on what actuated France in her participation in the American Revolution. No doubt, France was desirous of humiliating Great Britain and restoring her own prestige in Europe; but I do not feel so sure that it was not, also, part of her program to secure a controlling influence over the youthful United States and to prevent its expansion. Considering the relations at that time between Spain and France, taking into account the clear evidence (in Doniol, etc.) that France put forth earnest efforts to look after the interests of Spain rather than to permit America to secure boundaries necessary for her effective independent existence, and remembering the attitude of France in the years just before the American Revolution and in the administrations of Washington and Adams, I still think that Phillips, particularly, and partly Corwin and also Van Tyne, were more exculpatory of France in that period than I should be. Certainly, Vergennes did not "deserve an American statue." One at all familiar with the spirit of diplomacy in that period will be cautious in accepting the views of these professors; and no sufficient examination of the Spanish archives, and perhaps those of France, has yet been made, to settle the real relations between France and Spain. Even if France agreed not to invade, or attempt to possess, any part of North America, there was still, in view of the shifty character of the diplomats of the time, the possibility that Louisiana might be either acquired from Spain or given nominal independence under French control. The instructions to Genet, later, show that revolutionary France did not feel itself debarred from securing the independence of both Louisiana and Canada. It may be that Corwin is right in his analysis of the Vergennes *Memoir* on Louisiana. In my paper, I was concerned with the period of Washington and Adams, and I introduced this *Memoir* into the discussion without committing myself to it. Treatment of this period, however, was not essential to the bulk of my argument, and I still believe that the Spanish and French archives should be more carefully examined with reference to French policy in the matter.

After the close of the American Revolution, was "overseas colonization dropped out of sight" by France "until its house was set in order"? The period of Genet, Brissot, Collot, etc., would seem to belong to the years before France set its house in order. Certainly, I should not say that the shift of parties at the time of Genet "caused Louisiana to be *forgotten*."

But these are all minor questions (now quite out of my historical activities) that come to my mind in connection with your stimulating paper; and let me say, in closing, that I am very happy to know that you think I "first encouraged" you "to continue research." The habit of my seminary may account for the queries that accompany my admiration of your paper as a whole.

Very sincerely yours,

Not many months after receiving the flattering telegram from his friends in the Mississippi Valley Historical Association, Turner read Joseph Schafer's appreciative essay, "The Author of the Frontier Hypothesis," which appeared in the September 1931 issue of the *Wisconsin Magazine of History*.

TO JOSEPH SCHAFER

Carmel, California
R.F.D. 1, Box 195
[Sept., 1931]

Dear Schafer:

The September issue of the Wisconsin Historical Magazine, which arrived yesterday certainly gave me a good surprise, for I had so recently read your draft of a review of my New England and had no idea that you had any thing up your sleeve.

Although I know there is always a glamor about the days when one is finding his life work and rejoicing in the finding, I was particularly pleased that you could say such pleasant things about me, as I seemed to you in the days when I did my paper on the Frontier. Now that I am before long to "join the innumerable caravan," I look back on that young man with a perhaps pardonable indulgence and a sense of detachment that enables me to read your words without the blushing confusion that would be normal.

Be sure of one thing, I liked you from the earliest days of our companionship and believed in your future—justifiably, as you have proved!

We are leaving here in about a week for our Pasadena home, after a vacation that has been enjoyable in this lovely part of the Pacific coast. My wife has particularly enjoyed and profited by it. The other day Edgar Robinson blew in to my surprise and pleasure.

My wife and I wish to be remembered cordially to all your family.

With sincere thanks and appreciation,

Yours with warm regards
Frederick J Turner

Your references to my senior days & "orations," (excellent evidence of your research!) called out many memories! I'll send you a snap shot which will trouble you as a historian of my "gift of eternal youth"!

One of the last letters Turner wrote was to Carl Becker congratulating him on his American Historical Association presidential address, "Everyman His Own Historian."

TO CARL BECKER

January 14, 1932

Professor Carl Becker
Cornell University
Ithaca, New York

Dear Becker:

I have just been reading your Presidential Address with intense pleasure. Not only is it a characteristically fine piece of writing, but I can agree with the ideas contained in it. That I have been associated with you, is one of the real pleasures of my life. Your card of greeting from the meeting was very welcome.

Welcoming you to the fraternity of "retired presidents," I am, as ever,

Cordially yours,
Frederick J. Turner

Here are excerpts from Becker's reply, written, January 19, 1932:

I need not say that your judgment on what I write has always been of the highest import to me; and it is a great comfort to know that you approve of my address. Like most efforts at writing, this one left me when I was through, without any objective judgment of it. . . . it seemed to take very well at Minneapolis, and a number of good judges told me that it was good, so I think now that [if not as good as it could be?]* it is as good as I could make it.

Only a month before his death, while confined to bed because of illness, Turner dictated a letter of criticism to Archer B. Hulbert, a former student who wrote on transportation history and who had held the post of archivist for the Harvard Commission on Western History. Turner had reservations about the merits of Hulbert's fictionalized volume, a composite Gold Rush diary entitled, *The Forty Niners,* which had won a literary prize.

TO ARCHER B. HULBERT

February 2, 1932

Professor A. B. Hulbert
The Stewart Commission on Western History
310 Mining Exchange Building
Colorado Springs, Colorado

Dear Hulbert:

I had read with interest your *Forty-niners,* and had meant before this to congratulate you upon your having won the *Atlantic*'s prize. As you say in your statement about the critics, the new form that you have given to the book, as you intimate, has evidently got them guessing. Whether one who has read many of the original journals would feel the sense of reality, is doubtful, in my mind; but I can see that your unique experience in having gone through so vast a collection of

* Becker's brackets.

these journals, having traversed the ground yourself, and having worked out the trails so carefully, gives you an exceptional position for attempting such a composite picture. Perhaps because I am now one of the older generation, I must confess that the review by Nevins, the historian, seems to me to be more nearly in accord with my own impressions than are the reviews of your literary critics. The combination of fiction and history, even in skilful hands like yours, finds me somewhat unconvinced. Thank you for sending me the clipping, and believe me that I appreciate the excellence of your scholarship just the same.

I am still doing my dictation from my bed, due to the persistent refusal of the blood clot in my leg to permit me to get about much.

Mrs. Turner joins me in regards to you and your wife. I hope we shall see you out here this year.

Sincerely yours,

The following letter, which Turner dictated to his secretary, Merrill H. Crissey, was to be his last. It was addressed to Miss Marion Sheldon, a former student, advising her on reference materials for a biographical sketch of the New York political leader Silas Wright which she was preparing for the *Dictionary of American Biography*. Turner had recommended Miss Sheldon as an author to the editors of the *Dictionary of American Biography*. His reference here is to Ransom H. Gillet, *The Life and Times of Silas Wright* (2 vols., 1874).

TO MARION SHELDON

Henry E. Huntington Library
and Art Gallery San Marino, California
March 14, 1932

Miss Marion Sheldon
567 Potomac Avenue
Buffalo, New York

Dear Miss Sheldon:

Of course you know of the quotation in *Niles' Register* [Sept 4, 1847]* (Vol. LXXIII, p. 6) of an editorial from the *Union* on the

* Turner's brackets.

death of Silas Wright, giving a rather interesting estimate of his career; quoting a biographical sketch in the *Democratic Review;* noting that Ransom H. Gillet was engaged at the time in compiling the speeches and political writings of Wright; and quoting a letter of Gillet's in 1844, giving some reminiscences. On the chance that you may not have seen this, I venture to send this note.

Very sincerely yours,
Frederick J. Turner

# 7

## Epilogue: Turner's Accomplishments

The reader is likely to emerge from his perusal of Turner's letters with a deeper understanding of the qualities that contributed to his success as scholar and teacher than he might from the reading of books about the man. We cannot help but be impressed by the breadth of Turner's historical interests. His approach to research and the techniques he recommended in letters to students and colleagues were very advanced indeed. Particularly modern was the emphasis he placed on the use of statistical source material; Turner was one of the first historians to draw statistical data from related fields such as sociology, economics, and politics and to show its pertinence to his own investigations. Not least important, Turner's letters provide us with a self-portrait of an outstanding teacher.

Yet Turner is not one of the great letter writers: in this respect he fails to equal the historian Henry Adams, whose letters throw light upon a whole generation. Turner's letters, by comparison, have no special literary merit. In spite of the occasional sparkle of wit and the occasional metaphor, they are stylistically somewhat flat, lacking in variety. Their tone is a shade too professorial for elegance. Yet in all fairness we must remember that these letters were written with no special care and not, as far as we know, with publication in mind (although late in life Turner did exhibit an unexpected lack of modesty in annotating some of his correspondence for the use of his future biographer).

Moreover Turner's subject matter is limited almost entirely to matters connected with his profession—perhaps simply because most of his letters were addressed to historians. Turner never suggests that the world contains music, literature, and art in addition to history. Though we know he read widely during his student days and touched on cultural topics in his early correspondence with his wife, these broader cultural interests are almost completely absent from his correspondence. We find here little psychological or philosophical speculation, little bubbling over of high spirits and, for that matter, little evidence of real depression. Sometimes his letters are humorous, but applying literary standards, we must admit that his is not always the kind of humor that wears well. Moreover even if we accept the limited scope of these letters, even if we consider them simply as the informal writings of a historian, we are likely to find them somewhat disappointing: there is little that is really brilliant here, little that is new. Occasionally a position taken in a previously published work is clarified, or a new line of investigation suggested.

Turner's absorption in his work left little room for other concerns; this may partly explain the air of impersonality in many of his letters, even those written to old friends like Max Farrand. The tone in all his letters is kindly, thoughtful, warm, pleasant —but not more so to some correspondents than to others. As we read through the letters in this volume we gradually become aware that for Turner the natural medium for expression was not the letter at all—it was conversation. It was for this reason that Turner found his day-to-day contacts with his graduate students a source of such satisfaction. The feeling that important topics are best reserved for personal meetings and not dealt with in writing was shared by both Turner and Farrand. Some of the matters that they declined to take up in their letters were probably too involved for correspondence, and others dealt with matters that they were reluctant to put in writing. Neither of the two men evidenced any overwhelming belief in his ability to express himself fully in writing.

The limitations of these letters may be striking, but they are limitations of omission which in no way detract from the positive value of the letters. Their chief virtue is that they put before us a portrait of a very modern historian: not a literary man at all, but a thorough professional who approaches American history with an attitude taken over from the sciences. Indeed, no one could have been more offhanded in dismissing romantic folderol about frontiers of the Golden West.

Despite the limitations of these letters there shines through them the qualities that played a prime part in winning for Turner a place in the front rank of American historical scholars. The first of these qualities is his unquestioned devotion to his subject. His subtle mind delved under the surface of events to discover the fundamental issues. Despite the intractability of his material, he never ceased his efforts to get down on paper the fruit of his investigations. It is indeed no exaggeration to say that his whole life was spent in a great effort to throw light on the past. Everything else took second place. Thus he could not bring himself to accept an attractive and prestige-laden offer of a position at Princeton because the University's library was not well endowed with Midwestern material such as Turner found in profusion at Wisconsin: "I am conscious of the great advantage I get from a seminary of graduate students who bring home to me the spoils of the rich library day after day," Turner wrote to his friend Farrand in 1907. Whatever offers Turner received from the leading universities of his day, his first concern seemed always to be the library—would he be able to carry on his research? That this should have been Turner's primary concern in the face of his constantly precarious financial situation is some measure of his commitment to his work. Turner had no private income and had little expectation of extra earnings through publications. He was dependent on the modest salary of a university professor.

A second quality conveyed by Turner's letters is that of great kindness and sincerity. Often he found it necessary to discuss the personal and professional qualities of students and associates; yet nowhere among his preserved letters can one detect a jealous or malicious note or a tone of cynicism. Turner's occasional reservations about individuals were worded with the utmost care, and whatever could be said in a person's favor, Turner said it. His letters are full of praise, encouragement, and judicious advice, and his criticism was designed to injure the feelings of the recipient as little as possible. Just as Turner helped students on their professional way (and this long after they had left his seminar), so he encouraged the projected studies of students and colleagues with praise and expressions of confidence in the ability of the various authors to complete their projects successfully. Qualities such as these are rare; in a teacher they are invaluable. It was this side of Turner's personality (as much a part of the man as it was part of his letters) that drew to him the affection and gratitude of his students; and it is this side of his personality which is so fully and delightfully documented throughout the correspondence.

Yet another aspect of Turner's personality is illuminated by his letters. The reader becomes increasingly aware that the force which motivated Turner's efforts was less the intellectual satisfaction of doing a difficult job well than the emotional pleasure of having made more intelligible a portion of his country's past. His letters show that love of country was a driving force motivating Turner's studies. He was happiest when among the woods and lakes of the unspoiled interior, although he was full of admiration for the charm of New England and the wonders of California. "Southern California," Turner wrote in one of his letters (to Edward T. Hartman [February 1927]), "is wonderful even under rainy skies and I am deeply impressed with its spiritual possibilities. There is initiative and vitality and optimism, social and artistic construction at every center I see. It has a formative future in the nation. We love the fierce beauty of the desert, too." It was this commitment to America, this awareness of her beauty and appreciation of her historic past, that saved Turner from the aridity in which scholarship without love so often ends. The following lines from a letter to Carl Becker (June 5, 1899) reveal how, for Turner, history was no mere abstract entity but a reality rooted in the American countryside:

> The other day I took a train and trolly ride to an old favorite of mine, Conway, Mass., where my wife's family came from—It is a lovely ride through the stony hills. Later I took my wheel for a fifty mile run to, and back from Goshen. It is up hill for twenty five miles and coasting nearly all the way down! (This is not historically accurate.) The sharp contrast between New England's interior and the tidewater James is a delight to my historical feelings. We came to New England via the Lehigh Valley (& Wyoming valley) route—a former

channel of frontier migration. That too, was immensely stimulating. "Laurel crowned heights" mean more to me now than they once did, for I came over them. Good heights to take breath upon—glorious deep breaths—and then to leave.

In this brief conclusion we have been primarily concerned with Turner's total commitment to the calling of history, for which there is abundant evidence. We have also dealt in part with the powerful influence that Turner had upon his generation of American historians. The larger question of his dominant role in the study and teaching of history during and beyond this period calls for a separate volume with which I hope to conclude my studies on Turner.

# Bibliographical Note

### *The Turner Collection at the Henry E. Huntington Library*

Frederick Jackson Turner's correspondence at the Huntington Library is divided into three groups, each arranged chronologically: general correspondence, including certain miscellaneous materials; family correspondence; and correspondence with Mrs. Alice Forbes Perkins Hooper. Letters quoted in the foregoing text are housed in boxes numbered in the three series given below.

#### GENERAL CORRESPONDENCE
#### (HEH TU Boxes 1–63)

Box 1: 1879–94
Box 2: 1895–99
Box 3: 1900–02
Box 4: 1903–04
Box 5: 1905
Box 6: 1906 (Jan.–March)
Box 7: 1906 (April–Dec.)
Box 8: 1907 (Jan.–March)
Box 9: 1907 (April–June)
Box 9A: 1907 (July–Dec.)
Box 10: 1908 (Jan.–April)
Box 11: 1908 (May–Dec.)
Box 12: 1909 (Jan.–Sept.)
Box 13: 1909 (Oct.–Dec.)
Box 14: 1910 (Jan.–May)
Box 15: 1910 (June–Dec.)
Box 16: 1911 (Jan.–Dec.)
Box 17: 1912 (Jan.–May)
Box 18: 1912 (June–Dec.)
Box 19: 1913 (Jan.–May)
Box 20: 1913 (June–Oct.)
Box 20A: 1913 (Nov.–Dec.)
Box 21: 1914 (Jan.–July)
Box 22: 1914 (Aug.–Dec.)
Box 23: 1915 (Jan.–Feb.)
Box 24: 1915 (March–May)
Box 25: 1915 (June–Dec.)
Box 26: 1916 (Jan.–Dec.)
Box 27: 1917 (Jan.–Dec.)
Box 28: 1918 (Jan.–Dec.)
Box 29: 1919 (Jan.–Dec.)
Box 30: 1920 (Jan.–Dec.)
Box 31: 1921 and 1922
Box 32: 1923 (Jan.–Dec.)
Box 33: 1924 (Jan.–Dec.)
Box 34: 1925 (Jan.–June)
Box 34A: 1925 (July–Dec.)
Box 35: 1926 (Jan.–June)
Box 35A: 1926 (July–Dec.)
Box 36: 1927 (Jan.–June)
Box 37: 1927 (July–Dec.)
Box 38: 1928 (Jan.–March)
Box 39: 1928 (April–Aug.)
Box 40: 1928 (Sept.–Dec.)
Box 41: 1929 (Jan.–April)
Box 42: 1929 (May–Dec.)
Box 43: 1930 (Jan.–Feb.)
Box 44: 1930 (March–June)
Box 44A: 1930 (July–Dec.)
Box 45: 1931 (Jan.–June)
Box 46: 1931 (July–Dec.)
Box 47: 1932 (Jan.–March)

Box 48: 1932 (April–June 10)
Box 49: 1932 (June 11–Dec.)
Box 50: 1933 (Jan.–April)
Box 50A: 1933 (May–Dec.)
Box 51: 1934 (Jan.–Dec.)
Box 52: 1935–63
Box 53: 1907–33
Box 54: 1877–99
Box 55: 1900–10
Box 56: 1911–26
Box 57: 1927–55
Box 58: Photographs
Box 59: Ephemera (1880–1928)
Box 60: Ephemera (1929–47)
Fragmentary letters
Newspaper clippings
Box 61: Business papers, receipts, etc.
Box 62: Pocket diary pages
Scrapbook kept by Turner
Genealogical data
Miscellaneous sketches
Box 63: Correspondence to and from Henry Holt and Co.

FAMILY CORRESPONDENCE
(HEH TU Boxes A–K)

Box A: 1862–1887 (May)
Box B: 1887 (June–Dec.)
Box C: 1888 (Jan.–Sept.)
Box D: 1888 (Oct.)–1889 (July)
Box E: 1889 (Aug.)–1893
Box F: 1894–1904
Box G: 1905–10
Box H: 1911–13
Box I: 1914–21
Box J: 1922–26
Box K: 1927–39

TURNER-HOOPER CORRESPONDENCE
(HEH TU-H Boxes 1–8)

TU–H Box 1: 1910–12
TU–H Box 2: 1913–14
TU–H Box 3: 1915–17 (June)
TU–H Box 4: 1917 (July)–1919
TU–H Box 5: 1920–24
TU–H Box 6: 1925–26
TU–H Box 7: 1927–29
TU–H Box 8: 1930–44

This correspondence is supplemented by a group of seven microfilm reels: HEH MSS Film Reels numbered 452, 454, 476, 555, 560, 562, and 574, containing Turner material from the State Historical Society of Wisconsin, the University of Wisconsin, the Library of Congress, and other sources. Copies of most of the letters written by Turner and included on these reels have been incorporated into the larger boxed collection, but some of the letters written to him, for instance those from Richard T. Ely and J. Franklin Jameson, are on film but not in the main collection.

Other Turner correspondence is separately bound in manuscript volumes. These letters are listed under the name of the correspondent in the Turner Collection card index. TU Vol. I, Turner's "Red Book," contains letters from students and colleagues written to Turner at the time he left Wisconsin for Harvard. TU Vol. II, Turner's "Blue Book," contains letters from students and friends written to him at the time of a dinner in his honor given by his Harvard seminar students just before his retirement on May 24, 1924. Some fifty letters of condolence written to Mrs. Turner in 1932 following her husband's death are in TU Vol. V; and TU Vol. VIII contains Turner's correspondence relating to the beginnings of the *Dictionary of American Biography*. Correspondence and a diary of the early 1890s relating to Turner's children are in TU Vol. X. Other bound volumes of special interest are: TU Vol. III (1 and 2), Turner's commonplace books; TU Vols. XIII–XVIII, Turner's student notebooks; and TU Vol. XI, Mrs. Turner's journal of the Turner–Van Hise camping trip during the summer of 1908.

The Turner correspondence includes some 10,000 items. Far more extensive, however, are his research and lecture materials. Most of these are in manila folders, many of them labeled by Turner during his lifetime or by his former student Fulmer Mood, who helped to sort and classify the collection before it was opened to other scholars in 1960. In the early 1960s the present writer helped to identify and label a number of fragments and unpublished essays. These manuscripts are housed in eighteen oak file drawers and four steel drawers numbered File Drawers 1–22. Twelve more steel file drawers (File Drawers A–L) contain drafts of his last book, *The United States, 1830–1850,* and a collection of data culled from his research on the history of American society during this period. Turner's intellectual development can be traced in his large collection of 3″ × 5″ reference cards (3 × 5 File Drawers, 1–19). His early 3″ × 5″ reference cards, faded, dog-eared, and written in lavender ink, date back to the early 1890s. These cards, arranged chronologically under topics, record data and references on the development of American society from the colonial era to the 1920s. The card collection is supplemented by boxes of maps (many of them made by Turner himself), student theses, offprints, and lantern slides used for lectures.

Some 600 books and pamphlets in the Rare Book Department of the Huntington Library are the remains of Turner's large personal library. Almost all of these items contain his annotations, and many of them are extremely useful for investigating the influence on him of earlier writers. Here, for example, are annotated copies of the writings of Achille Loria, Hermann von Holst, Theodore Roosevelt, Henry George, Walter Bagehot, Johann Gustav Droysen, and a host of other authors including sociologists, geologists, geographers, and biologists. Here also is Turner's working copy of the *Guide to the Study and Reading of American History* (1912, edited with Edward Channing and Albert Bushnell Hart, filled with marginalia and pasted revisions.

A number of Turner's other books, with occasional notations in his handwriting, are scattered throughout the reference department collections at the Huntington Library, and a few of his copies of college textbooks in ancient and modern history are in the stacks of the Millikan Library of the California Institute of Technology, Pasadena, California.

In the Manuscripts Department at the Huntington Library are three unpublished descriptions of the Library's Turner Collection: "Turner's Papers, Miss [Gertrude] Ruhnka's List," 39 pages, and "Summary Report, Frederick Jackson Turner Collection" [Barbara P. Boucot], 2 pages, enclosed in a folder with "The Frederick Jackson Turner Papers in the Huntington Library," by Ray A. Billington, 1960, 26 pages. Much of the data in these manuscripts is incorporated into "The Frederick Jackson Turner Papers in the Huntington Library," by Ray A. Billington and Wilbur R. Jacobs, in *Arizona and the West,* 2 (1960), 73–77, which includes a brief description of the annotated Turner books and pamphlets owned by the Library. A short description of the Huntington's collection also appears in Wilbur R. Jacobs, ed., *Frederick Jackson Turner's Legacy: Unpublished Writings in American History* (San Marino, Calif., 1965), pp. 1–4. Two additional collections at the Huntington Library, the Max Farrand Papers and the John Martin Vincent Papers, contain references to Turner but none of his letters.

These descriptions of the Turner Collection and the subject and author card index to his letters made by the Manuscripts Department Staff at the Huntington Library were invaluable tools in preparing the present volume. Other books based on Turner manuscripts are being prepared for publication. Ray A. Billington and Walter Muir Whitehill are editing Turner's correspondence with Mrs. Alice Forbes Perkins Hooper, and Billington is editing a short series of letters that passed between Turner and Carl Becker and Merle Curti when these historians were writing essays about Turner in 1927 and 1931. Billington is also editing other letters which will be published in state history journals in Arizona and Utah.

*Turner's Published Writings*

Turner's most important published writings are briefly described in the first part of this book under "Turner's Life and Affairs." *The Frontier in American History* (New York, 1920, paperback reprint by Holt, Rinehart, and Winston, New York 1962) includes his seminal essay of 1893 on "The Significance of the Frontier in American History" and his American Historical Association presidential address of 1910, "Social Forces in American History," which sets forth his view of the processes of social evolution. The 1962 edition has a foreword by Ray A. Billington. *The Rise of the New West, 1819–1829* (New York, 1906; paperback reprint by Collier Books, New York, 1962) also has a foreword by Billington. *The Significance of Sections in American History* (New York, 1932) contains Turner's essay on "Problems in American History," which should be read in conjunction with the central essay in the book, "The Significance of the Section in American History." Peter Smith, Gloucester, Mass., has reprinted this volume and Turner's last book, *The United States, 1830–1850: The Nation and Its Sections* (New York, 1935; paperback reprint by W. W. Norton, New York 1965) as well as the other books listed above. *The Frontier and the Section,* ed. Ray A. Billington (Englewood Cliffs, N.J., 1961), includes three Turner essays of the early 1890s and one of his essays on sectionalism. Turner's doctoral dissertation, "The Character and Influence of the Indian Trade in Wisconsin: A Study of the Trading Post as an Institution," was first published in *Johns Hopkins University Studies in Historical and Political Science, 9* (Baltimore, 1891), 541–615. In slightly altered form this work was reprinted in *The Early Writings of Frederick Jackson Turner,* comp. Everett E. Edwards with an intro. by Fulmer Mood (Madison, 1938). Mood's lucid introductory essay to this volume deals with Turner's early years and provides a useful introduction to the writings published before 1893. An accompanying thirty-five page bibliography of Turner's writings, though incomplete, shows that Turner wrote a considerable number of minor articles for newspapers, encyclopedias, and other publications. Two more books should be mentioned here. Turner's *Reuben Gold Thwaites, A Memorial Address* (Madison,

1914, with annotated bibliography) is an eloquent tribute to an old friend. Turner was also an active member of the editorial committee that gathered together the essays and prepared the bibliography for *Essays and Monographs by William Francis Allen* (Boston, 1890).

In the 1940s Fulmer Mood republished a number of Turner's early writings that had appeared in newspapers. Mood and Everett E. Edwards edited "Frederick Jackson Turner's History of the Grignon Tract on the Portage and Wisconsin Rivers" for *Agricultural History, 17* (1943), 113–20, and Mood reprinted a speech of Turner's (originally published in a newspaper of 1896), "Frederick Jackson Turner's Address on Education in a United States without Free Lands," *Agricultural History, 23* (1949), 254–59, which includes a discussion of the safety valve concept and the frontier. Turner's early writings as a newspaper correspondent are examined in three additional articles by Fulmer Mood: "Radisson and Groseilliers, A Newly Recovered Essay by Frederick Jackson Turner," *Wisconsin Magazine of History, 33* (1950), 318–26; "Frederick Jackson Turner and the *Milwaukee Sentinel*, 1884," *Wisconsin Magazine of History, 34* (1950), 21–28; "Frederick Jackson Turner and the *Chicago Inter-Ocean*, 1885," *Wisconsin Magazine of History, 35* (1952), 188–95. In the first of these newspaper articles Turner deals with problems of historical evidence in tracing routes of early French explorers. In the latter two articles Turner comments on Wisconsin state politics in the 1880s. In "Frederick Jackson Turner's Notes on the Westward Movement, California and the Far West" (Wilbur R. Jacobs, ed., *Southern California Quarterly, 46* [1964], 161–68), appears the concept of the mountain states as constituting a backlash from the Pacific Coast. Drafts of an unpublished address by Turner are examined in Jacobs, "Research in Agricultural History, Turner's View in 1922," *Agricultural History, 42* (1968), 15–22. Jacobs' edition of *Frederick Jackson Turner's Legacy* contains a selection of twenty-one of his most valuable unpublished writings on American history.

A number of Turner's letters to Herbert Baxter Adams have been published in *Historical Scholarship in the United States, 1876–1901*, ed. W. Stull Holt (Baltimore, 1938), and several excerpts from Turner's letters are quoted in the notes in Elizabeth Donnan and Leo F. Stock, eds., *An Historian's World, Selections from the Correspondence of John Franklin Jameson* (Philadelphia, 1956). A letter from Turner to William F. Poole of May 10, 1893, suggesting O. G. Libby for the 1893 Chicago meeting program, appears in "A Sidelight on the Frontier Thesis: A New Turner Letter," ed. William L. Williamson, *The Newberry Library Bulletin, 3* (1953), 46–49. Wendell H. Stephenson in "The Influence of Woodrow Wilson on Frederick Jackson Turner," *Agricultural History, 19* (1945), 249–53, has published a letter of Turner's to William F. Dodd, October 17, 1919, dealing with Turner's early friendship with Wilson; and Fulmer Mood in his essay "The Origin, Evolution, and Application of the Sectional Concept, 1750–1900," in *Regionalism in America,* ed. Merrill Jensen (Madison, 1951), pp. 5–98, quotes Turner's letter on sectionalism (addressed to Walter Hines Page) of August 30, 1896.

*Contemporary Published Material*

A number of essays have been written by those who knew Turner well. Especially useful are those by colleagues and former students; these have tended to stress his abilities as thinker and teacher as well as to call attention to his efforts to draw the social sciences into the range of historical scholarship. Everett E. Edwards edited and published Ulrich Bonnell Phillips' "The Traits and Contributions of Frederick Jackson Turner," in *Agricultural History, 19* (1945), 21–23. Other sympathetic essays on Turner by Joseph Schafer, Avery Craven, and Merle Curti are republished in *Wisconsin Witness to Frederick Jackson Turner: A Collection of Essays on the Historian and the Thesis,* comp. O. Lawrence Burnette, Jr. (Madison, 1961), pp. 25–43, 100–16, 175–204. Outstanding essays on Turner by Craven and Curti are found in two other publications: Craven, "Frederick Jackson Turner," in *The Marcus W. Jernegan Essays in American Historiography,* ed. William T. Hutchinson (Chicago, 1932), pp. 252–70; and Curti, "The Section and the Frontier in American History: The Methodological Concepts of Frederick Jackson Turner," in Stuart A. Rice, ed., *Methods in Social Science, A Case Book* (Chicago, 1931), pp. 353–67. Fulmer Mood has written two penetrating essays on Turner's intellectual development: "Turner's Formative Period," in *Early Writings of Frederick Jackson Turner,* pp. 3–39, and "The Development of Frederick Jackson Turner as a Historical Thinker," *Publications of the Colonial Society of Massachusetts,* Vol. XXXIV, *Transactions, 1937–42* (Boston, 1943), pp. 283–352. Carl Becker's recollections of Turner as a teacher are contained in an informal essay, "Frederick Jackson Turner," in Howard W. Odum, ed., *American*

*Masters of Social Science* (New York, 1927), 273–318; the essay is reprinted in Becker, *Everyman His Own Historian: Essays on History and Politics* (New York, 1935), pp. 191–232. Two articles by Edward E. Dale, "Memories of Frederick Jackson Turner," *Mississippi Valley Historical Review, 30* (1943), 339–58, and "Turner—the Man and Teacher," *University of Kansas City Review, 17* (1951), 18–28, concentrate on Turner's Harvard years.

Three students of Turner's from his Wisconsin years have recorded their impressions of him: Edgar Eugene Robinson, "Frederick Jackson Turner," *North Dakota Historical Quarterly, 6* (1931–32), 259–61; Herbert Eugene Bolton, "Turner as I Remember Him," ed. Wilbur R. Jacobs, *Mid-America, 36* (1954), 54–61; and Homer C. Hockett, *The Critical Method in Historical Research and Writing* (New York, 1955), pp. 234–38. Lecture notes made by Hockett in Turner's class on the history of the West are quoted in Wilbur R. Jacobs, "Frederick Jackson Turner—Master Teacher," *Pacific Historical Review, 23* (1954), 54–61. Richard T. Ely's *Ground Under Our Feet, An Autobiography* (New York, 1938) contains several illuminating passages on Turner's activities at the University of Wisconsin, and two essays by Max Farrand describe Turner's twilight years and the influence he had upon fellow historians: "Frederick Jackson Turner at the Huntington Library," *Huntington Library Bulletin, 3*, (1933), 157–64, and "Frederick Jackson Turner, A Memoir," *Proceedings*, Massachusetts Historical Society, *65* (Boston, 1940), 432–40. Short additional Turner pieces are also based upon personal recollections: Louise Phelps Kellogg, "The Passing of a Great Teacher—Frederick Jackson Turner," *Historical Outlook, 23* (1932), 270–72; F[rederick] M[erk], [Frederick Jackson Turner,] *American Historical Review, 37* (1932), 823–24; Samuel Eliot Morison, "Frederick Jackson Turner," *Proceedings*, American Academy of Arts and Sciences, *68* (Boston, 1933), 685–86; Henry Morse Stephens, "Some Living American Historians," *World's Work, 4* (1902), 2316–27.

The sources consulted in the course of preparing the present work were not limited to writings by or about Turner. The catalogs of the University of Wisconsin for the 1880s and early 1890s contain useful descriptions of Turner's courses and seminaries. *The Annual Report of the American Historical Association for the Year 1893* (Washington, D.C., 1894), pp. 3–9, contains Herbert B. Adams "Report" on the proceedings of the 1893 program in Chicago. The Huntington Library Rare Book copy of this volume (Rare Book No. 263629) has annotations in Turner's handwriting in the margins of pages 199 to 227, where his essay, "The Significance of the Frontier in American History," is printed. In the margin opposite the description of the frontiersman's "inquisitiveness; that practical, inventive turn of mind" (p. 227), Turner wrote "wasteful and seeking quick results rather than conservation and permanence." Obviously Turner had second thoughts about the positive image of the frontiersman that he had drawn in his essay of 1893. *The World's Columbian Exposition Illustrated,* No. 22 (Chicago, 1892), includes photographs of exhibition buildings at the Fair and a description of the various "Congresses" held at the Art Institute building. Biographical data on faculty members and details on the development of historical studies and related fields at the University of Wisconsin are found in Reuben Gold Thwaites, ed., *The University of Wisconsin, Its History and Its Alumni with Historical and Descriptive Sketches of Madison* (Madison, 1900).

*Secondary Materials*

In the quarter century following Turner's death, occasional articles about the man and his work—especially criticism of his frontier theory—appeared in the academic journals; in the last decade the volume of Turnerean literature has steadily grown. Ray A. Billington's *America's Frontier Heritage* (New York, 1966) contains an astute analysis of the frontier theory based in part on Turner's correspondence. Wilbur R. Jacobs, ed., *Frederick Jackson Turner's Legacy* (San Marino, 1965) contains a brief biography of Turner; Turner's concern with general American history and social history is discussed in Jacobs, "Frederick Jackson Turner," *The American West, 1,* (1964), 32–35, 78–79. Turner's problems in writing history are examined in an expanded version of this essay in Jacobs et al., *Turner, Bolton, and Webb, Three Historians of the Frontier* (Seattle, 1965). Further analysis of Turner's difficulties as a writer may be found in Ray A. Billington, "Why Some Historians Rarely Write History, A Case Study of Frederick Jackson Turner," *Mississippi Valley Historical Review, 50* (1963), 3–27. Other recent essays by Billington—essays based upon careful study of Turner manuscripts—are "Young Fred Turner," *Wisconsin Magazine of History, 46* (1962), 38–48; "Frederick Jackson Turner and the Interpretation of American History," *California Social Science Review, 3* (1964), 7–16; "Manuscripts and the Biographer," *Manuscripts, 16* (1964), 30–35; "Frederick Jackson Turner Goes to Harvard," *Proceedings* of the Massachusetts Historical Society, *74* (Boston, 1962), 51–52. An early incident in Turner's professional life is the subject of Jacobs, "Wilson's First Battle at Princeton: The Chair for Turner," *Harvard Library Bulletin, 8* (1954), 74–87.

Recent appraisals of Turner's continuing influence in American historiography are to be found in John Higham et al., *History* (Englewood Cliffs, N.J., 1965) and in essays by Earl Pomeroy, John William Ward, and David Potter in *The Reconstruction of American History,* ed. John Higham (New York, 1962). Louis Hartz in *The Liberal Tradition in America* (New York, 1955) makes a number of questionable generalizations on Turner and his work, and emphasizes America's lack of a feudal heritage. The significance of Turnerean interpretations is stressed in two works on American Western history by Ray A. Billington: *The American Frontier,* Service Center for Teachers of History (2d ed. Washington, D.C., 1965) and *Westward Expansion, A History of the American Frontier* (3rd ed. New York, 1967). John A. Hawgood's prize-winning *America's Western Frontiers, The Exploration and Settlement of the Trans-Mississippi West* (New York, 1967) makes use of Turnerean interpretations and contains excellent bibliographical notes. Oscar O. Winther's perceptive chapter, "Trails, Rails, and Paddlewheels, and Frederick Jackson Turner," in John F. McDermott, ed., *The Frontier Re-examined* (Urbana, 1967), pp. 41–48, is based partly upon Turner manuscripts. The same author shows how the frontier theory is used in textbooks in "The Frontier Hypothesis and the Historian," *Social Education, 21* (1957), 294–98, and Turner as an interpreter of our traditions is the subject of John William Ward's "Cleric or Critic, The Intellectual in the University," *The American Scholar, 35* (1965–66), 101–13. William M. Tuttle attempts to link Turner with other writers in "Forerunners of Frederick Jackson Turner: Nineteenth Century British Conservatives and the Frontier Thesis," *Agricultural History, 41* (1967), 219–27. The influence of the Italian economist Achille Loria on Turner is treated in Lee Benson's *Turner and Beard, American Historical Writing Reconsidered* (New York, 1965). Merle Curti et al., *The Making of An American Community, A Case Study of Democracy in a Frontier County* (Stanford, 1959), uses data-processing techniques to evaluate the accumulated evidence; the study supports Turner's concept of the frontier Americanization process. Wilbur R. Jacobs' essay-review of this book stresses the pioneer quality of Turner's investigations into American social history (*Arizona and the West, 2* [1960], 294–99). Support for Turner's views on the significance of the frontier in the growth of American nationalism is to be found in Daniel J. Elazar, *The American Partnership: Intergovernmental Co-operation in the Nineteenth Century* . . . (Chicago, 1962), as well as in William T. Hutchinson's influential Mississippi Valley Historical Association presidential address, "Unite to Divide: Divide to Unite, The Shaping of American Federalism," *Mississippi Valley Historical Review, 46* (1959), 3–28.

Although most of the controversies involving Turner's theories had died down by the 1950s, critical opinions continued to be expressed. Louis B. Wright in *Culture on the Moving Frontier* (Bloomington, 1955) felt that Turner had drawn a too favorable picture of the colonial frontier, neglecting its more barbarous aspects. He also felt that Turner had paid insufficient attention to the persistence of English traditions in the South. The preoccupation of American historians with the frontier theory is the subject of critical comments by Peter Marshall in "The Fascination of the Frontier," *Bulletin,* British Association for American Studies, *1* (1960), 66–71. A polemic directed at Turner's concern with "primitivism" (echoing arguments set forth by Richard Hofstadter in "Turner and the Frontier Myth," *The American Scholar, 18* [1949], 433–43) appears in the appendix of Francis S. Philbrick, *The Rise of the New West, 1754–1830* (New York, 1965), pp. 379–88. Turner's work is criticized as an outgrowth of the Puritan covenant in another book, David Noble's *Historians against History, The Frontier Thesis and the National Covenant in American Historical Writing* (Minneapolis, 1966). Two excellent bibliographical essays on the Turner frontier theory controversy are: Walter Rundell, Jr., "Concepts of the 'Frontier and the West'," *Arizona and the West, 1* (1959), 13–41, and Gene M. Gressley, "The Turner Thesis —A Problem in Historiography," *Agricultural History, 32* (1958), 227–29.

A number of recent studies inspired by Turnerean ideas deal with subjects generally thought to be outside the historian's sphere—with psychology, sociology, and literature. Alan C. Beckman's provocative essay, "Hidden Themes in the Frontier Thesis: An Application of Psychoanalysis to Historiography," *Comparative Studies in Society and History, 8* (1966), 10–34, analyzes the frontier theory in terms of the "frontier-West-mother symbol complex." This theme has already been developed with a different emphasis as the "myth of the Garden" in Henry Nash Smith's brilliant *Virgin Land, The American West as Symbol and Myth* (Cambridge, 1950). Less convincing is Arthur K. Moore's *The Frontier Mind: A Cultural Analysis of the Kentucky Frontiersman* (Lexington, Kentucky, 1957) which devotes much space to a discussion of frontier barbarism. Rush Welter, "The Frontier West as an Image of American Society: Conservative Attitudes before the Civil War," *Mississippi Valley Historical Review,* 46 (1960), 593–614, shows that Easterners viewed the early frontier as a kind of middle-class utopia. Less valuable because of questionable generalizations is a survey of the influence of Turnerean thought on our literature: Edwin Fussell, *American Literature and the American West* (Princeton, N.J., 1965). Turner's concept of social evolution and his use of the great American forest as symbol are discussed in William Coleman, "Science and Symbol in the Turner Hypothesis," *American Historical Review, 82* (1966), 22–49. Turner's social Darwinism was also the theme of an earlier essay by Rudolf Freund, "Turner's Theory of Social Evolution," *Agricultural History, 19* (1945), 78–87. Wilbur R. Jacobs in "Turner's Methodology: Multiple Working Hypothesis or Ruling Theory?" *Journal of American History* 55 (1968), 853–63, argues that Turner confused scientific methodology with comparative, interdisciplinary approaches to research. Turner's lifelong concern with the interrelations of economics, history, sociology, and other fields is stressed in another essay by Jacobs, "Research in Agricultural History, Turner's View in 1922," *Agricultural History, 42* (1968), 15–22.

In recent years a number of articles have appeared disagreeing with certain aspects of Turner's interpretations but arguing for the adoption of revised versions of his theories. Turner's ideas on space, mobility, and migration, for instance, have inspired a whole series of exploratory essays. Robert F. Berkhofer, Jr., in "Space, Time, Culture, and the New Frontier," *Agricultural History, 38* (1964), 21–30, suggests that Turnerean theories of sectional expansion and social evolution were put forward as general doctrines or social laws that account for a wide range of historical phenomena. Earl Pomeroy, on the other hand, argues in his "Comments on Space, Time, and Culture and the New Frontier," *Agricultural History, 38* (1964), 31–33, that such concepts were put forward as mere hypotheses rather than basic social laws. Everett S. Lee in "The Turner Thesis Re-Examined," *The American Quarterly, 13* (1961), 77–83, stresses migration as a part of the American way of life. The mobility, or "M-Factor," is described by George Wilson Pierson is two articles: "The M-Factor in American History," *American Quarterly, 14* (1962), 275–89, and "A Restless Temper . . . ," *The American Historical Review, 69* (1964), 969–89. One of the early writers on theories of space and expansion and a penetrating critic of Turner's ideas was James C. Malin, who portrayed the frontier theory as a "closed-space" theory, an agrarian interpretation in an industrial age. Two of Malin's essays are "Mobility and History; Reflections on the Agricultural Policies of the United States in Relation to a Mechanized World," *Agricultural History, 17* (1943), 177–91, and "Space and History: Reflections on the Closed Space Doctrines of Turner and Mackinder and the Challenge of those Ideas by the Air Age," *Agricultural History, 18* (1944), 65–74 and 107–26. Turnerean themes of frontier mobility and free land are reevaluated in two influential books: David M. Potter, *People of Plenty, Economic Abundance and the American Character* (Chicago, 1954), and Walter Prescott Webb, *The Great Frontier* (Boston, 1952).

The doctrine of closed space and the safety-valve theory have triggered a succession of articles. These are appraised by an economist, Norman Simler, in "The Safety-Valve Doctrine Re-evaluated," *Agricultural History, 32* (1958), 250–57. Ellen von Nardroff summarizes Simler's views along with those of Fred Shannon, W. Stull Holt, Stanley Elkins, Eric McKitrick, and other writers in "The American Frontier as a Safety-Valve—The Life, Death, Reincarnation, and Justification of a Theory," *Agricultural History, 36* (1962), 123–42. Interpretations in this piece are questioned in still another article on the subject, Henry M. Littlefield, "Has the Safety-Valve Come Back to Life?" in *Agricultural History, 38* (1964), 47–49.

Merrill Jensen, ed., *Regionalism in America* (Madison, 1951), includes chapters on the concepts of section and frontier by Fulmer Mood, Vernon Carstenson, William B. Hesseltine, Howard W. Odum, and Merle Curti. This book helps clarify the relationship between the Turnerean concept of sectionalism and patterns of regionalism, and it illustrates how economics, politics, and geography are all relevant to the study of regional development. Clarence Ver Steeg in his survey of American colonial history, *The Formative Years, 1607–*

*1763* (New York, 1964), makes use of the Turnerean concept of the "Old West"; and John Richard Alden, *The First South* (Baton Rouge, 1961), stresses the role of the wilderness in the emergence of the South as a section. Ver Steeg in his essay "Historians and the Southern Colonies," in Ray A. Billington, ed., *The Reinterpretation of Early American History, Essays in Honor of John Edwin Pomfret* (San Marino, 1966), pp. 81–99, maintains that the ruling class in the South developed from among the settlers of the Old West. Edmund S. Morgan in an essay in the same volume, "Historians of Early New England," pp. 41–63, writes that Turner's emphasis on the West, reinforced by Beard's economic interpretation of history, had a stifling effect upon historical scholarship. Turner's responsibility for furthering the concept of geographical determinism in work on early American history is discussed in H. Roy Merrens' prize-winning essay, "Historical Geography and Early American History," *William and Mary Quarterly, 22* (1965), 529–48. Merrens, a geographer who reexamined a number of early American maps, was one of the first to question Turnerean concepts of the fall line. Turner's view of the frontier type is questioned by another geographer, James T. Lemon, in "The Agricultural Practices of National Groups in Eighteenth-Century Southeastern Pennsylvania," *The Geographical Review, 56* (1966), 467–96. Sigmund Diamond in "An Experiment in Feudalism," *William and Mary Quarterly, 18* (1961), 3–34, adopts the safety-valve idea to explain why plentiful land caused a labor shortage in colonial Canada. Ralph H. Brown, *Historical Geography* (New York, 1948), presents the best overall discussion of the geographical factors that influence frontier expansion and sectional growth.

The varying meanings that have been attached to the word "frontier" are discussed in John T. Juricek's "American Usage of the Word 'Frontier' from Colonial Times to Frederick Jackson Turner," *Proceedings,* American Philosophical Society, *110* (1966), 10–34. Further comment on Turner's use of the term is contained in Fulmer Mood's "Notes on the History of the Word Frontier," *Agricultural History, 22* (1948), 78–83, and in Mood, ed., "Little Known Fragments of Turner's Writings," *Wisconsin Magazine of History, 23* (1940), 338–41.

The frontier theory has also made an impact on foreign scholars. The University of Melbourne historian Norman Harper has published three readable articles on Turner and his theories: "The Rural and

Urban Frontiers," *Australian Journal of Science, 25* (1963), 321–34; "Frontier and Section, A Turner Myth?" *Historical Studies, Australia and New Zealand, 5* (1952), 135–53; "Turner the Historian: Hypothesis or Process?" *University of Kansas Review, 18* (1951), 76–86. Harper's essays show wide knowledge of Turner's writings, and the piece on "Rural and Urban Frontiers" is based on study of Turner manuscripts at the Huntington Library. The British historian Harry C. Allen makes an appreciative evaluation of Turner's writings in "F. J. Turner and the Frontier in American History," in H. C. Allen and C. P. Hill, eds., *British Essays in American History* (London, 1957), pp. 145–66. Allen points out resemblances between the American and Australian past in *Bush and Backwoods: A Comparison of the Frontier in Australia and the United States* (East Lansing, Mich., 1959). H. Hale Bellot, also a British historian, portrays Turner as the leader of a Midwestern school of historians who stressed environmental influences (*American History and American Historians* [Norman, Okla., 1952.]) Foreign scholars are given an excellent overview of Turner's basic ideas on the frontier in Robert E. Riegel's essay, "The American Frontier Theory," *Cahiers d'Histoire Mondiale, Journal of World History, Cuadernos de Historia Mundial, 3* (1956), 356–80.

In England and in continental Europe historians have tended to emphasize Turner's frontier theory, neglecting his writings on multiple causation and sectionalism. This one-sidedness is apparent in both Per Sveaas Anderson's *Westward Is the Course of Empires* (Oslo, 1956) and Ronald H. Beck's *Die Frontiertheorie von Frederick Jackson Turner* (Zurich, 1955). Soviet historians who write on American history tend to see evidence of capitalistic depravity in most events of the past. A. V. Efimov's studies on American history (described in Wilbur R. Jacobs and Edmond E. Masson, "History and Propaganda: Soviet Image of the American Past," *Mid-America, 46* [1964], 75–91), fall into this pattern. Efimov singles out Turner for specific criticism in " 'Svobodnye zemli Ameriki i istoricheskaia kontseptsiia F. D. Ternera" (Free Lands of America and the Historical Concept of F. J. Turner), *Iz istorii obshchestvennykh dvizhenii i mezhdunarodnykh otnoshenii* (From the History of Social Movement and International Relations) (Moscow, 1957), pp. 548–60. An English translation of a Soviet evaluation of Turner's ideas which originally appeared in No. 9 of Russia's leading historical journal,

*Voprosy istorii* (Problems of History), is to be found in *Soviet Review, 5* (1964), 22–38: N. N. Bolkhovitinov, "The Role of the 'Frontier' in the History of the U.S.A."

A number of American historians have examined the history of other nations in the light of Turnerean ideas. Paul F. Sharp sees parallel developments in foreign nations in "Three Frontiers: Some Comparative Studies of Canadian, American, and Australian Settlement," *The Pacific Historical Review, 24* (1955), 369–77. A. L. Burt carries the exploration of this theme further in "If Turner Had Looked at Canada, Australia, and New Zealand When He Wrote about the West," in Walker D. Wyman and Clifton B. Kroeber, eds., *The Frontier in Perspective* (Madison, 1957), 59–77, and in his Canadian Historical Association presidential address, "Broad Horizons," Canadian Historical Association, *Report* (1950), pp. 1–10. Peter Coleman compares New Zealand with America in "The New Zealand Frontier and the Turner Thesis," *Pacific Historical Review, 27* (1958), 221–37, and Donald W. Treadgold points out convincing parallels between the American and Russian frontier experiences in "Russian Expansion in the Light of Turner's Study of the American Frontier," *Agricultural History, 25* (1952), 147–52, and *The Great Siberian Migration* (Princeton, N.J., 1957). Lynn White, Jr., in a learned and witty essay criticizes Turner's environmental determinism and points to the survival of medieval customs on the frontier: "The Legacy of the Middle Ages in the American Wild West," *The American West, 3* (1966), 72–79, 95, reprinted from Volume 40 of *Speculum*. A severe critic of White's interpretations is Owen Ulph in his "The Legacy of the American Wild West in Medieval Scholarship," *The American West, 3* (1966), 50–52, 88–91. The relation of Turner's frontier theory to American expansionism and foreign policy is explored in Walter LeFeber, *The New Empire, An Interpretation of American Expansion, 1860–1898* (Ithaca, 1963), and in William A. Williams, "The Frontier Theme and American Foreign Policy," *Pacific Historical Review, 24* (1965), 379–95. Frederick Merk in *The Oregon Question: Essays in Anglo-American Diplomacy and Politics* (Cambridge, 1967) uses the concept of multiple hypotheses and that of the westward-moving frontier in his analysis of a complex question in American history. Turner's own belief that his theories might throw light on the causes of international conflicts and their avoidance is discussed by Wilbur R. Jacobs in *Uloga vojnij subkoba u Americkoj istoriji* (The Role of Military Conflict in American History), Jugo-slovenski-Americki Seminar (Novi Sad, Jugoslavia, 1965). Wilbur R. Jacobs, ed., *The Paxton Riots and the Frontier Theory* (Chicago, 1967), is a case study in sectional conflict.

A number of additional works, especially biographical studies of Turner's close associates, throw light on Turner's influence on the scholarly world. Some of these studies (for example Maurice M. Vance's able biography, *Charles Richard Van Hise, Scientist Progressive* [Madison, 1960]) help us to understand Turner's intellectual development and his interest in such special areas as geology and conservation. Readable biographical sketches of other associates—Lyman C. Draper, J. Franklin Jameson, Reuben Gold Thwaites, and Henry E. Huntington—are to be found in Clifford L. Lord, ed., *Keepers of the Past* (Chapel Hill, 1965). William B. Hesseltine's *Pioneer's Mission: The Story of Lyman Copeland Draper* (Madison, 1954) provides a more detailed account of Draper's work. *J. Franklin Jameson: A Tribute, Fourteen Contributors,* ed. Ruth A. Fisher and William L. Fox (Washington, D.C., 1965), and Waldo G. Leland's excellent essay on Jameson in the *Dictionary of American Biography,* Supplement II (New York, 1958), pp. 339–344, supplies background material on Turner's work with Jameson in the American Historical Association. Jacob E. Cooke's *Frederic Bancroft, Historian* (Norman, Oklahoma, 1957), pp. 98–102, is an authoritative account of Frederic Bancroft's side of the American Historical Association reform-movement controversy. Burleigh Taylor Wilkins provides a well-documented account of Turner's influence on one of his best students during his formative years: *Carl Becker, A Biographical Study in American Intellectual History* (Cambridge, Mass., 1961). Turner himself praised the accuracy of William E. Dodd's account of his early associations with Wilson in *Woodrow Wilson and His Work* (New York, 1920). Benjamin F. Rader, *The Academic Mind and Reform: The Influence of Richard T. Ely in American Life* (Lexington, 1966) describes Ely's "golden years" at Johns Hopkins and Ely's "heresy trial" at Wisconsin in 1894. An account of this episode and of Turner's prominent role as a leader in academic life at Madison is contained in the excellent two-volume *The University of Wisconsin, A History, 1848–1925* (Madison, 1949) by Merle Curti and Vernon Carstenson. William Francis Raney, *Wisconsin, A Story of Progress* (New York, 1940) names William F. Allen and Turner as two intellectual leaders of the state. Turner's contribution to the growth of the Harvard Department of History is briefly sketched in an essay on the history department by Ephraim Emerton and Samuel Eliot Morison in Morison, ed., *The Development of Harvard University Since the Inauguration of President Eliot, 1869–1929* (Cambridge, Mass., 1930), 150–78. Morison's chapter on "The Lowell Administration" in his *Three Centuries of Harvard* (Cambridge, 1946) provides a frame of reference for many Turner letters written after 1910.

Turner's life and work are assessed in Charles A. Beard, *The American Spirit, A Study of the Idea of Civilization in the United States* (New York, 1942), pp. 360–64. Beard points to the misconceptions to which the frontier theory has given rise, but he also recognizes Turner's role in stimulating interdisciplinary studies. This appraisal is in sharp contrast to Beard's earlier review of *The Frontier in American History* in *The New Republic, 25* (1920–21), 349–50, a biting attack on Turner for neglecting urban development and class conflicts. Turner is identified with the "new historians" in Harry Elmer Barnes, *A History of Historical Writing* (Norman, Oklahoma, 1937), and in an earlier work, *The New History and the Social Studies* (New York, 1925). Barnes' perceptive essay on James Harvey Robinson in Howard W. Odum, ed., *American Masters of Social Science* (New York, 1927), pp. 321–408, reveals that in their basic approach to historical study Robinson and Turner had much in common.

Two of the best surveys of modern American historical writing give Turner a prominent place in the development of historical thought: Michael Kraus, in *The Writing of American History* (Norman, Oklahoma, 1953), pp. 271–314, regards Turner as the leader of a school of frontier and sectional historians, and Harvey Wish, in *The American Historian, A Social-Intellectual History of the Writing of the American Past* (New York, 1960), pp. 181–208, devotes a chapter to Turner and the frontier, arguing that no other writer has had greater influence in shaping the writing of American history in the twentieth century. An astringent review of a series of newspaper articles by Turner on immigration published in the *Chicago Record-Herald* from August to October 1901 is to be found in Edward N. Saveth, *American Historians and European Immigrants* (New York, 1948), pp. 122–49. Two recent volumes edited by Saveth, *American History and the Social Sciences* (New York, 1964) and *Understanding the American Past* (Boston, 1965), stress Turner's influence in developing concepts of sectionalism, nationalism, and democracy. Robert Allen Skotheim in *American Intellectual Histories and Historians* (Princeton, 1966) deals briefly with Turner but concentrates attention on two of Turner's students, Merle Curti and Carl Becker, whom he regards as leaders of the progressive tradition. Turnerean ideas are sympathetically treated in a discussion of urban and cultural frontiers by John C. Parish in *The Persistence of the Westward Movement and Other Essays,* ed. Louis Knott Koontz (Berkeley, 1943), but Richard Wade, *The Urban Frontier and the Rise of Western Cities, 1790–1830* (Cambridge, 1939) ignores the frontier theory in explaining Western urban growth. Rex W. Strickland, *The Turner Thesis and the Dry World* (El Paso, 1960), shows that problems arise in applying the frontier theory to arid regions. Earl Pomeroy in "Toward A Reorientation of Western History: Continuity and Environment," *Mississippi Valley Historical Review, 41* (1955), 579–600, maintains that Turnerean interpretations have led to environmental determinism in recent writings on Western American history, and Gilman Ostrander, "Turner and the Germ Theory," *Agricultural History, 38* (1964), 21–30, argues that Turner, despite the stress he placed on the frontier as an influence in American life, never abandoned the idea that Americans were strongly influenced by their European heritage. Turner's contributions to a variety of historical topics including the city, robber barons, immigration, and populism are discussed in Donald Sheehan and Harold C. Syrett, *Essays in American Historiography, Papers Presented in Honor of Allan Nevins* (New York, 1960). A number of the most important articles dealing with Turner's frontier theory are in two paperback booklets: Ray A. Billington, ed., *The Frontier Thesis, Valid Interpretation of American History?* (New York, 1966), and George Rogers Taylor, ed., *The Role of the Frontier in American History* (rev. ed. Boston, 1956). Perhaps the most important recognition of Turner's work is to be found in the numerous references to his writings in *The Harvard Guide to American History* (Cambridge, Mass., 1954), ed. Oscar Handlin and others. Significantly, *The Harvard Guide to American History* is dedicated to Turner and his colleagues, Edward Channing and Albert Bushnell Hart, "who blazed the way" with their pioneering *Guide to the Study and Reading of American History* (Boston, 1912).

# Index


Abbott, Wilbur C., 209–10
Academic freedom. *See* Freedom, academic
Adams, Brooks, 53
Adams, Charles Francis, 53
Adams, Charles Kendall (president of the University of Wisconsin), 1, 26, 29, 31–33, 95
Adams, George, 204
Adams, Henry, 52–54, 177, 184, 251
Adams, Herbert Baxter, 1–3, 10–11, 16, 21–24, 43, 60, 69, 73–76, 80–83, 85–86, 135, 197–98
Adams, James Truslow, 141, 171
Adams, John, administration of, 58, 91, 245–46
Adams, John Quincy, administration of, 53, 119
Africa, 172, 236
Agricultural Institutes, 82–84
Agriculture, College of, in Logan, Utah, 156, 232
Agriculture, history of, 59, 68, 120, 129, 155
Allegheny region, and westward movement, 92, 119, 142–43, 151
Allen, William F. (early mentor to Turner), 7, 11–12, 21–22, 24, 26, 49, 60, 68, 73–74, 78, 86, 124, 130–32
Almack, John C., 163
Alvord, Clarence W., 59, 110–11, 154–55, 223–24
American Antiquarian Society, 56
*American Commonwealth, The* (Bryce), 133
American Council of Learned Societies, The, 17–18, 117
*American Geographical Review,* 168–70
American Historical Association, 56, 60, 111, 130, 162, 164, 198, 232, 247; and Historical Manuscripts Commission, 17; meetings held by, 1, 24, 48, 50, 134; prizes offered by, 44; reform movement in, 16–17, 49–50; Turner elected president of, 13, 193
*American Historical Review,* 15–16, 56, 58–59, 141, 162, 172, 183, 195, 209, 240; reforms in, 110. *See also* Turner
*American Masters of Social Science* (Odum) 175
*American Nation Series, The* (Hart, ed.), 45
Americanism, 4
Americanization, confusion over meaning of, 153
Andrews, Charles M., 10, 85, 132, 186
Anglo-American civilization, study of, 66, 117–18
Archives and archivists, 58, 92, 102, 129, 216–17, 245–46, 248
Armstrong, H. M., 138
Art Institute Building (Chicago), 2
Athletics, intercollegiate, reform in, 37–40
*Atlantic Migration, 1607–1860, The* (Hansen), 158
*Atlantic Monthly, The,* 31–32, 57–58, 70, 209; prizes offered by, 248; Turner writes for, 10–11
Autobiography: C. F. Adams, 53; Henry Adams, 52–54

Bagehot, Walter, 10
Balance of power, and sections, 108
Bancroft, Frederic, 15–16; and reform movement in American Historical Association, 49–51
Bancroft, George, 8
Bancroft, Hubert H., 107

Bancroft Library, The, 91, 93–94
Banks and banking, 140
Barnes, Harry Elmer, 58, 114–15, 124, 176, 231–32
Beard, Charles A., 58, 125, 152, 163, 228, 230
Beaux, Cecilia, 241–42
Becker, Carl, 20, 46, 125, 134–35, 143, 175, 185–86, 196, 200–01, 206–10, 219, 221, 239, 247–48, 254–55; doctoral program of, 88–90, 99; evaluation of Turner by, 67; and A. A. Young, 14
Bellamy, Edward, 132
Beloit College, 115
Benton, Thomas Hart, 150
Bidgood, Lee, 59
Birge, Edward A., 90
Blackmar, Frank W., 85
Blair, Helen, 59
Blaisdell, James A. (president of Pomona College), 64–65
Bohemian Club, 109
Bolshevism, 160
Bolton, Herbert E., 106–07, 146–48, 215–16
Book-reviewing, 8, 125–26, 152, 172–73, 195–96, 248
Boston, Mass., 14, 77, 237–38
*Boston Merchants and the Non-Importation Movement* (Andrews), 186
Bowen, Clarence, 164
Bowman, Isaiah, 168–72
Bristol, Edward N., 37, 42, 87–88, 186–88
Brown University, 150
Bryce, James, Viscount, 133
Buck, Solon J., 103
Buffinton, Arthur H., 69, 114–15, 188, 195, 221–29
Bullock, Charles Jesse, 165–66

Calhoun, John C., 137–38, 153
California, State of, 51, 62–65, 117, 205, 214, 233–34, 239, 254; earthquake in, 37
California, University of, 74, 93, 101, 106–07, 146, 233; professorship offered to Turner, 46
California Institute of Technology, 118, 240
Cambridge, Mass., 13, 47–48, 146, 162, 213
Camp Alexander, 42
Camp, Dr. Walter, 225
Canada, 170, 172, 236, 246
Capitalism, American, 125, 153
Carnegie Foundation, 65, 118, 189
Carnegie Institution, 17, 50–51, 112, 143, 216
Census Bureau, reports of, 3, 11, 150, 169–71, 191, 214
Chamberlin, Thomas C. (president of University of Wisconsin), 23–24, 26, 80–81, 84
Channing, Edward, 13, 54, 56, 100, 141, 221, 231
Chautauqua movement, 73–75
Chicago, Ill., 2, 7, 11, 32, 51, 234
Chicago, University of, 27, 86–87, 103, 137, 141, 172, 196, 205; competition with University of Wisconsin, 12; intercollegiate sports at, 38, 40; library of, 29; professorship offered to Turner, 90–91
Chicago World's Fair, 1–2
Civil War, study of, 92, 119, 121, 144, 148–49
Civilization, Anglo-American, 66, 117–18; evolution of, 72; western, 168
Clark, Anna M., 189
Clark, Champ, 144
Clark, Victor S., 147
Clay, Henry, 142, 150
Clubs, 14, 51, 77. *See also* specific clubs by name
Coffin, Victor, 26–27
Colonial Society of Massachusetts, 14, 226, 240
Colonization: theory of, 159, 198, 202–03, 235–36, 245–46; of West, 3, 46–47
Colorado, State of, 7, 43, 62

Colorado, University of, 203, 248
Columbia University, 89, 129, 143, 149, 230
Coolidge, Archibald C., 72, 102–03, 217
Common man, 9
Commons, John R., 133–34
Commonwealth Fund of New York, 64–65, 111
Community conformity, 156
Comte, Auguste, 8–9
Conformity, danger of, 156
Congressional documents and records, 66, 72, 92, 120, 170, 190, 230
Connecticut, 202
Connor, Robert D. W., 147
*Conquest of the Southwest, The* (Henderson), 59
Conscription, 144
*Conservation of Natural Resources in the United States, The* (Van Hise), 47–48
Constitution: English, 77; Roman, 75; of the United States, 77, 140, 215
Constitutional Convention, 157
Cornell University, 210, 219
Correspondence university, idea for, 74–75
Corwin, Edward S., 245–46
Cosmos Club, 51
Craven, Avery, 177
Creeds and dogmas, 9
Creel Bureau, and World War I, 127
Crissey, Merrill H., 196, 249
Croly, Herbert, 135
Culture, in America, 4, 30, 90, 112, 126, 156, 165, 233, 251–52
Cunliffe, John William, 47
Curti, Merle, 6, 20, 70, 115–17, 122, 126, 177, 236–42
*Cyclopedia of Government, A* (McLaughlin and Hart), 56

Daenell, Ernst, 55–56
Dana, Richard Henry, 128, 139
Darwin, Charles, theories of, 8–10
Davis, Jefferson, 137–38
*Decline of Aristocracy in the Politics of New York, The* (Fox), 228–29
Democracy: American, 109, 133–34, 159–60, 168, 189, compared with European, 168–69; Andrew Jackson type of, 213; backwoods, 168; ideals of, 145, 150–51; and the press, 151; and pro-slavery, 140; spread of, 8, 73, 162
*Democratic Machine 1850–1854, The* (Nichols), 228, 230
Democratic party, 7, 137, 214
*Democratic Review*, 249
Determinism, 126, 142, 230
"Development of American Society, The" (Turner), 127
Dewey, John, 126
*Dial, The*, 199
*Dictionary of American Biography, The*, 17–18, 249
*Division and Reunion* (Wilson), 196, 198–99
Doctoral programs, 68–69, 88, 90, 99. *See also* Education; Graduate training
Documents, collections of, 29, 58–59, 66, 72, 85, 92–93, 120–21
Dodd, William E., 137–38, 189
"Dominant Forces in Western Life" (Turner), 31
Douglas, Walter B., 106
Draper, Lyman C., and collection of manuscript materials, 7–8, 60, 93, 181–83
Droysen, Johann Gustav, 114
Duluth, Minn., 43

*Early Writings of Frederick Jackson Turner* (Mood), 178
Earthquake of *1906*, 37
East (geographical region), 58, 82, 102, 191
*Economic Interpretation of the Constitution* (Beard), 58
Economics: development of, 56–58, 61, 72, 120, 169; factor in American history, 11–12, 45, 86–88, 94, 99, 129,

Economics (*cont.*)
154, 161, 171, 177, 201, 251; force of, 5, 150–51; reform in, 125–26
Education, 58, 122, 131, 146; and American university system, 174–75; basic needs of, 95–99; higher, 82–83; popular, 66–74, 82, 113–14, 125. *See also* Graduate training
*Education of Henry Adams, The* (Adams), 52–54
Edwards, Everett E., 241
Electoral system, 141
Ely, Richard T., 11–12, 59–60, 75–76, 80, 86
Emerson, Guy, 59
Emerson, Ralph Waldo, 8, 53, 165
Emerton, Ephraim, 24, 54
Emigration, 130–32, 160
Emotional force, in religion, 9
England, 58, 81, 124, 128, 141, 144–45, 159–62, 201, 236, 245
Entertainment, and Chautauqua assemblies, 74
*Epic of American History* (Adams), 171
Epoch Series, 206
Erick, wilderness guide, 41–42
*Essays in American History Dedicated to Frederick Jackson Turner,* 59, 134, 208
Ethnic groups, 61
Europe, 143, 145, 158, 168; democracy in, 168–69; influence of, 155, 160–62; institutional history of, 11, 60; libraries in, 161; social inequalities in, 3; and United States, 156–57; visited by Turner, 32–35
Evolution, social, 9
Examiner Club, 49
Extension movement, 69, 82–84, 86, 99

Facts, historical, Becker and Turner's view of, 206–08
Farrand, Beatrice Cadwallader Jones, 51–52, 64, 242
Farrand, Max (director of Huntington Library), 6, 12–13, 16–19, 35–37,
Farrand, Max (*cont.*)
44–47, 51–52, 62–72, 91–94, 98–99, 111, 113, 122–23, 127, 143–46, 178–80, 184–85, 195, 202–06, 210–12, 215, 240–41, 252–53
Fäy, Bernard, 14
Federalism, 140
Federalist party, 151
Fellowships, graduate, 200–01
Ferguson, William Scott, 230
*First Alleghany Explorations* (Alvord and Bidgood), 59
Fish, Carl Russell, 147
Fishing, recreational aspects of. *See* Turner
Fishing Club of Boston, 14
Fiske, John, 3, 57, 202
Foerster, Norman, 165
Folk-Moot, 75
Football. *See* Intercollegiate athletics
Ford, A. C., 59
Ford, Guy Stanton, 167, 187–88
Ford, H. J., 59
Foreign languages, graduate study requirements of, 78, 80, 89–90
Foreign relations, study of, 58, 76
Fort William, 41
*Forty Niners, The* (Hulbert), 248
Foundations, private, and philanthropy, 71, 111–12.
Fox, Dixon Ryan, 126, 129, 149–50, 228, 230
*Framing of the Constitution, The* (Farrand), 215
France, 58, 129, 145, 221, 228, 236, 245–46
Franklin, Benjamin, 8, 21
*Franklin in France* (Hale), 75–76
Freedom, academic, 9, 12–13
Frontier, and westward movement, 58, 60, 62, 125, 134–35, 166–67, 169, 235
*Frontier in American History, The* (Turner), 19, 54, 125, 152, 186–87, 219
Frontier theory, 3, 8, 11, 20, 54, 56–58, 125–27, 134–35, 154–55, 177–

Frontier theory (*cont.*)
78, 242–44, 247; modification of, 4; criticism of, 163–67
Frontiersmen, 4
*Fur Trade in Wisconsin, The* (Turner), 56, 130, 132

Garfield, Harry Augustus (president of Williams College), 227
Garrison, George P., 45
*General Sociology* (Small), 58
Geography, in relation to sectionalism, 58, 61, 72, 107, 126–27, 129, 135, 154–55, 164, 177, 190–91, 228
Geology, 151, 177
George, Henry, 11
Germ theory of American history, 11
Germany, 81, 141, 143, 145, 172; attitude toward U.S. in, 160–62; "Germanizing" influence of settlers from, 21, 131–32, 153, 158–59, 236; methods of historical research in, 7
*Gewerbe Schulen,* 84
Gibbon, Edward, 200
Gillet, Ransom H., 249–50
Gochenour, Merl Longfellow, 212–13
Graduate training, study programs of, 68–70, 73, 87–91, 100–03, 114, 122, 195–96, 200–01, 221, 223, 226–29, 234–38, 253. *See also* Doctoral programs
Great Lakes Region, 130
Great Plains, and westward movement, 109, 189
Greeley, Horace, 133
Green, John Richard, 8, 198, 201
Gridiron Club, 148
Grignon, Augustin, 182
*Guide to the Study and Reading of American History* (Channing, Hart, Turner), 13, 56

Hale, Edward Everett, 3, 57, 75–76
Hale, George Ellery, 64, 66, 118–19, 199
Hancock Point, Me. (summer home of Turner), 15, 19, 142, 237–38
Hanford, Thomas, 62
Hansen, Marcus Lee, 117–19, 158–60, 162
Harding, Warren G., administration of, 7
Harrison, William Henry, administration of, 150
Hart, Albert Bushnell, 13, 56, 58, 85, 100, 184–85
Hartman, Edward T., 141, 254
Harvard Commission on Western History, 13, 101–05, 139, 216, 241, 248
Harvard group, 63
Harvard University, 24, 50–54, 57, 67, 71, 77, 99, 105, 117, 122–23, 137, 167–68, 205–06, 210, 218, 221, 234–35; alumni of, 216; library of, 101–03, 230–01, 240. *See also* Turner
Harvard University Bulletin, 50, 55
Harvard University Press, 242–43
Haskins, Charles Homer (colleague of Turner), 2, 10, 13, 26, 30, 33, 48, 66, 87, 91, 157–58, 162, 199–200 209, 211, 220, 226
Hay, John, 53
Hazen, Charles D., 147
Heeren, Arnold H. L., 75–76
Henderson, Archibald, 59
Hendrickson, George, 204–05
Herbart Society, 57–58
Hibbard, Benjamin Horace, 59
Hill, Adams, 53
Hillard, G. S., 119
Historical Manuscripts Commission, 17
*Historical Outlook,* 163
History: agricultural, 59, 68, 120, 129, 155, 238; American, 8, 26, 28–30, 44–46, 56, 58, 60, 69, 76–77, 85, 87–88, 91–92, 94, 102, 112, 118–19, 121, 125, 128, 135, 144, 146, 153, 158, 164–65, 168, 170–71, 180, 187–88, 202, 219, 236, 239, 252; ancient, 128, 139, 200; church, 76; classical 87; colonial, 87, 99, 119, 176, 210, 235; constitutional, 85, 120, 133; contemporary, 128, 136, 139, 143;

History (*cont.*)
diplomatic, 177; economic, 85, 121, 125, 133, 164, 178, 239; English, 121, 200; European, 8, 24, 26–27, 60, 88, 91, 94, 139, 146, 200, 208, 239; general, 79; industrial, 87; institutional, 11, 26–27, 60, 87, 133, 177; intellectual, 126, 237; literary, 165; local, 7, 82, 92; medieval, 8, 56, 60, 66, 92, 100, 155, 225; modern, 92, 124, 210, 225; narrative, 71–72; New England, 141, 202–03; Northwest, 77, 197; Oriental, 74, 225; Pacific Coast, 110; political, 120, 133, 164, 177, 239; scientific, 112; social, 8–10, 124–25, 133, 162, 164, 178, 239; Southwest, 110; transportation, 248; Western, 8, 27, 45, 55–56, 60, 82, 101, 103, 105–06, 155, 163, 168, 197, 203, 234
—as a flow, 128; methodology of, 20; philosophy of, 207; teaching of, 54; traditional approach to, 178. *See also* Frontier theory; Germ theory of American history; Multiple hypothesis, concept of; Nationalism; Political parties; Politics; Safety-valve theory; Turner, F. J.; United States
*History of the American Frontier, The* (Paxson), 203
*History of the American People* (Wilson), 195
*History of Historical Writing, A* (Barnes), 124
"History of the Grignon Tract on the Portage of the Fox and Wisconsin Rivers" (Turner), 182
Hockett, Homer C., 116–17, 186, 196, 208
Hodder, Frank H., 209–10
Holst, Hermann von, 61, 86–87, 137
Holt, Henry, and Company, 37, 183, 186–90
Holyoke, Mass., 27
Hooper, Alice Forbes Perkins, 12–14, 101, 241–42
Hoover, Herbert, administration of, 166
Hosmer, James K., 202
Howard, George E., 133
Huizinga, Johann, 55–56
Hulbert, Archer B., 248–49
Hull, Charles H., 147
Humanities, the, 72, 112
Hunt, Gaillard, 147
"Hunter Type, The" (unpublished essay by Turner), 4
Huntington, Henry E., 64, 66, 72, 118–19, 121; Library and Art Gallery, 18–19, 62–63, 65–66, 71, 117–21, 130, 166–67, 178, 196–97, 239–41
Hutchins, Harry Burns, 210

Illinois, University of, 39, 103, 110
Immigration, and westward movement, 3, 117–18, 145, 150, 158–59, 162, 236
Imperialism, 226, 228
*Indian Trade in Wisconsin* (Turner's M.A. thesis and doctoral dissertation), 7
*Indian Tribes of the Upper Mississippi Valley* (Blair), 59
Indians, policies for, 42, 59, 61, 76, 103, 108, 130, 140, 163–64, 245
Individualism, 156, 163
Industrialization, 83–84, 87, 109, 120, 135, 137, 164
Institute of International Education, 18
Intercollegiate athletics, 37–40
Interdisciplinary studies, 11–12, 114, 124–27, 128–30, 133, 134–35, 232–33.
International political parties, and world peace, 128, 140, 156–57
*International Socialist Review*, 57
Interstate Commerce Commission, 142
*Introduction to Local Constitutional History, An* (Howard), 133
Iowa, State University of, 113–14, 230
Irish in Marquette County, 131
Ise, John, 59
Italy, visited by Turner, 34

Jackson, Andrew, administration of, 61
James, James A., 13, 38–40, 46, 69

Jameson, J. Franklin, 2, 16, 49–51, 85, 99, 135, 183, 209, 211, 230
Jaqua, Ernest James, 64–65
Jastrow, Joseph, 47–49
Jefferson, Thomas, administration of, 222
Johns Hopkins University, 11, 16, 26, 56, 63, 69, 73, 75, 81, 86, 186, 200; graduates of, 85; instruction at, 2, 60, 78–79. *See also* Turner
Jordan, David Starr (president of Stanford University), 69
*Journal of American History, The,* 110
Junior colleges, 69
Justin Winsor Prize, 44

Kansas, University of, 88–89, 208
Kellogg, Louise Phelps, 194, 243–45
King, Philip (football coach), 38–39
Knight, George M., 130–31
Krey, August C., 100

Labberton, Robert H., 80
Labor movement, 125, 134, 140, 150, 152, 213
La Follette, Philip Fox, 166
La Follette, Robert M., 136–37, 166
Lake Nipigon, 43
Lake Superior, 40
Land, free, 135, 153–54, 163; grants of, 131; policy on, 134, 235; tenure of, 155; unsettled, 165
Land companies, 236; and westward movement, 236
Law, the, 82, 126
League of Nations, 151, 156–57, 228
Lectures, Turner's use of, in teaching, 3, 106–09, 156, 175–76, 197, 214–15
Leisure time, useful employment of, 113, 115, 126, 130, 150–51, 161, 174–75, 184, 214
Leland, Waldo G., 17–18, 143–44, 147
Libby, Orin Grant, 1–2, 27
Libraries: European, 161; high school, 88; research facilities of, 18, 77, 82–83, 85, 90–91, 101, 116, 253; Turner's view of, in American intellectual life, 70–73; university, 71, 92. *See also* specific libraries by name
Library of Congress, 2, 72, 120, 229, 240
*Life and Times of Silas Wright, The,* 249–50
*List of References on the History of the West* (Turner and Merk), 171
Literature, and relation to history, 8, 58, 94, 126, 165, 201, 239, 249, 251
Locofoco movement, 150
Lodge, Henry Cabot, 54
Longmans, Green and Company, 197
*Looking Backward* (Bellamy), 133
Loria, Achille, 11
Los Angeles, Calif., 63, 66, 233; library in, 119–21
Louisiana, 246
Lowell, Abbott Lawrence (president of Harvard University), 50, 122

McAdoo, Eleanor Wilson, 30
McLaughlin, Andrew C., 56, 58, 141–42
MacVeagh, Lincoln, 188–90
Madison, Wisc., 11–12, 18, 27–31, 35, 39, 47, 59, 77, 83, 156, 211, 230
Maps and charts, as research aids, 60, 80, 102–03, 149–50, 156, 191–92, 199
Martin, Thomas P., 104–05, 216–17
Marx, Charles David, 83–84
Mason, George, 222
Massachusetts Historical Society, 14, 233, 240
Meany, Edmond S., 52–53
Mechanics Institutes, 83–84
*Memoirs* (J. Q. Adams), 53
*Memoirs and Correspondence of Jeremiah Mason* (Hillard), 119
Merk, Frederick, 71, 168–69, 171, 174, 234, 242
Merriman, Roger Bigelow, 47
*Mesaba, S. S.,* 33
*Methods in Social Science* (Rice, 122
Mexico, 138
Meyers, Philip Van Ness, 80

Michigan, University of, 38–40, 208, 210
Migrations, and westward movement, 155, 255. *See also* Immigration
Mill, John Stuart, 75
Millikan, Robert A., 62–63, 118
Minnesota, University of, 38, 167, 218, 224, 235
*Mississippi Question, 1795–1803, The* (Whitaker), 233
Mississippi Valley, 27, 92–93, 108–09, 150
*Mississippi Valley in British Politics, The* (Alvord), 154
*Mississippi Valley Historical Review, The,* 110, 194, 212, 240, 243–44, 246
Missouri Historical Society, 106
Mommsen, Theodor, 200
Monarchism, 160
Monroe, James, administration of, 179
Mood, Fulmer, 178, 234–35
Morison, Samuel Eliot, 232–33
Mormons, and development of the West, 234
Multiple hypothesis, concept of, 4–5, 124–26, 154–56, 238–39
Munroe, William Bennett, 100
Music, 251
Muzzey, David S., 126

Napoleonic Wars, 149
National Board for Historical Service, Turner a member of, 17, 127, 143–48
Nationalism, 8, 141–43
Negroes, 61. *See also* Slavery
Nevins, Allan, 248
New England, 48, 53, 56, 61–62, 93, 133, 141, 169, 191, 202–03, 227–28, 246, 254
*New Frontier, The* (Emerson), 59
*New History and the Social Studies, The* (Barnes), 176, 231
*New Republic,* 125, 152
New School for Social Research. *See* Turner
*New Viewpoints in American History* (Schlesinger), 153–54
"New West" (Turner), 56
New York City, 28, 152
New York State, 74, 126
*New York Times,* 172
Newspapers, as research aids, 61, 72, 92, 95, 104, 120, 129, 136, 150–51, 161, 218, 229
Nichols, Roy F., 228, 230
Niles' *Register,* 249
Nipigon River, 40–41, 43, 205
Nobel Prize, 62
Normal Schools, training at, 69–70
North (geographical region), 61, 191
North Carolina, University of, 165
Northwestern University, 38–39

Odum, Howard W., 67, 175
Ohio State University, 186, 228
Ohio Valley, 101, 108
"Old West, The" (Turner), 108
Oliver Mining Company, 41
Olsen, Nils, 59
Ontario, 40
Oregon, University of, 106
Osgood, Herbert L., 210
"Outline Studies in the History of the Northwest" (Turner), 56
*Oxford History of the United States, 1783–1917* (Morison), 232

Pacific Coast, 92–93, 102, 108–09, 156, 110, 203, 234, 247
Pacifism, 145–46
Page, Walter H., 57
Parish, John Carl, 18
Parkman, Francis, 8, 57, 107, 174, 216
Particularism, 198
Party politics, 228, 230–31. *See also* Political institutions; Political parties
Pasadena, Calif. (retirement home of Turner), 18, 19, 63, 65, 118, 247
Patriotism. *See* Turner
Patronage, power of, 50
Patten, Simon Nelson, 130–31
Pattengill, Albert Henderson, 38–39

Paullin, Charles O., 178, 190–91
Paxson, Frederic Logan, 203, 217
Peace, international, and international political parties, 128, 140, 156–57
Peace Movement, 238
Pennsylvania, University of, 233
Pessimism, of the Adams family, 53, 70
Phi Beta Kappa, 4, 117, 150
Philanthropic foundations, 71, 111–12
Phillips, Paul C., 245
Phillips, Ulrich B., 175
Philosophy, 126
"Physiographic provinces," settlers in, 4
Pierce, Roger, 217
*Pioneer Fringe, The* (Bowman), 169–70, 172
Pittsburgh, University of, 212
Planning, governmental, need for, after closing of frontier, 125
Ploetz, Carl, 80
*Political History of the Public Lands from 1840 to 1862, The* (Stephenson), 59, 218
Political institutions, 81, 155
Political parties, 108, 136–37, 140, 150–51, 157, 213–14, 228, 230–31; international parties and peace, 128, 140, 156–57
Political science, study of, 86, 88, 94, 99, 201–02
*Political Science Review*, 214
*Political and Sectional Influence of the Public Lands 1828–1842, The* (Wellington), 59
Politics, 61, 72, 108–09, 124, 126, 155, 171, 251; forces of, 5–6; international, 128–29; national, 136–38; in Ohio, 228–30; social interpretation of, 59; university, 37–40; in Wisconsin, 2, 48
Polk, James K., administration of, 137
Pomona College, 64–65
Poole, William F., 1
Population, density of, 157
Porlier, Louis B., 181
Port Arthur, Mich., 43
Portage, Wisc., 6, 22, 61, 182
*Portage State Register*, 182
Pound, Arthur, 113
*Premises of Political Economy, The* (Patten), 130
Press, the, 146, 148. *See also* Newspapers
Princeton University, 199; library of, 28, 253. *See also* Turner
Pritchett, Henry Smith, 118
"Problems in American History" (Turner), 1, 56, 178
"Problems of the West" (Turner), 57
Professionalism in sports, 37–40
Progressive movement, 136, 151, 213–14
Progressive party, 166
*Promise of American Life, The* (Croly), 112, 135
Propaganda, and World War I, 144
Provincialism, 90
Pryor, Roger A., 137–38
Public Record Office (England), 159–61
Public school system, 69, 82–84, 96–98, 131–32
Publications, importance of, 224–27; Turner's problems in producing, 45, 174–77
Pulitzer Prize. *See* Turner
Putnam, Herbert, 120

Quaife, Milo M., 104–05, 153, 155

Radcliffe College, 48
Railroads, 62, 131, 142, 235–36
Rainy River, 41
Rangeley Lakes, 47
*Records of the Federal Convention of 1787* (Farrand), 211
Reform: and American Historical Association, 16–17, 49–50, 110; in athletics, 39–40; in economics, 125–26; political, 134. *See also* Turner
Religion, 8–9, 28, 58, 72, 74, 126, 132, 152, 234, 239

Republican Party, 7, 61, 137, 150–51, 214, 230
Research: German scientific, 7; methods of, 63, 127, 129; necessity for, 13, 19, 102–03, 116, 118–21, 147–48, 159–61, 176, 178–79, 181, 190, 215–16, 234; and original source material, 7, 68, 70–73, 75–76, 79, 85, 102–03, 107, 129, 174–75
Revolution, American, 108, 129, 144, 168, 176, 183, 245–46
Revolution, French, 160, 246
Rhodes, James Ford, 71, 179, 184
Rice, Stuart A., 122, 241–42
*Rise of the New West, 1819–1829, The* (Turner), 19, 58, 108, 184–85
Robinson, Edgar Eugene, 128, 136–37, 156, 213, 247
Robinson, James Harvey, 125–26
Rocky Mountains, 7, 93–94, 143, 189, 203
Roosevelt, Theodore, and frontier theory, 4, 54, 57, 60–61, 107, 134, 137
Roseboom, Eugene H., 228–29
Russia, 145, 172

Safety-valve theory, 125
*Saturday Review of Literature,* 165
Schafer, Joseph, 166–67, 194, 202–03, 246–47
Schlesinger, Arthur M., 19–20, 69, 71, 113–14, 126, 129, 153–55, 158, 163–64, 230, 235–37
Scholarship, ideals of, 8, 60
Schools. *See* Education; Public school system
Schouler, James, 2
Science, 112, 126
Scientific inquiry, method of, 9, 21
*Scribners Magazine,* 119
Scudder, Horace, 57
Secrist, Horace, 152
Sectionalism: and frontier rivalries, 4, 108; and westward movement, 134–35, 141–43, 154–55, 178, 190–91
"Sectionalism in American History" (Turner), 141
Sections: federation of, 58; hypothesis of, 60, 126–27, 135, 157–58, 163
"Sections and the Nation" (Turner), 114, 168
Self-government, 99
Sellery, George Clark, 196–97
Seminars: Adams, 10–11; Becker, 135, 209; Ely, 75; Haskins, 200; Johns Hopkins University, 74; method of study, 77, 148–49, 161–62; Turner, 12–13, 44–45, 48, 57–60, 69, 100, 193, 197, 246, 253
Shad, Robert O., 18
Sheldon, Marion, 132, 249–50
Shop Club, 14
*Short History of the English People* (Green), 198
Shotwell, James T., 143, 149
Sierra Club, 106
Sierra Nevada Mountains, 119
"Significance of the Frontier in American History" (Turner), 1–3, 56
"Significance of History" (Turner), 124–25
"Significance of the Mississippi Valley in American History" (Turner), 212
"Significance of the Section in American History, The" (Turner), 156
Skinner, Constance Lindsay, 7, 54–57, 177
Slaughter, Moses S., 33, 47, 49, 52
Slavery, controversy of, 8, 61, 92, 140, 142, 151, 153, 198
Slichter, Charles S., 33–34, 47–49, 122
Small, Albion W., 10, 38, 58, 85
"Social and Economic History of the United States" (Turner), 155
Social evolution, 9
"Social Forces in American History" (Turner), 5, 45, 114–15, 130, 132, 134–35
Social foundations in American history, 56–61, 87, 129, 177
Social Science Research Council, The, 159, 241
Social sciences, 72, 114–15, 127, 167, 231–32

Socialism, 12, 101, 165–66
Society, American, 99, 112, 167, 179; industrial, 70; institutional, 3, 7, 9–10; modern, 124, 132; traits of, 165, 169, 171; western, 105
Sociology, 10, 38, 88, 122, 126, 251
Source material in research, original. *See* Research
South (geographical region), 60–61, 103, 130, 137, 141, 191, 198
South America, 170, 172, 236
Spain, 58, 108, 129, 245–46
*Spanish American Frontier, 1783–1795, The* (Whitaker), 233
Spencer, Herbert, 8–9, 24
Spofford, Ainsworth R., 2
Stagg, Amos Alonzo, 38–39
Stanford University, 44, 69, 156, 204–05, 213–14; library of, 35. *See also* Turner
State sovereignty, 58
*Statesmen of the Old South* (Dodd), 137
Statistical data, as aid in research, 11, 151, 157, 178, 251
Steffens, Lincoln, 99
Stephens, Henry Morse, 101–02, 106–07
Stephenson, George M., 59, 218–19
Stewart Commission on History, 248
Supreme Court, decisions of, 85
Sutro Library, 91, 94
Switzerland, visited by Turner, 34

Tariffs, 136–37, 140, 153
Taylor, Henry Charles, 59
Taylor, Henry Osborn, 54
Teaching, methodology of, 75–81
*Texas in the Middle of the Eighteenth Century* (Bolton), 215
Texas, University of, 45, 100
Textbooks, writing and use of, 85, 95–96, 126, 176, 181, 183, 185–86, 188–90, 197, 230
Thomas, Carl C., 62–63
Thompson, James Westfall, 172
Thursday Club of Boston, 14
Thwaites, Reuben Gold, 2–3, 7, 23–24, 59–61, 81, 107, 153, 155, 197, 206
Town and Gown Club, 47, 49, 205
Toynbee, Arnold, 75
Traditionalism, in education, 8, 31, 101, 157, 175, 178
Trans-Allegheny movement, 108
Transportation, 51, 158
Treaties, 85, 103
Turner, Andrew Jackson, 6–7, 23, 34, 36, 62
Turner, Caroline Mae Sherwood, 11, 14, 16, 19, 22, 28–35, 49, 52, 94, 136, 156, 167, 196, 205, 211, 213, 234, 237, 247, 249, 252
Turner, Dorothy Kinsley, 17, 26, 33–34, 42–43, 52, 136, 205–06
Turner, Frederick Jackson: on academic freedom, 12–13; on Adams family, 53–54; H. B. Adams' influence on, 1–3, 10–11, 16, 43, 60, 69, 135, 197–98; Allen's guidance of, 7–8, 11–12, 24, 26, 49, 60, 86; and American Historical Association, 1–3, 13, 48–51, 114–15, 134, 193, 232; and *American Historical Review,* 15–17, 49–50, 110; Bancroft's accusations against, 15–16, 49–51; Becker's evaluation of, 67; biographical notes on, 6–11, 14, 18–19, 54–60, 155; on books and book reviewing, 79, 195–96; and University of California, 46, 106; at Carnegie Institution, 17, 216; on the Chautauqua movement, 74–75; and University of Chicago, 12, 90–91; club memberships of, 14, 47, 49, 51, 77, 106, 109; and Colonial Society of Massachusetts, 14; commitment to history of, 5, 7, 20, 77–80, 124–25, 128–29, 143–44, 147–50, 193–95, 255; commonplace notebook of, 9; criticism by, 126, 141, 170–71, 195–97, 210–13, 219, 233–35, 244–45, 248–49; criticism of, 12, 113, 125, 152–53, 163–65, 170–71, 210–11;

Turner, Frederick Jackson (*cont.*)
cultural standards of, 8, 26, 30, 251–52; and democracy, 8; and Draper, 8; on economics, 11–12; editorial policies of, 110–11; educational concerns of, 60, 66–74; 82, 95–99, 113–14, 122–23, 125, 146–47; on emigration, 130–32; and ethnic groups, 61; European travels of, 32–35; family life of, 2, 6–7, 12, 23, 26, 28, 35–36; "fertilize and spiritualize" expression of, 82, 134; financial problems of, 37, 40, 65, 96–97, 184, 189, 253; fishing activities of, 14–15, 18, 21, 42–43, 47, 62, 136, 187, 205, 211, 238–39; frontier hypothesis of, 3–4, 8, 11, 20, 54, 56–58, 125–27, 134–35, 154–55, 163–67, 177–78, 242–44, 247; genealogy of, 6, 14, 62; on "Germanizing" influence, 21, 131–32, 153; on graduate instruction, 68–70, 73, 87–91, 253; and Hancock Point vacations, 15, 19, 142, 237–38; and Harvard Commission on Western History, 13, 101–05, 139, 216, 241, 248; Harvard University years of, 13–14, 18, 44–51, 62–63, 100–01, 114, 117, 141, 156, 164; health of, 28, 66, 162, 166, 169, 172, 188, 223, 237, 248–49; humor of, 51–52, 251; influence of, 12–13, 20, 153–54, 176–77, 193, 251–52; on intercollegiate athletics, 37–40; interdisciplinary program of, 11–12; and Johns Hopkins University, 1, 10, 21, 60, 67–68, 73–74, 81, 130; on languages, 74, 78, 80; later years of, 228–29; on League of Nations, 156–57; lecturing abilities of, 3, 8, 156, 197, 214–15; leisure time of, 115, 174–75, 184, 214; on libraries, 18, 25, 27, 29, 31, 35–37, 45–46, 63, 71–73, 77, 82–83, 85, 88–95, 101–07, 116, 118–19, 253; literary ability of, 251; M.A. thesis of, 7; on National Board for Historical Service, 17, 127, 143–48;

Turner, Frederick Jackson (*cont.*)
on nationalism, 8; and New School for Social Research, 126; as a newspaper correspondent, 6–7; outside interests of, 96–98; patriotism of, 3, 17, 127–28, 152, 202; personality of, 9, 14–15, 23, 176–77, 252–55; on philanthropic foundations, 71, 111–12; on philosophy, 8–9; physical characteristics of, 14–15; on politics, 6, 37–39, 48, 136–38; and Princeton University, 11, 25–31; publisher of, 37, 183, 186–90; wins Pulitzer Prize, 19, 203; and reforms, 12; on religion, 8–9, 28; on research, 13, 19, 29–30, 44–47, 68, 70–75, 85, 87, 90–95, 102–05, 116, 127, 129, 147–48, 158-59, 174, 176–79, 181–88, 190–91, 194–95, 215–16, 234; retirement years of, 189, 228–30; rhetoric and oratory instructor, 7; on salaries, 25, 27, 30–31, 36, 44, 48, 65, 81, 97, 122; scholarly attainments of, 2, 60, 81, 110, 124, 147–49, 175, 180–82, 194–95, 203, 211, 220, 249, 251, 254; "scientific inquiry" of, 21; sectional hypothesis of, 126–27, 134, 141–43, 154–55, 157–58, 178–79, 190–91; and seminar studies, 12–13, 44–45, 48, 57, 59–60, 69, 193, 197, 246, 253; sensitivity of, 178–81; shortcomings of, 212; and slavery controversy, 8; on social forces, 7, 9, 126–27, 134–35, 162; social life of, 12–13, 112–13; and Stanford University, 35–37, 91, 94–95, 98; on statistical data, 151, 157, 178, 251; students of, 1, 12, 20, 26, 35, 44–45, 59, 66, 69–71, 85, 100–01, 103, 106, 114–17, 126, 129, 134, 136, 146, 158, 166–68, 176–77, 186, 188, 193–98, 206, 208–09, 212–19, 238–39, 248–49, 251–54, 200–01, 228, 231, 242; teaching methods of, 66–67, 75–81, 87, 113–14, 175–76, 181, 188–89, 206–07, 234–35, 238; on textbooks, 85–88, 95–96, 176, 188–

Turner, Frederick Jackson (*cont.*)
90, 197, 230; traditional approach of, 8; and university extension program, 69–71, 74–75, 81–84, 86, 99; vacation trips of, 15, 33–34, 40–44, 47, 254; and Van Hise, 12, 44–45; and westward movement, 107–09, 130, 170, 177–79, 189; and Wilson, 10, 23, 26–31; at University of Wisconsin, 1, 6–7, 12–13, 22–25, 44–46, 59–60, 67, 81, 86, 94–95, 175, 204–05, 231; and "Wisconsin School" of history, 12, 45, 86, 155, 175; and World War I, 127–28, 143–44; writings by, 1, 10–11, 17–19, 21, 31, 37, 45, 48, 56–59, 115–16, 129–30, 141, 171, 174–78, 181–87, 212. *See also* Frontier theory; Huntington Library
—correspondence with: H. B. Adams, 21–23, 73, 81, 83–86; Allen, 21, 68, 74–75, 78, 124, 130–32; Alvord, 110–11; Andrews, 186; Barnes, 231–32; Beard, 152; Becker, 46, 88–89, 134–35, 143, 175, 185–86, 196, 200–02, 219–20, 239, 247–48, 254–55; Bolton, 146–48; Bowman, 170–72; Bristol, 37, 87–88, 186–87; Buffinton, 114–15, 188, 221–27; Channing, 100; Clark, 189; Commons, 133–34; Coolidge, 72, 102–06; Curti, 6, 70, 115–17, 177, 236–39; Dana, 128; Dodd, 137–38, 189; Douglas, 106; Ely, 12, 86–87; family members, 2, 17, 34–35; Farrand, 6, 35–37, 44–47, 51–52, 64–72, 91, 92–94, 98–99, 111–13, 119, 122, 127, 143–46, 178–79, 184–85, 202–06, 210–11, 240–41; Foerster, 165; G. S. Ford, 187–88; Fox, 129, 149–50; Gochenour, 212–13; Hansen, 117–19, 158–59, 162; Hart, 100, 185; Hartman, 141, 254; Haskins, 157–58; Hockett, 116–17, 186, 208; Hooper, 14; Hulbert, 248–49; James, 38–40, 46, 69–70; Jameson, 16–17, 49–51, 183; Jastrow, 47–49; Kellogg, 244–45; Krey, 100–01; McLaughlin, 141–42; MacVeagh, 188–90; Martin, 216–17; Meany, 52–54; Merk, 168–69, 174; Mood, 235–36; Morison, 232–33; Pattengill, 38–39; Paullin, 178, 190–91; Paxson, 203, 217–18; Poole, 1; Porlier, 181–82; Quaife, 104–05; E. E. Robinson, 136–37, 156–57; J. H. Robinson, 125–26; Roseboom, 228–29; Schafer, 246–47; Schlesinger, 20, 69, 113–14, 129, 163–64, 230; Sellery, 196–97; Sheldon, 249–50; Skinner, 7, 54–57, 177; Small, 38; Stephens, 101–02; Stephenson, 218–19; Van Hise, 32–33, 44–45, 95, 208–10; Whitaker, 233–34; Wilson, 24–32, 70, 95–98, 181, 197–200
Turner, Helen M., 2
Turner, Jackson Allen, 26, 32
Turner, Mae Sherwood, 26, 32, 42
Turner, Mary Hanford, 6, 34–36

Uniformity, tendencies toward, 156
Unitarianism, 28
United States: aid to higher education, 74–75; capitalism in, 160–61; culture in, 112, 165; democracy in, 145, 159, 168, 189; development of, 133, 141–42, 171, 233; and immigration, 145; industrial history of, 88–89, 233; labor policy in, 134; national spirit in, 3, 5, 57–58, 189, 191; physiographic provinces of, 203; politics in, 81, 127, 136–38, 157; public documents of, 66, 92, 120, 190; relations with Europe, 11, 156–57; rural life in, 189; social forces in, 112, 130–32, 158, 167, 179, 233
United States Geological Surveys, 199
*United States, 1830–1850: The Nation and Its Sections, The* (Turner), 18, 19, 58, 190, 219, 230
University extension movement. *See* Turner
Urban centers, development of, 129

Utah, 231–34
Utah State Agricultural College, 156, 232

Vacation wilderness trip by Turner, 40–43. *See also* Turner
Van Buren, Martin, administration of, 100
Van Hise, Charles (president of the University of Wisconsin), 12, 32, 39, 42–48, 61, 68, 95
Van Hise, Hilda, 34, 40–41
Van Tyne, Claude H., 208–10, 245
Vincent, John Martin, 56
Virginia, 169
Virginia Company, The, 236
Voting, patterns of, 129, 156

Walker, Francis A., 3–4, 150
Washington, D.C., 51, 76, 120, 199, 216, 221, 230
Washington, George, administration of, 58, 245–46
Washington, University of, 52, 105–06
Washington University (St. Louis), 201
Waters, Willard O., 120
Wellington, R. G., 59
Wells, Edgar H., 216–17
Wesleyan University (Connecticut), 23
West: colonization of, 3, 46–47, 236, 252; concept of, 4, 61, 77, 134–35, 142; creative activity in, 30; Far, 156; influence of, 107, 125, 137, 153, 191, 197; Middle, 93, 143, 159, 191, 203; sectional rivalries in, 4; study of, 56–57, 102
"West as a Field for Historical Study, The" (Turner), 60
Western Insurgents, political movement in Wisconsin, 136
"Western State-Making in the Revolutionary Era" (Turner), 183
*Westward Extension, The* (Garrison), 45
Westward movement, influence of in American history, 107–09, 130, 170, 177, 179, 189
Whig Party, 150–52, 230
Whitaker, Arthur P., 233–34
Whitman, Walt, 165
Widener, Harry Elkins, Memorial Library, 102
Williams, Harry L., 38
Williams College, 114, 188, 195, 221, 227
Wilson, Woodrow: at Johns Hopkins University, 10, 16; associations with Turner, 23–25, 32, 60, 70, 78, 81, 85, 142, 151, 181, 189, 195–200, 233; offers Princeton professorship to Turner, 26–31; as President, 7, 53, 148, 160
Wilson Observatory, 118
*Winning of the West, The* (Roosevelt), 4
Winslow, John Bradley, 47
Winsor, Justin, 2, 57, 60–61, 107, 202
Wisconsin: Indian trade in, 7; legislative policies in, 36, 45, 51, 94–95, 98–99, 104, 130–31, 136–37
Wisconsin, University of, 56, 123, 134, 196–97, 199, 206; Board of Regents of, 11–13, 24, 26, 29–31, 44–46, 68, 94–95, 99; competition with University of Chicago, 12; doctoral program at, 88–90; Dorothy Turner matriculates at, 43; instruction at, 14, 77–78; intercollegiate athletics at, 37–40; library facilities of, 25, 31, 36, 45–46, 73, 90–94, 104, 240, 253; student body of, 6–7, 59–60. *See also* Turner
Wisconsin Academy of Arts and Sciences, 152
Wisconsin Magazine of History, 55, 156, 246
Wisconsin "school" of history. *See* Turner
Wisconsin State Historical Library, research facilities of, 27, 82, 86–87, 91–94

Wisconsin State Historical Society, manuscript collections of, 7–8, 60, 72–73, 81–82, 154, 166, 181, 217
Wisconsin University Bulletin, 89, 99, 200, 203
World War I, 124, 127, 143–44, 164
*Writings in Economics* (Bullock), 166
Wright, Benjamin F., 167–69
Wright, Silas, 249
Wylie, George, 95

*Yale Review,* 114, 167–68
Yale University, 43–44, 98, 111, 204–05, 209; library facilities of, 44
Yankee element, 53, 56, 61–62
Yost, Fielding Harris, 38–39
Young, Allyn A., 14
Young Women's Christian Association, 189

*Zeitgeist,* and historical concepts, 159